Sedona

AN EASY-TO-USE GUIDE
FOR 120 HIKING TRAILS and LOOP
HIKES IN SEDONA, ARIZONA

FEATURING
20 FAVORITE HIKING TRAILS
and LOOP HIKES

by
William Bohan

Non-liability Statement

The author has taken every precaution to ensure that the information contained within is up-to-date, accurate and reflects trail conditions when this guide was printed. However, trail conditions frequently change because of weather, Forest Service activity or other causes. The included GPS data were obtained from a Garmin model 60CSx GPS unit. Because the location, elevation and track data are only as accurate as the sensitivity of the GPS unit, some inaccuracies may be present. Everyone, including users of GPS data, is urged to use common sense when hiking. Always stay on the trail. The author, publisher, contributors, and all those involved in the preparation of this guide, either directly or indirectly, disclaim any liability for injuries, accidents, and damages whatsoever that may occur to those using this guide. You are responsible for your health and safety while hiking the trails.

Acknowledgments

The author would like to acknowledge several individuals for their contributions to this guide. They are:

Lorna Thompson and Nancy Williams for editing this work; Brenda Andrusyszyn, Michelle Barrett, Carole Bell, Wade Bell, David Butler, Ruth Butler, Barbara Lewis, Peg Likens, Tom Likens, Barbara Livermont, Gary Livermont, Cindy Parker, Rene' Ragan, Rick Ragan, Jim Rostedt, Kathy Rostedt, Gary Stouder, Barrie Thomas, Grace Thomas, Darryl Thompson, Lorna Thompson and Marjorie Whitton for their companionship while hiking the trails.

© Copyright William Bohan 2020 - 2024

All rights reserved
No portion of this guide may be reproduced in whole or in part by any means (with the exception of short quotes for the purpose of review), without the express permission of the author. v 1.18

Front Cover Photo: Taken on Brins Mesa

Table of Contents

Acknowledgments	2
Features of this Guide	4
QR Code Technology	4
Definition of Cumulative Ascent	4
Hiking Time	4
Trail Popularity	4
In-Out Hikes vs. Loop Hikes	4
Trailhead Shuttle Service	5
Vortex Information	6
Safe Hiking Tips	7
Definition of the "Y"	7
Master Hiking Trail/Loop Hike Locator	8–9
Sedona Average Weather & Sunrise/Sunset Data	10
GPS Data	10
Photographic Hotspots	10
Red Rock Pass Fee Program	11
Alphabetical List of Included Hiking Trails/Loop Hikes	12–14
Alphabetical List of Included Loop Hikes	14–15
List of 20 Favorite Hiking Trails/Loop Hikes	15
Hiking Trails/Loop Hikes Rated by Difficulty	16–17
Hiking Trails/Loop Hikes Listed by Feature	17
Shaded Hiking Trails/Loop Hikes for Hot Weather	17
Hiking Trails/Loop Hikes for Muddy Conditions	17
Trail Descriptions	18–165
Trail Waypoint GPS Data	166–176
Beyond the Hike	177–178
Other Titles by the Author	178
Index	179
Hiking Record	180

Features of This Guide

The Sedona Hiking Guide contains all the information you need to have a wonderful hiking experience in Sedona, Arizona. It includes the best, but not all trails in the Sedona area. Driving distances shown on the maps are from the "Y." The trail descriptions give you the highlights of each trail, what to watch for and where to take the best photos. A representative photo of each trail and easy-to-understand maps are included. GPS coordinates of the trailhead parking areas for each trail/loop are included in the Trailhead Directions section. You'll find all the trail waypoint GPS data in a separate section at the end of this guide. And information on the Trailhead Shuttle Service to popular trails is included.

QR Code Technology

Because of space limitations, only one representative photograph from each trail is included in this guide. But by using QR code technology, you can scan the QR code found near each trail map which will give you access to additional color photos of each trail.

Definition of Cumulative Ascent

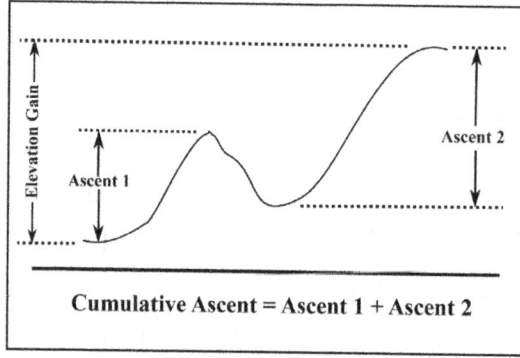

Sedona hiking trails are not flat, but rather rise and fall over their length. You'll find cumulative ascent rather than elevation change on each trail/loop map. Cumulative ascent reflects the total of all the ups of the trail. The greater the cumulative ascent, the more difficult the trail becomes. Elevation change reflects the difference between the lowest and highest elevations of the trail. Cumulative ascent is always greater than the elevation change.

Hiking Time

Hiking time is estimated based on a hiking speed of between 1.5 and 2 miles per hour. Trails that have greater cumulative ascent are at the lower end of that range to allow for stops to catch your breath. Hiking time doesn't include stops for snacks, photographs, meditation, etc.

Trail Popularity

A popular trail is indicated by 4 🚶🚶🚶🚶 symbols. You'll find just one 🚶 symbol for a trail that isn't used very often. You should expect crowds on trails with 4 hiker symbols and likely won't encounter other hikers on a trail that has just one hiker symbol. Weekends in Sedona bring more hikers to the trails and holidays can be especially busy.

In-Out Hikes vs. Loop Hikes

For an in-out hike (e.g. Fay Canyon), you'll hike a trail for a distance then retrace your steps to return to the trailhead. A loop hike is a circular hike using either a single trail (e.g. Baldwin Loop) or a combination of several trails and you essentially won't retrace your steps as you return to the trailhead.

4

Trailhead Shuttle Service

A free trailhead shuttle service has been launched to help alleviate trailhead parking lot overcrowding at the Soldier Pass, Dry Creek, Mescal, Cathedral Rock and Little Horse trailheads. The shuttles operate Thursday, Friday, Saturday and Sunday from 8:00 am to 6:30 pm and on additional days during busy times. The shuttles are free and a Red Rock Pass is not required to hike. Restrooms are available at each shuttle park and ride lot. Parking is prohibited at the Cathedral Rock and Soldier Pass trailheads when the shuttles are running. There are three trailhead park and ride shuttle parking lots.

The **West SR89A Park & Ride** lot located at 905 Upper Red Rock Loop Road has shuttles serving the **Mescal** (number **3** on the map below) and **Dry Creek** (number **2** on the map below) trailheads

The **Posse Grounds Park & Ride** lot located at 20 Carruth Drive, off of Soldiers Pass Road has shuttles serving the **Soldier Pass (1)** and **Dry Creek (2)** trailheads. This Park & Ride lot can also be used to access the shared use path alongside Soldiers Pass Road so that you can hike about 1 mile to the **Soldier Pass** trailhead (see Soldier Pass Trail).

The **North SR 179 Park & Ride** lot located at 1294 SR 179, off of Bowstring Drive has shuttles serving the **Cathedral Rock (4)** and **Little Horse (5)** trailheads.

Complete information about the trailhead shuttles, including real-time departure information is available at www.SedonaShuttle.com. You can also download the Transloc App from Google Play and the App Store for real-time departure information.

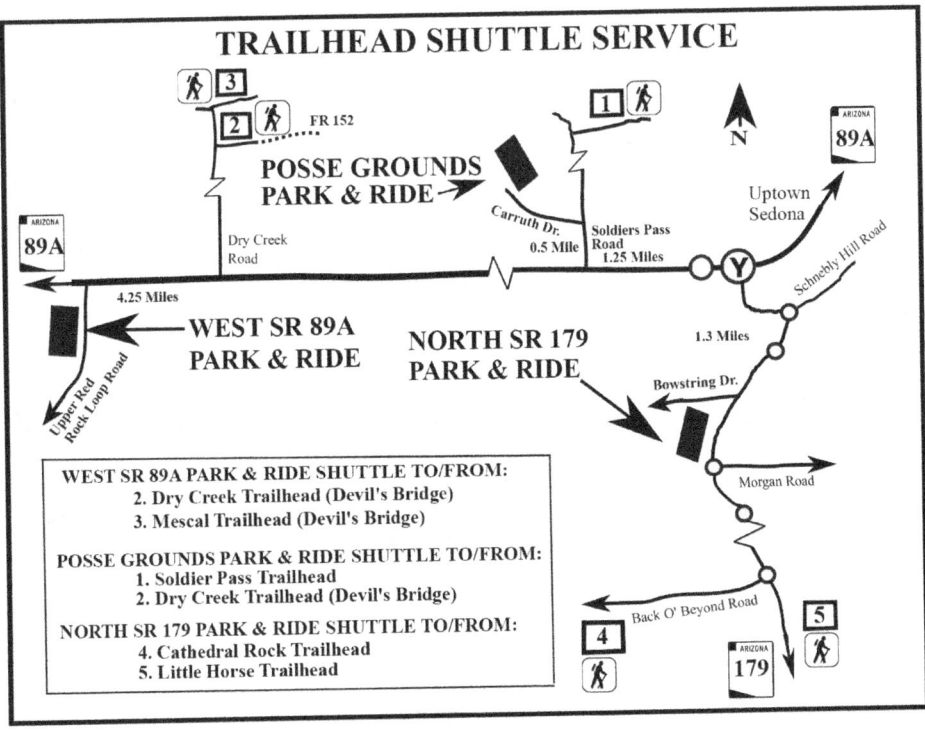

Vortex Information

If you come to Sedona with the thought of visiting a vortex or two, you are not alone. It's estimated that more than half of Sedona visitors are interested in experiencing the power of vortexes (vortices). There are four well known Sedona vortexes: Airport, Bell Rock, Boynton Canyon, and Cathedral Rock. All four locations are described in this guidebook. There are other areas, several of which are shown below, that are considered by some to be powerful vortex areas. I suggest that you approach each vortex without preconceived ideas of what you may experience and just let the experience happen. If nothing else, you'll enjoy some of Sedona's finest views.

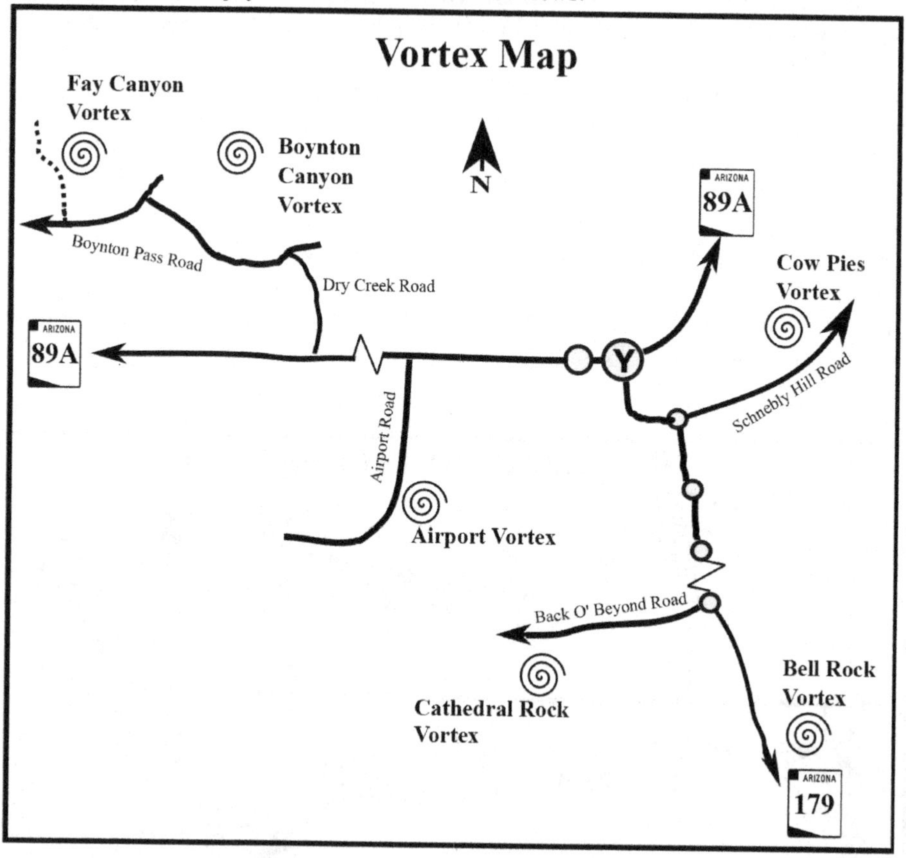

Vortex Map

If you'd like additional information on the four well known vortexes, plus information on the location of 10 lesser known power spots where vortex energy has been reported, you might be interested in *Hiking the Vortexes, a* book that is available at many Sedona retailers or scan the code below.

Safe Hiking Tips

The stunning, unique red rock formations, moderate temperatures, low humidity and close proximity to the trails make hiking in Sedona an experience unlike anywhere else in the world. But hiking is not without risk. It is very important to be prepared, even for a day hike. Bring enough water to stay hydrated and drink water throughout the hike. In addition:

- Check the weather before you begin hiking and reschedule your hike if inclement weather is predicted. Do not hike if trails are slippery or icy.
- Wear a hat and sunscreen and take along a wind breaker or light raincoat
- Bring hiking poles as they may help with balance on the uneven trails
- Wear hiking boots or sturdy walking shoes with good grip as the trails can be uneven, rocky and slippery
- Carry a first-aid kit, a fully charged cell phone (although many hiking trails do not have cell phone service), flashlight, compass, hiking guide, map, portable GPS unit, rescue whistle, pocketknife and a snack
- Hike with at least one other person and complete the hike before sunset
- If you must hike alone, let someone know where you'll be hiking and leave a note in your vehicle stating where you intend to hike and when you expect to return
- Trailhead parking areas can be the target of thieves so don't leave valuables in your vehicle
- Stay on the designated trail. Most rescues are for hikers who have left the trail to "explore"
- Downhill hikers have the right-of-way in most instances because footing is more tenuous downhill than uphill. If hiking uphill, step aside and let downhill hikers pass
- Mountain bikers are supposed to yield to all trail users, but use common sense and step aside when appropriate
- There is no trash service in the forest. Take out anything you bring in. "Take nothing but pictures, leave nothing but footprints"

Definition of the "Y"

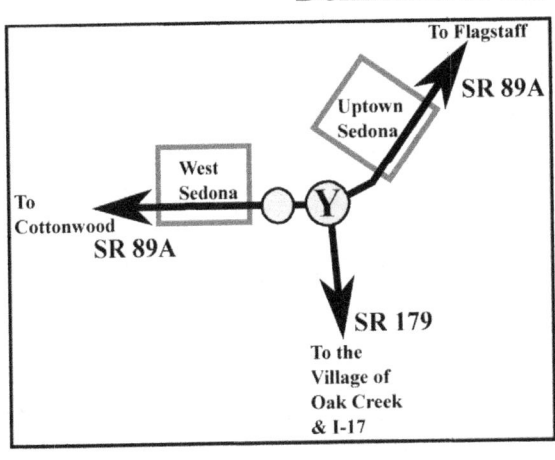

If you obtain directions from a Sedona local, chances they will give you those directions referencing something called the "Y." The "Y" is used as the reference point in this guidebook also. The "Y" is the traffic circle at the intersection of State Route (SR) 89A and SR 179, which is west of Uptown Sedona and east of West Sedona. All of the driving distances shown on the maps are from the "Y."

Master Map of Trails/

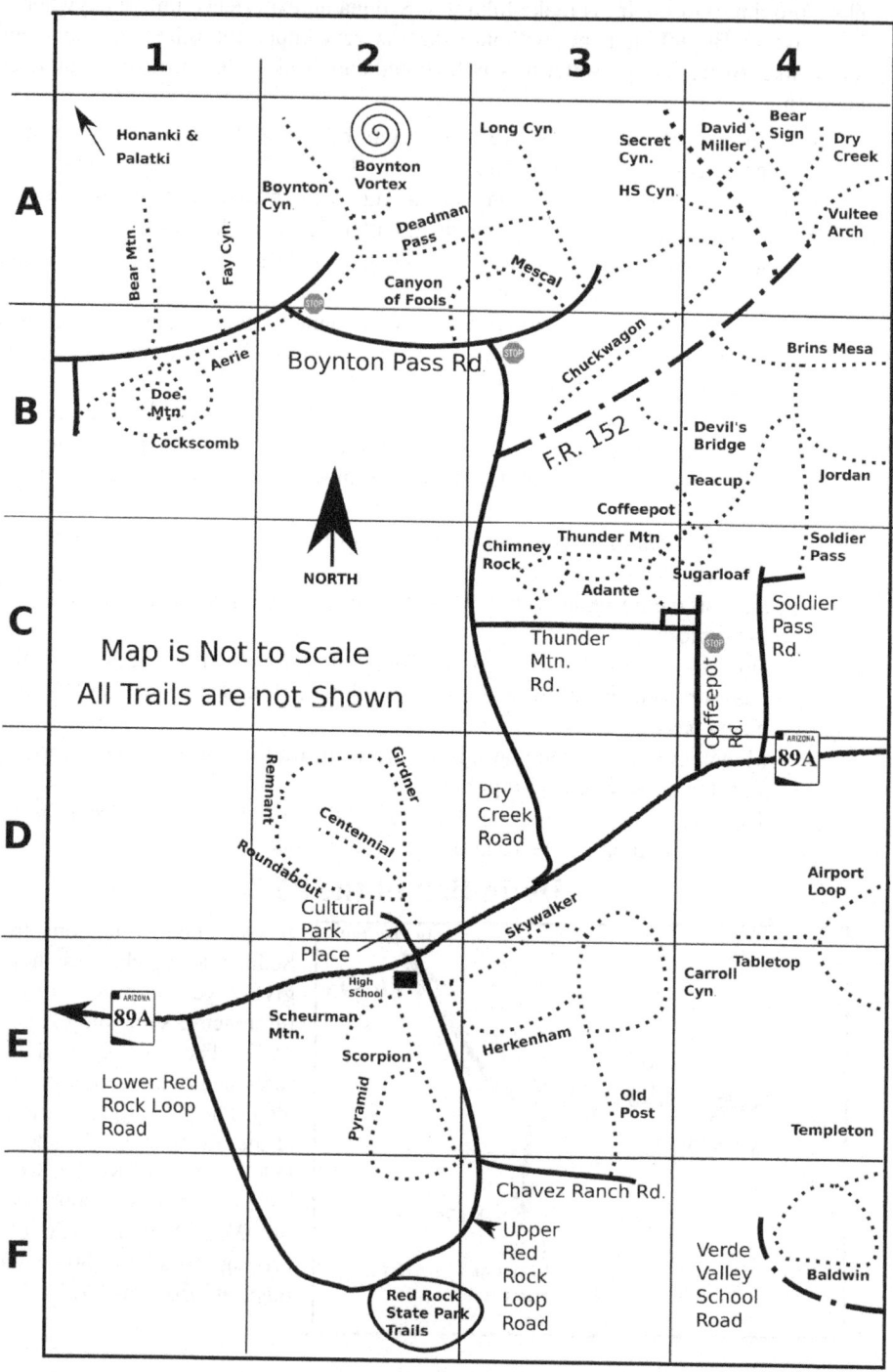

Loops Closest to Sedona

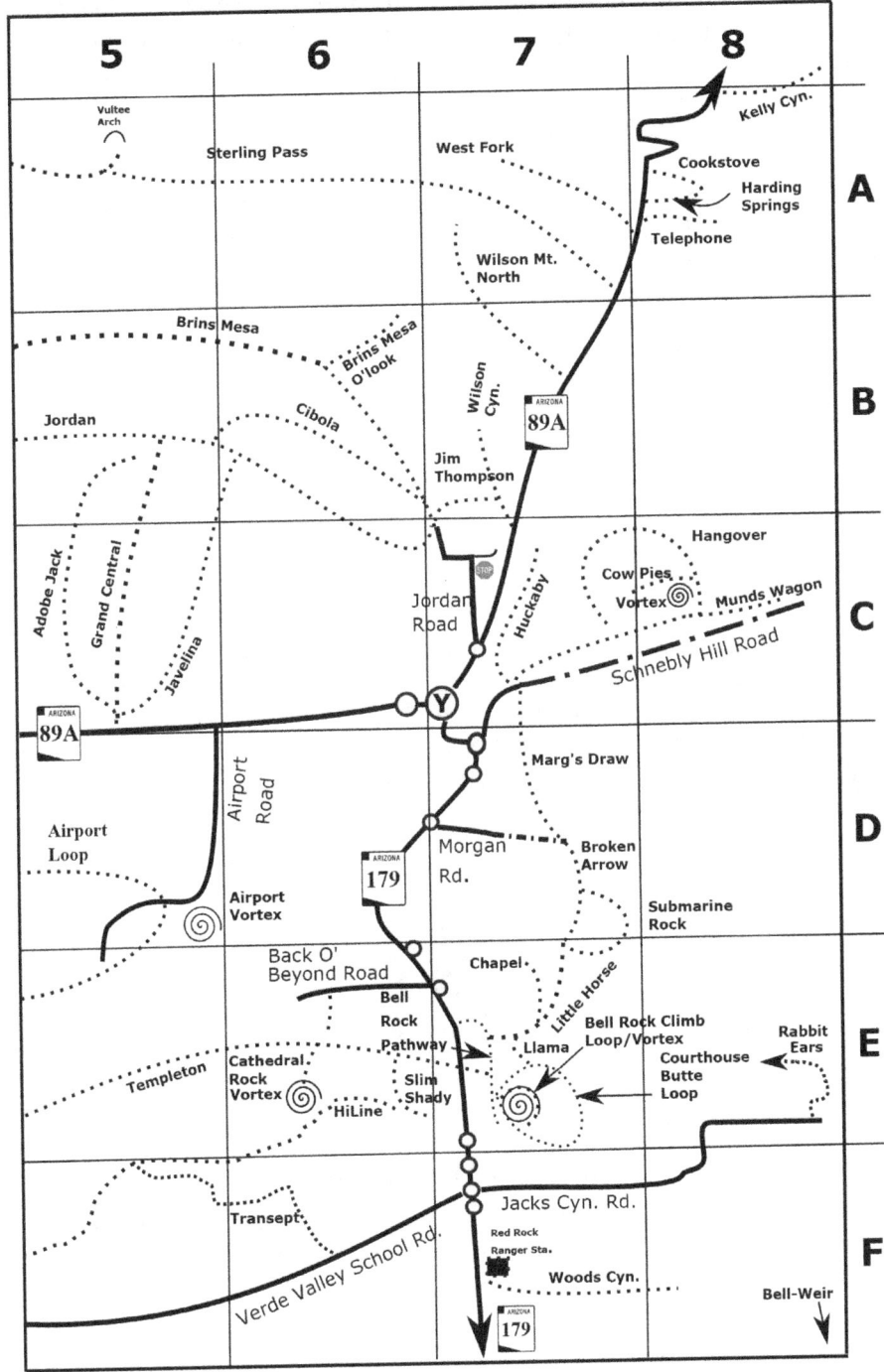

Sedona Average Weather & Sunrise/Sunset Data

	Temperature (°F) High	Low	Precipitation (Inches)	Sunrise (1st of	Sunset Month)
January	55	30	1.7	7:35 AM	5:39 PM
February	59	32	1.5	7:13 AM	6:10 PM
March	63	35	1.7	6:37 AM	6:36 PM
April	72	42	1.2	5:55 AM	7:00 PM
May	81	49	0.6	5:23 AM	7:24 PM
June	91	57	0.5	5:13 AM	7:43 PM
July	95	65	1.9	5:25 AM	7:41 PM
August	92	64	2.4	5:48 AM	7:15 PM
September	88	58	1.5	6:10 AM	6:33 PM
October	78	48	1.1	6:33 AM	5:52 PM
November	65	37	1.3	7:02 AM	5:22 PM
December	56	30	1.7	7:27 AM	5:18 PM
Average	75	46	1.4		

GPS Data

When you read the trail descriptions, you will find numbers in brackets such as {1}, {2} etc. These numbers refer to points of interest shown on the maps and mentioned in the trail descriptions. The GPS coordinates as well as the elevation for each waypoint shown on the maps are included at the end of this guidebook.

GPS data for your portable GPS unit in the universal gpx format for the trails contained in this guidebook are available at: https://greatsedonahikes.com/gps/gps.html or scan the code below.

Photographic Hotspots

You'll find camera symbols  on many of the maps. While photographic opportunities are remarkable on all the trails, the camera symbol indicates some of the best locations to take photos of the red rocks or other interesting scenery.

10

Red Rock Pass Fee Program

If you park on the National Forest around Sedona, you may need to display a Recreation Pass. If you stop temporarily on the National Forest to take a photo remaining near your vehicle, you probably don't need to display a Recreation Pass.

A Recreation Pass is required for trailhead parking for many of the trails listed in this guide. It is also required for the Bootlegger, Banjo Bill, Halfway and Encinoso picnic areas in Oak Creek Canyon. Additionally, there are 3 special fee areas: Crescent Moon Ranch/Red Rock Crossing, West Fork Trail (Call O' the Canyon), and Grasshopper Point Picnic Area. Each area charges a separate, unique fee. Developed campgrounds have their own fees.

A Recreation Pass is: 1) A National Parks Pass, also known as a Federal Interagency Annual Pass 2) A Senior Pass, also known as a Federal Interagency Senior Pass available to U.S. residents 62 years of age and older 3) A Federal Interagency Access Pass issued to individuals with permanent disabilities 4) A Red Rock Pass (described below).

If you do not have any of the above Federal Interagency Passes, you may display a **Red Rock Pass**, available for sale at many Sedona-area businesses, the Red Rock Ranger Station Visitor Center, the Sedona Chamber of Commerce Uptown Visitor Center and selected trailheads. The Red Rock Pass is available as a $5 Daily Pass, a $15 Weekly Pass, a $20 Annual Pass, or a $40 Grand Annual Pass. The machines located at the trailheads accept credit cards or cash ($1, $5 and $10) and only issue Daily or Weekly Red Rock Passes.

- The $5 Daily Red Rock Pass permits you to park on the National Forest for one calendar day. It expires at midnight. It <u>does not include</u> the additional parking fees at the 3 special fee areas.
- The $15 Weekly Red Rock Pass permits you to park on the National Forest for 7 consecutive days. It <u>does not include</u> the additional parking fees at the 3 special fee areas.
- The $20 Annual Red Rock Pass permits you to park on the National Forest for 12 consecutive months. It <u>does not include</u> the additional parking fees at the 3 special fee areas.
- The $40 Grand Annual Pass permits you to park on the National Forest and <u>includes</u> the additional parking fees at the 3 special fee areas for 12 consecutive months. It is available at the Red Rock Ranger Station and the Sedona Chamber of Commerce Uptown Visitor Center.

The Red Rock Pass Program changes periodically For the latest information, check http://www.fs.usda.gov/main/coconino/passes-permits/recreation or scan the code below.

To hike the trails at the Red Rock State Park, you'll pay a separate additional admission fee at the entrance station.

Alphabetical List of Included Hiking Trails/Loop Hikes

Hiking Trail/Loop Hike	Location (See pgs. 8-9)	Page
Adobe Jack	C-5	134
Adobe Jack/Javelina Loop	C-5	134
Andante	C-3	148
Aerie	B-1	18
Airport Loop	D-4	20
Airport Vortex	D-6	120
Apache Fire (RRSP)	F-2	118
Baby Bell	E-7	100
Bail	E-7	102
Baldwin Loop ★	F-4	22
Bear Mountain ★	A-1	24
Bear Sign	A-4	26
Bell Rock Climb and Vortex	E-7	28
Bell Rock Loop ★	E-7	30
Bell Rock Pathway	E-6	32
Bell Rock Pathway/Templeton Loop	E-6	32
Bell Rock Vortex	E-7	28
Bell/Weir	F-8	34
Boynton Canyon ★	A-2	36
Boynton Canyon Vortex	A-2	36
Brins Mesa	B-4	38
Brins Mesa Overlook ★	B-6	40
Brins Mesa/Soldier Pass Loop ★	B-5	42
Broken Arrow	D-7	44
Broken Arrow/Submarine Rock Loop ★	D-7	44
Bunkhouse (RRSP)	F-2	118
Canyon of Fools	A-2	46
Canyon of Fools/Mescal Loop	A-2	46
Carroll Canyon	E-4	112
Cathedral Rock and Vortex ★	E-6	48
Centennial	D-2	154
Chapel	E-7	98
Chimney Rock Lower Loop	C-3	50
Chimney Rock Pass Loop ★	C-3	52
Chuckwagon In-Out	B-3	54
Chuckwagon Loop	B-3	56
Cibola Pass	B-6	58
Cibola Pass/Jordan Loop	B-6	58
Cockscomb	B-1	60
Cockscomb/Aerie Loop	B-1	60
Coconino	E-6	130
Coffeepot	B-3	62
Cookstove to Harding Springs	A-8	64

★ symbol = Favorite Trail/Loop
(RRSP) = Trail at the Red Rock State Park

Alphabetical List of Included Hiking Trails/Loop Hikes (Cont'd)

Hiking Trail/Loop Hike	Location (See pgs. 8-9)	Page
Courthouse Butte Alternate Loop	E-8	66
Courthouse Butte Loop	E-8	68
Cow Pies	C-7	70
Coyote Ridge (RRSP)	F-2	118
Crusty	C-5	134
David Miller	A-4	126
Devil's Bridge ★	B-4	72
Doe Mountain ★	B-1	74
Dry Creek	A-4	76
Eagle's Nest (RRSP)	F-2	118
Easy Breezy	E-6	88
Fay Canyon ★	A-1	78
Grand Central	C-5	136
Grand Central/Javelina Loop	C-5	136
Girdner	D-2	156
Hangover In-Out	C-8	80
Hangover/Munds Wagon Loop	C-8	80
Harding Springs	A-8	64
Herkenham	E-3	128
Hermit	E-6	130
HiLine ★	E-6	82
Honanki Heritage Site	A-1	84
HS Canyon	A-3	86
HT	E-7	88
HT-Easy Breezy Loop	E-7	88
Huckaby	C-7	90
Javelina	C-5	134 & 136
Javelina (RRSP)	F-2	118
Jim Thompson	B-7	92
Jordan	B-5	94
Kelly Canyon	A-8	96
Kisva (RRSP)	F-2	118
Little Horse ★	E-7	98
Little Rock	E-8	116
Llama	E-7	102
Llama/Baby Bell Loop	E-7	100
Llama/Bail Loop	E-7	102
Llama/Little Horse Loop	E-7	102
Long Canyon	A-3	104
Marg's Draw	D-7	106
Mescal	A-3	108
Mescal/Long Canyon Loop ★	A-3	108
Munds Wagon	C-8	110
Old Post	E-3	112
Old Post/Carroll Canyon Loop	E-3	112

★ symbol = Favorite Trail/Loop
(RRSP) = Trail at the Red Rock State Park

Alphabetical List of Included Hiking Trails/Loop Hikes (Cont'd)

Hiking Trail/Loop Hike	Location (See pgs. 8-9)	Page
Palatki Heritage Site	A-1	84
Power Line Plunge	C-5	134
Pyramid/Scorpion Loop	E-2	114
Rabbit Ears	E-8	116
Rector Connector	E-7	30
Scheurman Mountain Vista ★	E-2	120
Scorpion	E-2	122
Secret Canyon	A-3	124
Secret Canyon/Bear Sign Loop	A-4	126
Sedona View	D-5	20
Skywalker	D-3	128
Skywalker/Herkenham Loop	D-3	128
Slim Shady	E-6	130
Slim Shady/Hermit Loop	E-6	130
Smoke (RRSP)	F-2	118
Soldier Pass ★	C-4	132
Sterling Pass to Vultee Arch	A-6	138
Sugarloaf	C-4	140
Tabletop	E-4	20
Teacup	B-4	142
Telephone	A-8	144
Templeton	E-5	146
Thunder Mountain	C-3	148
Thunder Mountain/Andante Loop ★	C-3	148
Transept	F-6	150
Vultee Arch	A-4	152
West Fork ★	A-7	158
Wilson Canyon ★	B-7	160
Wilson Mountain North	A-7	162
Woods Canyon	F-7	164
Yavapai Ridge (RRSP)	F-2	118
Yucca	A-2	46

Alphabetical List of Included Loop Hikes

Loop	Challenge Level	Page
Adobe Jack/Javelina Loop	Moderate	134
Airport Loop	Moderate	20
Baldwin Loop ★	Moderate	22
Bell Rock Loop ★	Easy	30
Bell Rock Pathway/Templeton Loop	Moderate	32
Brins Mesa/Soldier Pass Loop ★	Moderate	42
Broken Arrow/Submarine Rock Loop ★	Moderate	44
Canyon of Fools/Mescal Loop	Easy/Moderate	46
Chimney Rock Lower Loop	Easy	50
Chimney Rock Pass Loop ★	Easy	52

★ symbol = Favorite Trail/Loop
(RRSP) = Trail at the Red Rock State Park

Alphabetical List of Included Loop Hikes (Cont'd)

Loop	Challenge Level	Page
Chuckwagon Loop	Moderate	56
Cibola Pass/Jordan Loop	Easy/Moderate	58
Cockscomb/Aerie Loop	Moderate	60
Courthouse Butte Alternate Loop	Moderate	66
Courthouse Butte Loop	Moderate	68
Grand Central/Javelina Loop	Moderate	136
Girdner/Remnant/Roundabout Loop	Moderate	156
Hangover/Munds Wagon Loop	Hard	80
HT/Easy Breezy Loop	Moderate	88
Llama/Baby Bell Loop	Easy	100
Llama/Bail Loop	Moderate	102
Llama/Little Horse Loop	Moderate	102
Mescal/Long Canyon Loop ★	Moderate	108
Old Post/Carroll Canyon Loop	Moderate	112
Pyramid/Scorpion Loop	Moderate	114
Secret Canyon/Bear Sign Loop	Hard	126
Skywalker/Herkenham Loop	Moderate	128
Slim Shady/Hermit Loop	Moderate	130
Thunder Mountain/Andante Loop ★	Moderate	148

List of 20 Favorite Hiking Trails/Loop Hikes

Hiking Trail/Loop Hike	Location (See pgs. 8-9)	Page
Easy		
Bell Rock Loop ★	E-7	30
Chimney Rock Pass Loop ★	C-3	52
Fay Canyon ★	A-1	78
Moderate		
Baldwin Loop ★	F-4	22
Boynton Canyon ★	A-2	36
Brins Mesa Overlook ★	B-6	40
Brins Mesa/Soldier Pass Loop ★	B-5	42
Broken Arrow ★	D-7	44
Devil's Bridge ★	B-4	72
Doe Mountain ★	B-1	74
HiLine ★	E-6	82
Little Horse ★	E-7	98
Mescal/Long Canyon Loop ★	A-3	108
Scheurman Mountain Vista ★	E-2	120
Soldier Pass ★	C-4	132
Thunder Mountain/Andante Loop ★	C-3	148
West Fork ★	A-7	158
Wilson Canyon ★	B-7	160
Hard		
Bear Mountain ★	A-1	24
Cathedral Rock and Vortex ★	E-6	48

★ symbol = Favorite Trail/Loop

Hiking Trails/Loop Hikes Listed By Difficulty

Easy

	Page		Page
Airport Vortex	20	Crusty	134
Baby Bell	100	Fay Canyon (not to arch)	78
Bail	102	Hermit	130
Bell Rock Climb and Vortex	28	Honanki Heritage Site	84
Bell Rock Loop	30	Kisva	118
Boynton Canyon Vortex	36	Llama/Baby Bell Loop	100
Centennial	154	Llama/Bail Loop	102
Chapel	98	Palatki Heritage Site	84
Chimney Rock Lower Loop	50	Rector Connector	30
Chimney Rock Pass Loop	52	Slim Shady	130
Cibola Pass	58	Slim Shady/Hermit Loop	130
Cibola Pass/Jordan Loop	58	Smoke	118
Coconino	130	Tabletop	20
Coffeepot	62	Yucca	46
Cow Pies	70		

Easy to Moderate

	Page		Page
Andante	148	Kelly Canyon	96
Cibola Pass/Soldier Pass/Jordan	58	Llama	102
Dry Creek	76	Marg's Draw	106
Fay Canyon (to the arch)	78	Pyramid/Scorpion Loop	114
Jordan	94	Vultee Arch	152

Moderate

	Page		Page
Adobe Jack	134	Easy Breezy	88
Adobe Jack/Javelina Loop	134	Grand Central	136
Aerie	18	Grand Central/Javelina Loop	136
Airport Loop	20	Gridner	156
Apache Fire	118	Hangover In-Out	80
Baldwin Loop	22	Herkenham	128
Bear Sign	26	HiLine	82
Bell Rock Pathway	32	HS Canyon	86
Bell Rock Pathway/Templeton Loop	32	HT	88
Bell/Weir	34	HT/Easy Breezy Loop	88
Boynton Canyon	36	Huckaby	90
Brins Mesa	38	Javelina	134 & 136
Brins Mesa Overlook	40	Javelina (Red Rock State Park)	118
Brins Mesa/Soldier Pass Loop	42	Jim Thompson	92
Broken Arrow	44	Little Horse	98
Broken Arrow/Submarine Loop	44	Little Rock	116
Canyon of Fools	46	Llama/Little Horse Loop	102
Canyon of Fools/Mescal Loop	46	Long Canyon	104
Carroll Canyon	112	Mescal	108
Chuckwagon In-Out	54	Mescal/Long Canyon Loop	108
Chuckwagon Loop	56	Munds Wagon	110
Cockscomb	60	Old Post	112
Cockscomb/Aerie Loop	60	Old Post/Carroll Canyon Loop	112
Courthouse Butte Alternate Loop	66	Power Line Plunge	134
Courthouse Butte Loop	68	Rabbit Ears	116
Coyote Ridge	118	Remnant	156
Devil's Bridge	72	Roundabout	156
Doe Mountain	74	Scheurman Mountain Vista	120

Moderate (Cont'd)

	Page		Page
Scorpion	122	Templeton	146
Secret Canyon	124	Thunder Mountain	148
Sedona View	20	Thunder Mountain/Andante Loop	148
Skywalker	128	Transept	150
Skywalker/Herkenham Loop	128	West Fork	158
Slim Shady/Hermit Loop	130	Wilson Canyon	160
Soldier Pass	132	Woods Canyon	164
Sugarloaf	140	Yavapai Ridge	118
Teacup	142		

Hard

Bear Mountain	24	Harding Springs	64
Cathedral Rock and Vortex	48	Secret Canyon/Bear Sign Loop	126
Cookstove to Harding Springs	64	Sterling Pass to Vultee Arch	138
David Miller	126	Telephone	144
Eagle's Nest	118	Wilson Mountain North	162
Hangover/Munds Wagon Loop	80		

Hiking Trails/Loop Hikes Listed By Feature

To/Near Arches   **Vortex Areas**

Devil's Bridge	72	Airport Vortex	20
Fay Canyon	78	Bell Rock Vortex	28
Soldier Pass	132	Boynton Canyon Vortex	36
Vultee Arch	152	Cathedral Rock Vortex	48
		Cowpies Vortex	70
		Fay Canyon Vortex	78

To/Near Water   **Indian Ruins**

Baldwin Loop	22	Boynton Canyon	36
Bell/Weir	34	Honanki Heritage Site	84
Huckaby	90	Palatki Heritage Site	84
Templeton	146		
West Fork	158		

Shaded Hiking Trails/Loop Hikes for Hot Weather

The following trails provide partial shade and may be suitable for summer hiking. But be sure to take extra water when hiking in the summer.

Bear Sign	26	Long Canyon (after 1 mile)	104
Boynton Canyon	36	Munds Wagon	110
Cibola Pass	58	Sterling Pass	138
Cookstove to Harding Springs	64	Telephone	144
Devil's Bridge	72	Vultee Arch	152
Dry Creek	76	West Fork	158
HS Canyon	86	Wilson Canyon	160
Kelly Canyon	96		

Hiking Trails/Loop Hikes for Muddy Conditions

After rain or snow, the following trails may be suitable for hiking. Do not hike if thunderstorm, lightning or flash flood warnings are present.

Baldwin Loop	22	Little Horse	98
Boynton Canyon	36	Llama	102
Courthouse Butte Alternate Loop	66	Marg's Draw	106
Courthouse Butte Loop	68	Scheurman Mountain Vista	120
Doe Mountain	74	Templeton	146
Fay Canyon	78	Wilson Canyon	160

17

Aerie Trail

Summary: An in-out hike across the north side of Doe Mountain with great views of Doe Mountain, Bear Mountain, Fay Canyon and Boynton Canyon

Challenge Level: Moderate

Hiking Distance: 2.9 miles each way from the Aerie parking area to the Boynton Canyon parking area or 5.8 miles round trip

Hiking Time: About 3 hours round trip

Trail Popularity:

Trailhead Directions: From the "Y" roundabout (see page 7), drive west toward Cottonwood on SR 89A about 3 miles. Turn right onto Dry Creek Road. Stay on Dry Creek Road to a stop sign (about 3 miles) then turn left onto Boynton Pass Road. Proceed about 1.6 miles to a stop sign. Turn left and continue on Boynton Pass Road. Drive about 2.5 miles then turn left onto Aerie Road, which is about 0.5 mile past the Doe Mountain/Bear Mountain parking area on the left side of Boynton Pass Road. Follow Aerie Road then take the right fork to the parking area {1}. (34°53.139'N; 111°52.194'W) This parking area also serves the Cockscomb/Aerie Loop.

Description: The trail begins near the signboard at the west end of the parking lot. About 100 feet south of the parking area is a trail sign. Turn left (east) to hike the Aerie Trail across the north side of Doe Mountain all the way to the Boynton Canyon parking area.

You'll cross Aerie Drive, which leads to The Aerie subdivision, then you'll come to the Doe Mountain Trail {2} after 0.8 mile. The Aerie Trail takes a slight jog here at the intersection with the Doe Mountain Trail but is well-marked. You'll bend to the right then to the left as you hike around the northeast side of Doe Mountain. Next you'll intersect the Cockscomb Trail after 2.5 miles {3} then cross Boynton Canyon Road {4} on your 2.9 mile hike to the Boynton Canyon parking area {5}.

You'll have excellent views of Doe Mountain, Bear Mountain, Fay Canyon and Boynton Canyon. You may encounter some mountain bikers on the trail as you hike toward and return from the Boynton Canyon Trail parking area. The Boynton Canyon Trail parking area has a toilet.

Color Photos: Scan the QR code below for additional color photos of this trail

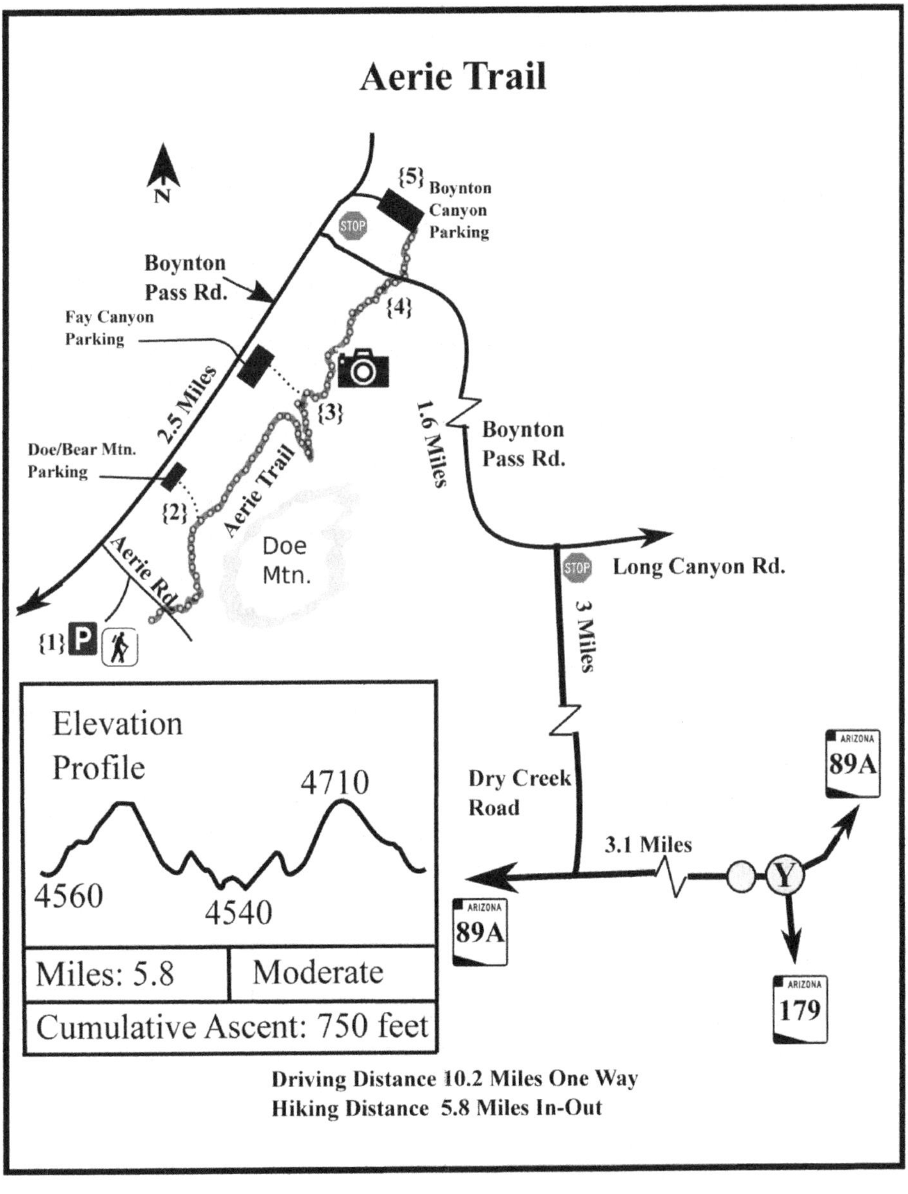

Aerie Trail

Miles: 5.8 | Moderate
Cumulative Ascent: 750 feet

Driving Distance 10.2 Miles One Way
Hiking Distance 5.8 Miles In-Out

Airport Loop and Airport Vortex

Summary: A loop hike that circles the Sedona Airport with nice views all around and a chance to visit one of Sedona's famous vortexes

Challenge Level: Easy for the vortex hike; Moderate for the loop hike

Hiking Distance: From the Airport Road parking area {1} less than 0.25 mile round trip for the vortex; about 3.3 miles for the loop hike, add another 1 mile if you hike the Tabletop Trail. Add 1.2 miles to all the above mileages if you hike from the Sedona View parking area {2}.

Hiking Time: From the Airport Road parking area, about ½ hour round trip for the vortex; about 2 hours for the Airport Loop hike: add ½ hour for the Tabletop Trail. From the Sedona View parking area, add 1 hour to the above estimated hiking times.

Trail Popularity: For the vortex: 🚶🚶🚶🚶 For the loop hike: 🚶🚶

Trailhead Directions: There are two ways to access this trail. From the "Y" roundabout (see page 7), drive west toward Cottonwood on SR 89A for 1 mile then turn left onto Airport Road, which is the first traffic light west of the "Y." The primary trailhead is located approximately 0.5 mile up Airport Road on the left {1}. (34°51.345'N; 111°46.804'W) There is parking for 10 vehicles plus one handicapped spot here.

If the parking lot is full, continue on for 0.6 mile then turn left into the Scenic Overlook parking area. The Sedona View trailhead is at the northeast corner of the parking area {2}. (34°51.196'N; 111°47.372'W) There is a $3 parking fee at this parking area.

Description: If you park on Airport Road {1}, you can easily reach one of Sedona's famous vortexes. From the parking area continue past the first sign then follow the main trail east until you come to a second sign in about 200 feet {3}. Turn left here then follow the trail to Overlook Point for a short distance then make a right turn to climb up about 50 feet to the overlook. The top of the rock formation is Overlook Point and is considered to be the vortex {4}. (Additional information on vortexes can be found on page 6.) From the Scenic View parking area {2}, hike the Sedona View Trail downhill for 0.6 mile. Continue past the intersection with the Airport Loop Trail to the intersection with the sign for Overlook Point {3} to go to the vortex {4}.

As you hike the Airport Loop Trail, there are good views all around. On the east, there are great views of Twin Buttes and, to the south, Cathedral Rock. Be sure to hike the 0.5 mile Tabletop Trail at the southwest end of the runway {5} to the end of the mesa {6} for a spectacular view of Sedona's Pyramid. Return to the Airport Loop Trail where after 0.6 mile you'll intersect the Bandit Trail {7} and have nice views of Chimney Rock, Thunder Mountain and Coffeepot Rock on the north side of the loop. You'll cross Airport Road to return to the parking area.

Note: This trail is very rocky and has narrow sections with large drop offs.

Color Photos: Scan the QR code below for additional color photos of this trail

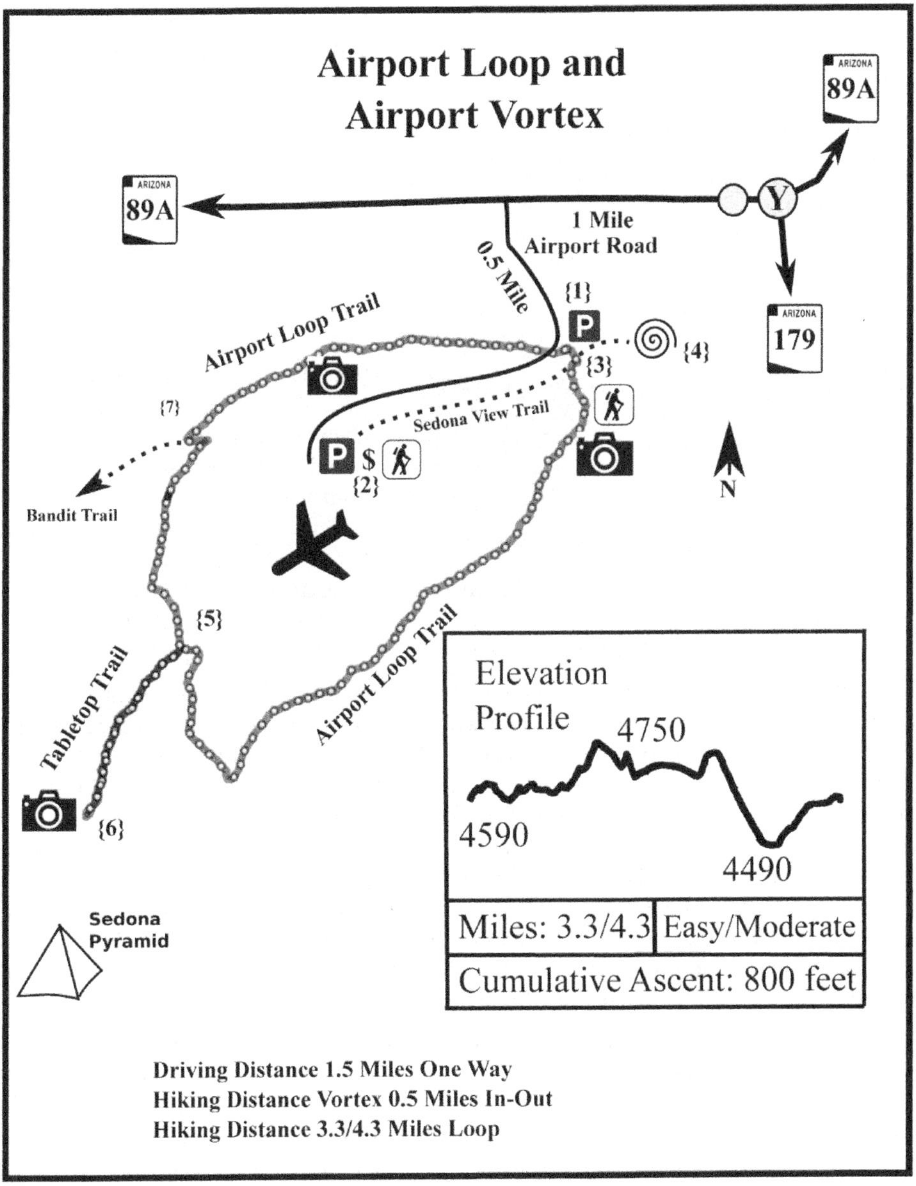

Airport Loop and Airport Vortex

Driving Distance 1.5 Miles One Way
Hiking Distance Vortex 0.5 Miles In-Out
Hiking Distance 3.3/4.3 Miles Loop

Baldwin Loop ★

Summary: A favorite loop trail at the base of Cathedral Rock offering some excellent views with an optional short side trip to the banks of Oak Creek

Challenge Level: Moderate

Hiking Distance: About a 2.7 mile loop

Hiking Time: About 1½ hours round trip

Trail Popularity:

Trailhead Directions: The trailhead is located on the unpaved portion of Verde Valley School Road. From the "Y" roundabout (see page 7), drive south on SR 179 about 7 miles to the Jacks Canyon/Verde Valley School Road roundabout then take the first exit onto Verde Valley School Road. At 4 miles, you'll pass the Turkey Creek parking area on your left {10} and at 4.5 miles you'll see the Baldwin Trail parking area on the left (west) side of Verde Valley School Road {1}. (34°49.309'N; 111°48.493'W) The trailhead is across the road from the north end of the parking area. There are toilets at the parking area.

Description: Named for Andrew Baldwin, one of the individuals who bought Crescent Moon Ranch in 1936, the Baldwin Loop Trail circles an unnamed red rock butte and provides excellent views of Cathedral Rock. After crossing the road, you'll come to a signboard {2}. You can hike the Baldwin Trail in either clockwise or counter clockwise direction. If you hike in the clockwise direction, you'll intersect a social trail in 0.3 mile {3} and the Templeton Trail after 0.5 mile {4}. Take a side trip by hiking east on the Templeton Trail until it is beside Oak Creek. After 0.2 mile, look across Oak Creek to see Buddha Beach, where visitors use river rock to build amazing stacked structures {5}. Periodically, floods knock the structures down, but they are usually quickly rebuilt. You may be lucky and see hundreds of buddhas. If you continue east on the Templeton Trail for 0.8 mile, you'll intersect the Cathedral Rock Trail.

Return to the Baldwin Loop Trail intersection then turn left to continue around the tall red rock butte. You'll pass some excellent places to stop and enjoy the views {6}{8} on your loop. You'll intersect the HiLine Trail {7}, which is a popular mountain biking trail, and a spur off of the Baldwin Loop Trail {9} that leads across Verde Valley School Road to the Turkey Creek Trail parking area {10}. For the best photos of Cathedral Rock, do this hike later in the day.

Color Photos: Scan the QR code below for additional color photos of this trail

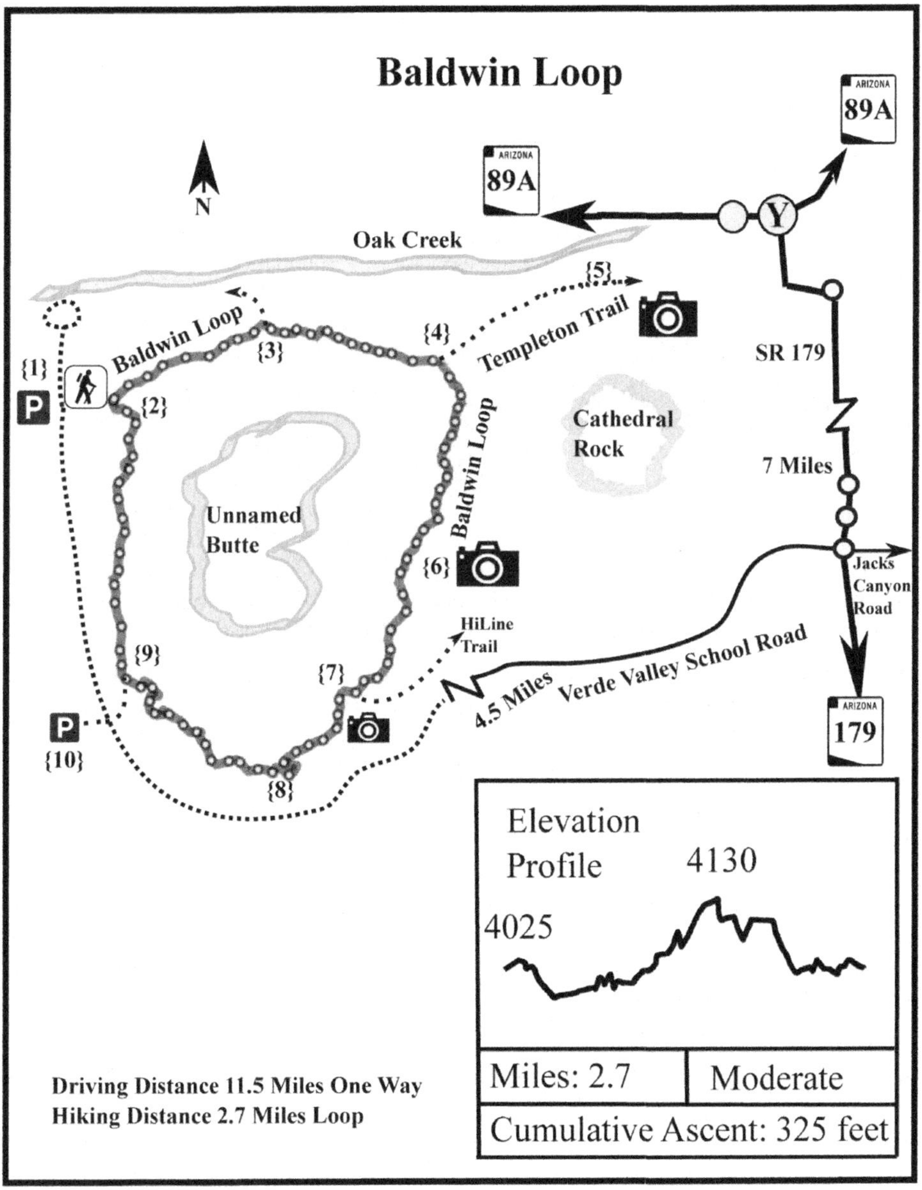

Baldwin Loop

Driving Distance 11.5 Miles One Way
Hiking Distance 2.7 Miles Loop

Miles: 2.7 | Moderate
Cumulative Ascent: 325 feet

Bear Mountain Trail ★

Summary: A favorite strenuous, sunny, in-out hike with excellent red rock views

Challenge Level: Hard

Hiking Distance: About 2.4 miles each way to the top of Bear Mountain or 4.8 miles round trip

Hiking Time: About 4 hours round trip

Trail Popularity: 🚶🚶

Trailhead Directions: From the "Y" roundabout (see page 7), drive west toward Cottonwood on SR 89A about 3 miles. Turn right onto Dry Creek Road. Stay on Dry Creek Road to a stop sign (about 3 miles) then turn left onto Boynton Pass Road. Proceed about 1.6 miles to a stop sign. Turn left and continue on Boynton Pass Road. The trailhead parking {1} is the second parking area on the left side, about 1.8 miles from the stop sign. (34°53.596'N; 111°51.945'W) This parking area also serves the Doe Mountain Trail. The Bear Mountain Trail begins across the road from the parking area. There are toilets at the parking area.

Description: Bear Mountain provides fantastic views of near and far red rock formations. You'll be hiking a trail with a cumulative ascent of some 2100 feet. This makes Bear Mountain a hard hike.

After crossing the road and stepping over a low fence, you first cross a series of three deep washes and enter a meadow-like landscape. After 0.3 mile, you begin the climb up the mountain. Throughout the hike, be sure to look around to enjoy the great views. After 0.7 mile you'll come to a huge rock beside the trail {2}.

At 1.2 miles, you'll come to a flat area {3} and soon have to scramble up in a narrow slot. At 1.4 miles, you'll reach a summit {4} then begin a series of descents and ascents. At 2 miles, you'll come to a large area of slick rock {5}, soon followed by a natural stopping place and photo opportunity at elevation 6150 feet {6}.

To reach the very top of Bear Mountain, you'll hike an additional 0.4 mile with ascents and descents. From the top of Bear Mountain {7}, look north and you can see the San Francisco Peaks northwest of Flagstaff.

Note: The trail is fairly easy to follow and there are usually cairns placed by other hikers. The trail is rocky with exposed and extreme drop-offs in some parts — watch your footing. Take extra water in the summer as there is limited shade and it can be a hot hike.

Color Photos: Scan the QR code below for additional color photos of this trail

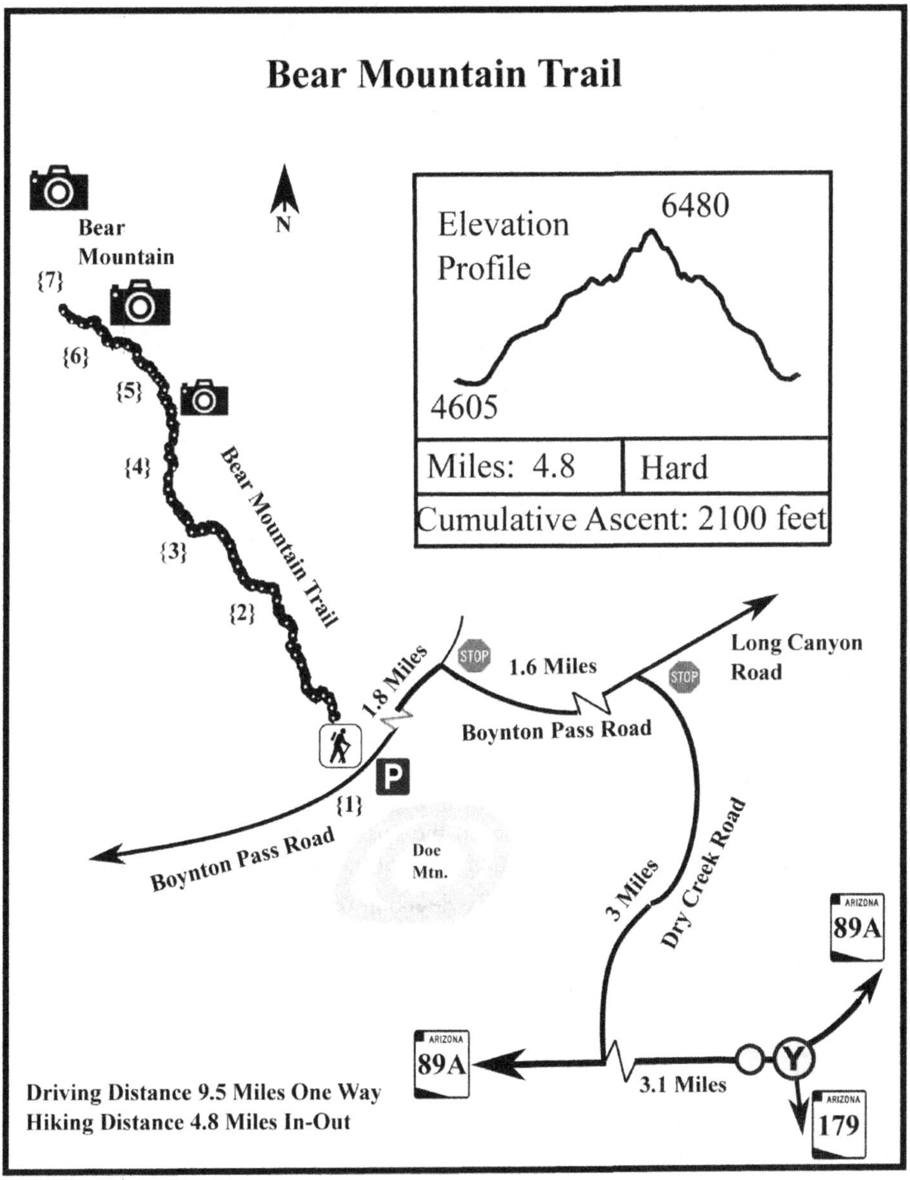

Bear Mountain Trail

Elevation Profile
6480
4605

| Miles: 4.8 | Hard |

Cumulative Ascent: 2100 feet

Bear Mountain {7}
{6}
{5}
{4}
Bear Mountain Trail
{3}
{2}
1.8 Miles
{1}
Boynton Pass Road
1.6 Miles
Boynton Pass Road
Long Canyon Road
Doe Mtn.
Dry Creek Road
3 Miles
ARIZONA 89A
3.1 Miles
ARIZONA 89A
ARIZONA 179

Driving Distance 9.5 Miles One Way
Hiking Distance 4.8 Miles In-Out

Bear Sign Trail

Summary: A beautiful in-out hike in a forested red rock canyon

Challenge Level: Moderate

Hiking Distance: About 3 miles each way or 6 miles round trip

Hiking Time: About 4 hours round trip

Trail Popularity:

Trailhead Directions: From the "Y" roundabout (see page 7), drive west toward Cottonwood on SR 89A about 3 miles. Turn right onto Dry Creek Road. Stay on Dry Creek Road for 2 miles then turn right onto Forest Road (FR) 152. Proceed to the end of FR 152 (about 4.5 miles) to the parking area on the left {1}. (34°56.236'N; 111°47.678'W) This parking area also serves the Dry Creek and Vultee Arch Trails.

Note: FR 152 is an extremely rough road beyond the 0.2 mile paved section; a high clearance vehicle and 4WD are strongly recommended.

Description: This trail was once a Favorite Trail. But because the access road (FR 152) is so difficult to navigate, it was removed from the list of favorites. It is seldom used so the trail will likely be somewhat overgrown with logs and other obstacles you must navigate. But the feeling of being alone on the forest, in the wilderness is wonderful. And you'll find many wildflowers at certain times of the year.

After you park, proceed in a northwesterly direction on the Dry Creek Trail. You'll be hiking in the forest so there is shade. The trail is relatively flat at the start then begins a gentle climb. After about 0.6 mile, you'll come to a fork where the Dry Creek Trail goes to the right and the Bear Sign Trail begins to the left {2}. Grizzly bears reportedly roamed the area until the 1930s; you may actually see signs of black bear along the trail.

Hike some 2.8 miles to the intersection of the David Miller Trail {3}. A short, but steep hike up the David Miller Trail about 0.2 mile provides a lovely view from the saddle of the ridge between Bear Sign and Secret Canyons {4}. If you'd like to hike a 6.6 mile loop, see Secret Canyon/Bear Sign Loop.

Color Photos: Scan the QR code below for additional color photos of this trail

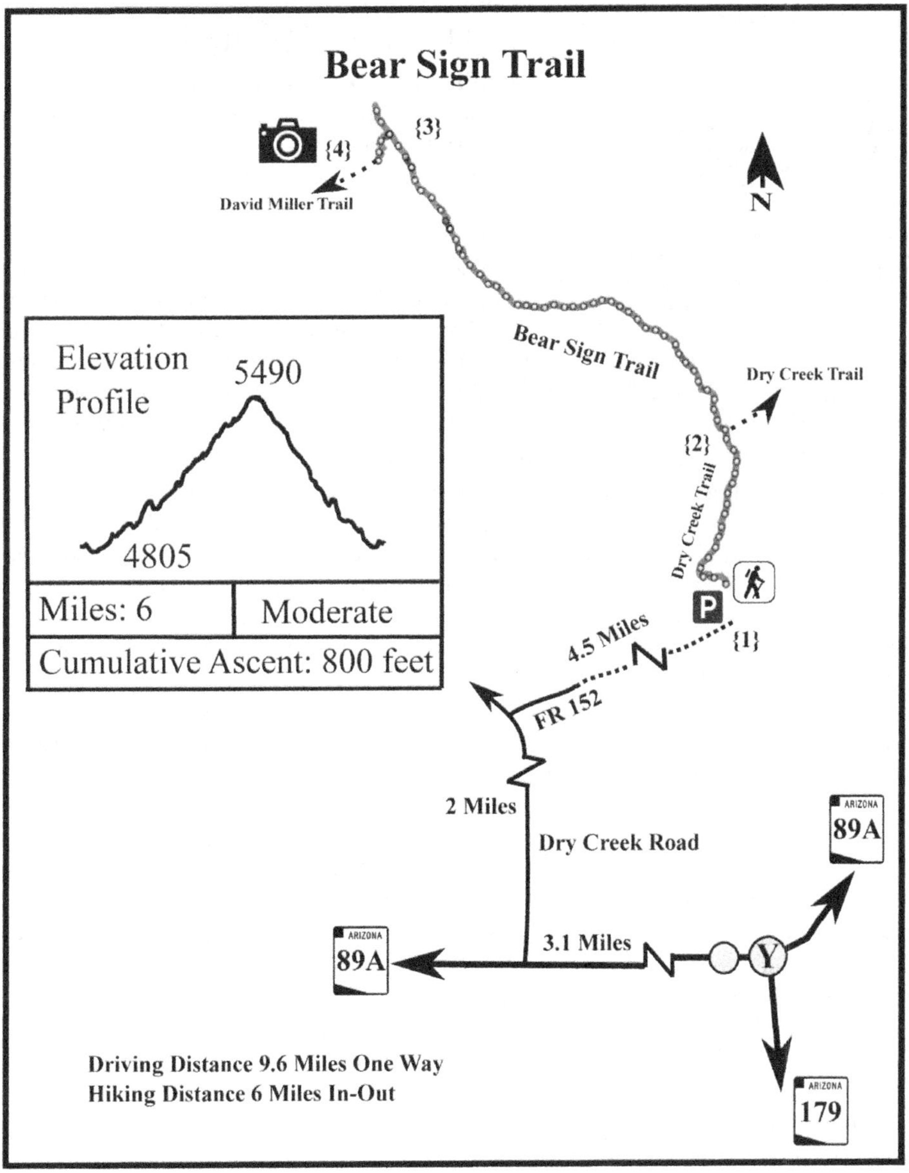

Bear Sign Trail

Elevation Profile: 5490 / 4805

Miles: 6	Moderate
Cumulative Ascent: 800 feet	

Driving Distance 9.6 Miles One Way
Hiking Distance 6 Miles In-Out

Bell Rock Climb and Bell Rock Vortex

Summary: Explore a famous Sedona rock formation and perhaps experience some vortex energy

Challenge Level: Easy but watch your footing

Hiking Distance: About 1.2 miles round trip

Hiking Time: About 1 hour round trip

Trail Popularity: 🚶🚶🚶🚶🚶

Trailhead Directions: From the "Y" roundabout (see page 7), drive south on SR 179 for about 5 miles to the parking area. After you drive about 3.2 miles, just past the Back O' Beyond roundabout, SR 179 becomes a divided highway. Continue driving south. About 1.8 miles beyond the Back O' Beyond roundabout, southbound SR 179 adds a passing lane on the left. From the passing lane, turn left at the sign for the Court House Vista parking area {1}. (34°48.350'N; 111°46.009'W) Before you turn, you'll see Bell Rock ahead of you on the left side of SR 179. This parking area also serves the Bell Rock Loop, Courthouse Butte Loop, Templeton and Llama Trails. There are toilets at the parking area. The trail starts just beyond the interpretive signboard.

Description: After you park in the Court House Vista parking area, walk past the interpretive signboard then proceed straight ahead on the Bell Rock Trail. Follow it for 0.2 mile to the intersection with the Bell Rock Pathway (BRP) Trail {2}. Continue straight ahead then make a slight left onto the Bell Rock Climb. In about 0.1 mile (and after climbing up about 65 feet), you'll intersect the Rector Connector Trail {3}. Make a right turn then continue to follow Bell Rock Climb and you'll shortly come to a large relatively flat area {4}.

You'll note that Bell Rock Climb goes to the left and right. If you go left, you'll go the east side of Bell Rock and have excellent views of Lee Mountain and Courthouse Butte. The trail becomes very narrow with large drop offs so I recommend you turn around after about 0.1 mile {5}. But take a few minutes to enjoy the views. Then return to where you came up on Bell Rock Climb and proceed to the west on the large flat area. Vortex energy has been reported all over Bell Rock so you may feel the energy. (Additional information on vortexes can be found on page 6.)

After about 0.8 mile, you'll come to a cairn and see that just beyond the cairn, there is a trail on the slick rock continuing around Bell Rock {6}. If you want to climb up to a vortex area known as the Meditation Perch, follow the slick rock around Bell Rock and you'll see the Meditation Perch ahead {7}. After you visit Meditation Perch, return to the cairn {6} then make a left turn to descend Bell Rock. You'll see Bell Rock Pathway below so make a right turn {8} then follow Bell Rock Pathway for 0.1 mile then make a left turn onto to the Bell Rock Trail {2} to return to the parking area {1}.

Note: You'll see several cairns above you high up on Bell Rock. A scramble up to these cairns requires steep climbs on smooth rocks. If you attempt, be extremely careful.

Color Photos: Scan the QR code below for additional color photos of this trail

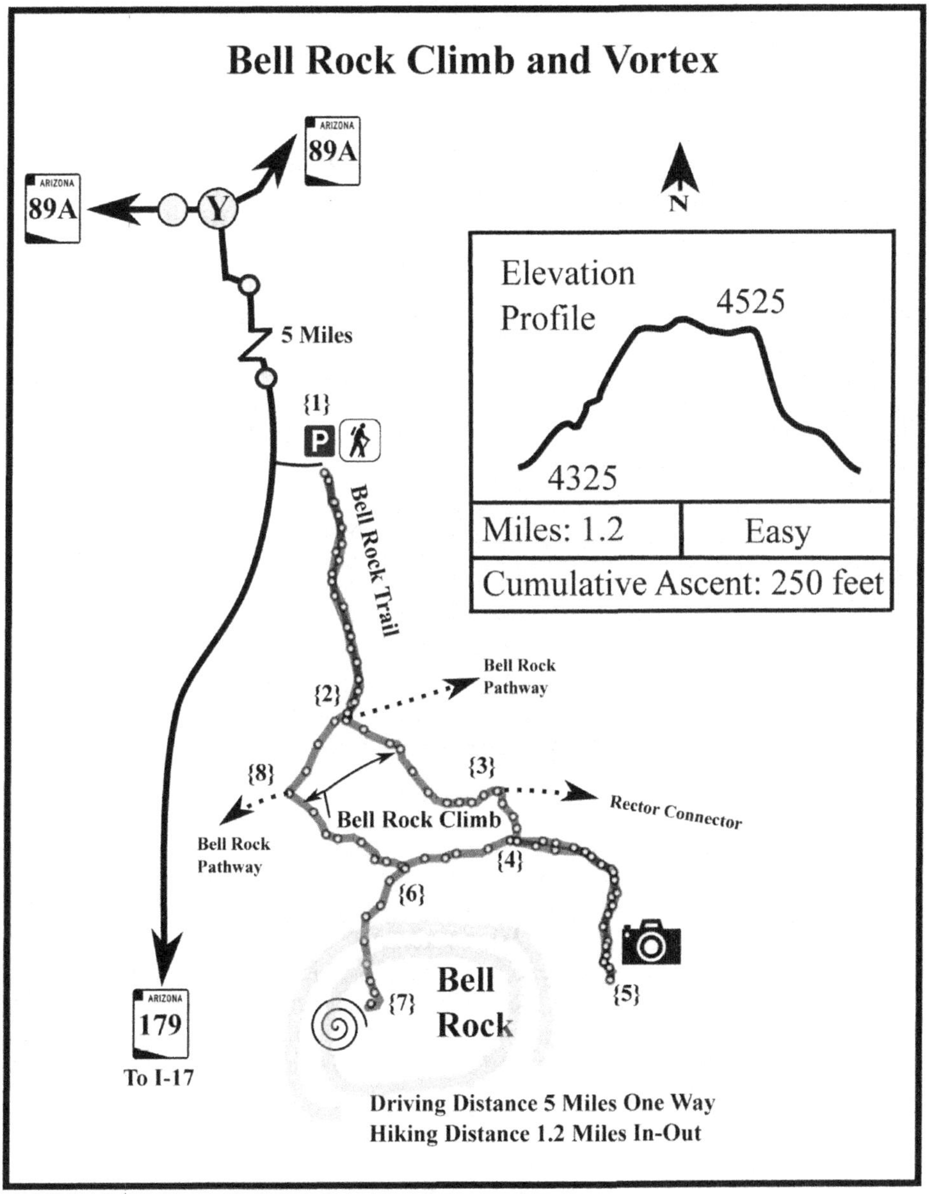

Bell Rock Climb and Vortex

Driving Distance 5 Miles One Way
Hiking Distance 1.2 Miles In-Out

29

Bell Rock Loop ★

Summary: A favorite easy loop hike that circles Bell Rock

Challenge Level: Easy

Hiking Distance: About 1.9 miles loop

Hiking Time: About 1 hour round trip

Trail Popularity:

Trailhead Directions: From the "Y" roundabout (see page 7), drive south on SR 179 for about 5 miles to the parking area. After you drive about 3.2 miles, just past the Back O' Beyond roundabout, SR 179 becomes a divided highway. Continue driving south. About 1.8 miles beyond the Back O' Beyond roundabout, southbound SR 179 adds a passing lane on the left. From the passing lane, turn left at the sign for the Court House Vista parking area {1}. (34°48.350'N; 111°46.009'W) Before you turn, you'll see Bell Rock ahead of you on the left side of SR 179. This parking area also serves the Bell Rock Climb, Courthouse Butte Loop, Templeton and Llama Trails. There are toilets at the parking area. The trail starts just beyond the interpretive signboard.

Description: After you park in the Court House Vista parking area, walk past the interpretive signboard then proceed straight ahead on the Bell Rock Trail. Follow it for 0.2 mile to the intersection with the Bell Rock Pathway (BRP) Trail {2}. Continue straight ahead and make a slight left onto the Bell Rock Climb to hike the loop in a clockwise direction. In about 0.1 mile (and after climbing up about 65 feet), you'll intersect the Rector Connector Trail {3}. Make a left turn here then continue on the Rector Connector Trail. You'll come to a nice view area in about another 0.1 mile {4} then the trail makes a left turn {5}. The views from the Rector Connector Trail are very nice throughout its length. At 1 mile, you'll intersect the Big Park Loop Trail {6}. Make a right turn then follow it for another 0.2 mile then make another right turn onto Bell Rock Pathway {7}.

Proceed on the Bell Rock Pathway for another 0.6 mile and you'll come to the western end of the Bell Rock Climb {8}. Continue on for another 0.1 mile then turn left onto the Bell Rock Trail {2} back to the parking lot {1}. If you don't mind a steep descent, hike the loop in the counterclockwise direction.

Color Photos: Scan the QR code below for additional color photos of this trail

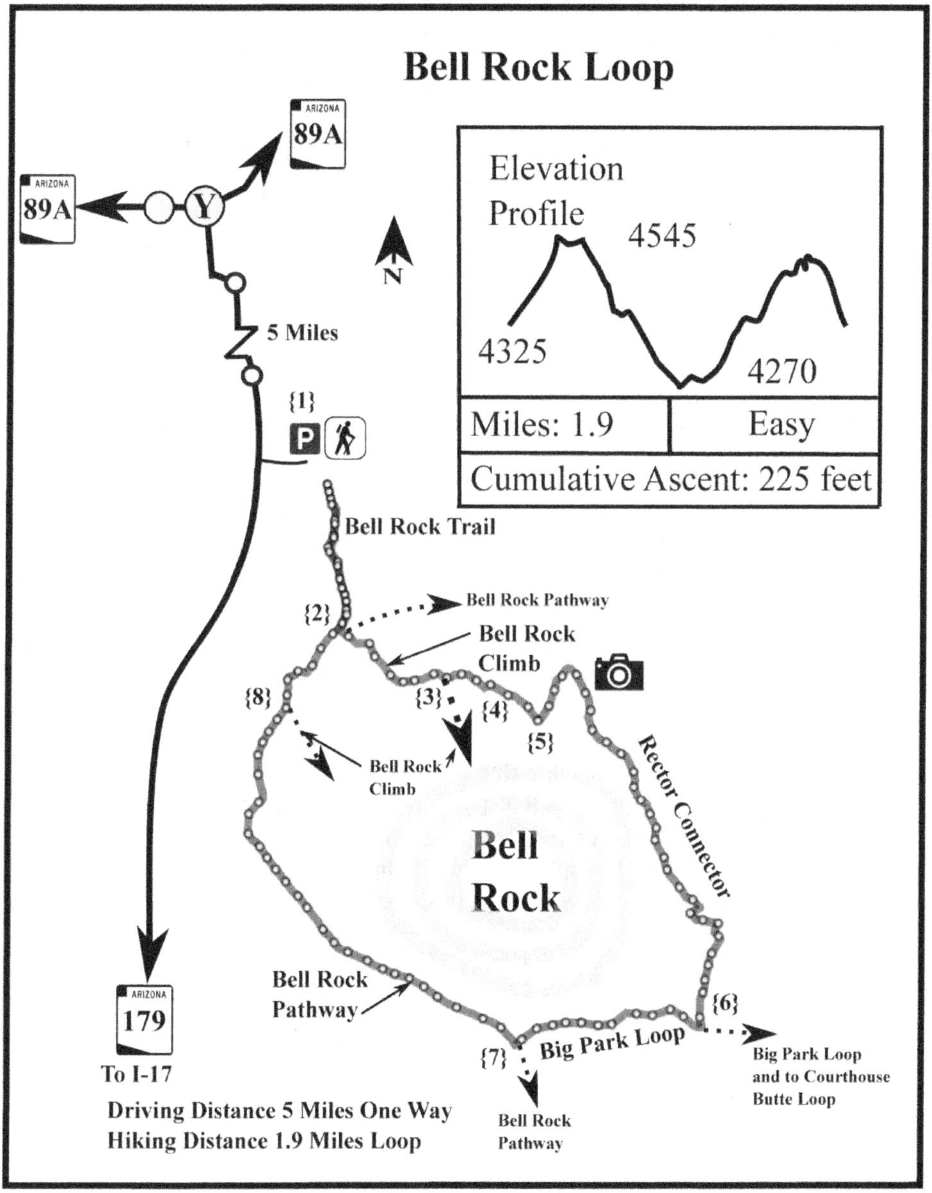

Bell Rock Loop

Elevation Profile	4545
4325	4270
Miles: 1.9	Easy
Cumulative Ascent: 225 feet	

Driving Distance 5 Miles One Way
Hiking Distance 1.9 Miles Loop

31

Bell Rock Pathway/Templeton Loop

Summary: A loop hike with views of many of Sedona's rock formations

Challenge Level: Moderate

Hiking Distance: About 4.1 miles loop

Hiking Time: About 2 1/2 hours round trip

Trail Popularity:

Trailhead Directions: From the "Y" roundabout (see page 7), drive south on SR 179 about 3.5 miles. Just past the Back O' Beyond roundabout, you'll see a Scenic View sign and a hiking sign on the right side of SR 179 and a left turn lane on the left. Turn left here then proceed to the parking area {1}. (34°49.433'N; 111°46.555'W) The parking area also serves the HT/Easy Breezy Loop and Little Horse Trail. There are toilets at the parking area. Parking is limited at these popular trails. Rather than attempting to park at the trailhead, a better choice is to take the shuttle **(see Trailhead Shuttle Service page 5)** if the parking area is full.

Description: Go past the interpretive signboard then proceed south on the Bell Rock Pathway. You'll intersect the Little Horse trail after 0.3 mile on the left {2}. In another 0.2 mile, you'll cross a footbridge and see the HT Trail sign on the right {3}. You'll be returning on the HT Trail. As you continue on the Bell Rock Pathway, you are rewarded with excellent views of Lee Mountain, Bell Rock and Courthouse Butte.

You'll intersect the Bail Trail {4} after 1.2 miles on the left. After 1.75 miles, you'll intersect the Templeton Trail on the right {5}. Turn right here onto the Templeton Trail. Follow the Templeton Trail beneath both the northbound and southbound lanes of SR 179 then you'll intersect the Easy Breezy Trail for the first time {6}. Continue on the Templeton Trail.

Look around for excellent views of Bell Rock, Courthouse Butte, Lee Mountain, Cathedral Rock and many other red rock formations. At 2.4 miles, you'll intersect the Easy Breezy Trail a second time {7}. At 2.75 miles, you'll have the best view of Cathedral Rock {8}. At 3 miles, you'll intersect the HT Trail on your right {9}. Turn right here then follow the HT Trail. You'll intersect the Easy Breezy Trail once again {10} then continue beneath both the southbound and northbound lanes of SR 179 until you intersect the Bell Rock Pathway {3} at 3.6 miles.

Make a left turn onto Bell Rock Pathway then follow it 0.5 mile back to the parking area {1}.

Color Photos: Scan the QR code below for additional color photos of this trail

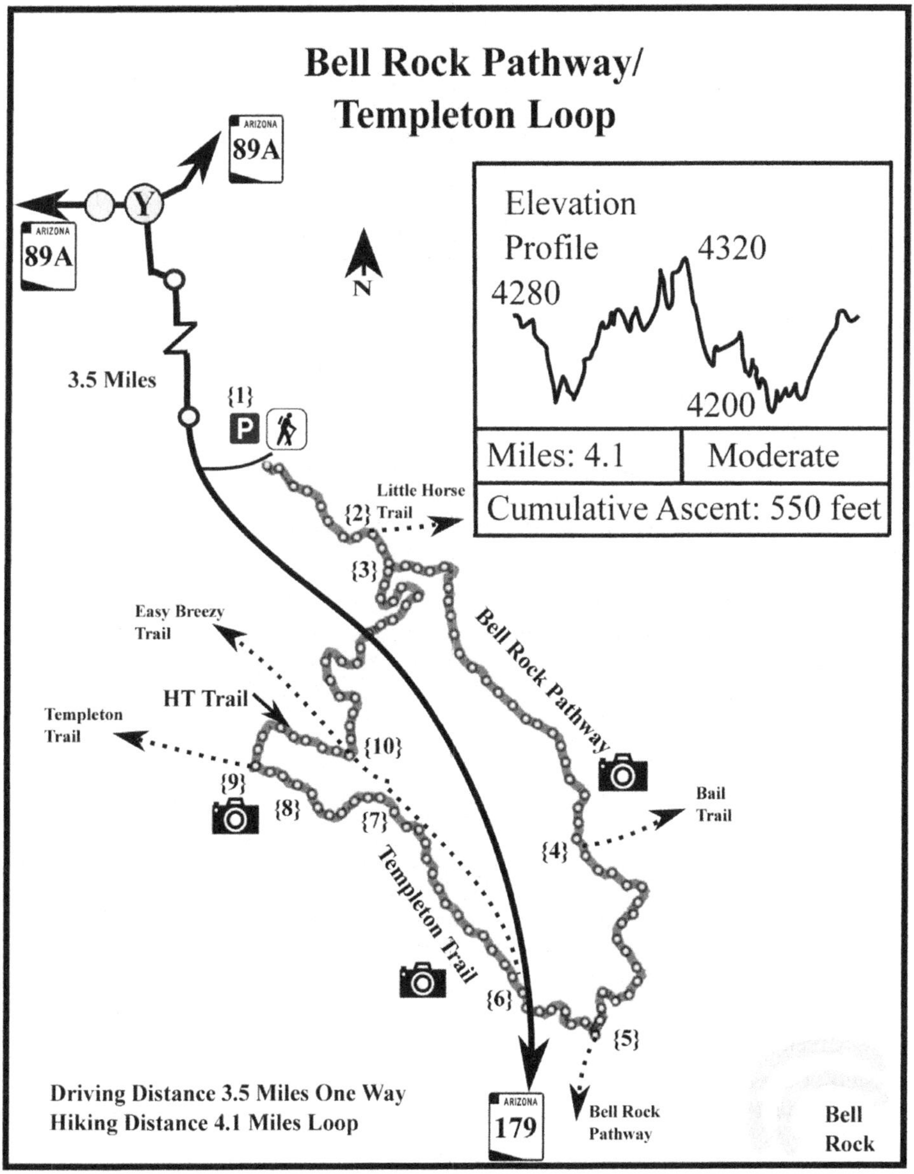

Bell Rock Pathway/ Templeton Loop

Elevation Profile 4280 4320 4200

Miles: 4.1 | Moderate

Cumulative Ascent: 550 feet

Driving Distance 3.5 Miles One Way
Hiking Distance 4.1 Miles Loop

33

Bell/Weir Trail

Summary: A sunny in-out trail that follows the path of Wet Beaver Creek with stops at a weir (a low dam) and a swimming hole

Challenge Level: Moderate

Hiking Distance: About 2.7 miles each way to the weir or 5.4 miles round trip; about 3.6 miles each way to the swimming hole or 7.2 miles round trip

Hiking Time: About 3 hours round trip to the weir; about 4 hours round trip to the swimming hole

Trail Popularity:

Trailhead Directions: From the "Y" roundabout (see page 7), drive south on SR 179 about 14.8 miles until it intersects Interstate 17. Continue under I-17 then proceed straight on Forest Road 618 for 2 miles then turn left at the sign for the Beaver Creek Work Center. Follow the road a short distance to the parking area {1}. (34°40.457'N; 111°42.795'W) There are toilets at the trailhead.

Description: This can be a very hot hike in the summer as there is no shade for most of the hike. To reach the Weir Trail, go through the gate at the parking area then follow the sometimes rocky Bell Trail east along Wet Beaver Creek. About a mile from the parking area, look for a large rock on the left covered with petroglyphs placed there by Native Americans hundreds of years ago {2}.

You will come across several trails as you hike along. The first one is the White Mesa Trail at about 1.75 miles {3}, followed by the Apache Maid Trail at 2.25 miles {4}. After 2.4 miles, you'll come to a large signboard and a fork {5}. Go right for 0.3 mile on the Weir Trail to reach the weir {6}. This is a good spot to take a break in the shade then return to the parking area for a 5.4 mile hike.

If you wish to visit a swimming hole known locally as The Crack, return to the fork in the trail {5} then continue to the east on the Bell Trail for about 1 mile to a sign for Bell Crossing {7}. The red rock views are very good along this part of the trail but there are places where the trail is narrow and there are large drop-offs. You'll see and hear Wet Beaver Creek on the right below.

Turn left at the sign then follow the faint trail north for 0.2 mile to The Crack {8}. At The Crack, Wet Beaver Creek is quite deep and this spot is a local favorite place for swimming.

Color Photos: Scan the QR code below for additional color photos of this trail

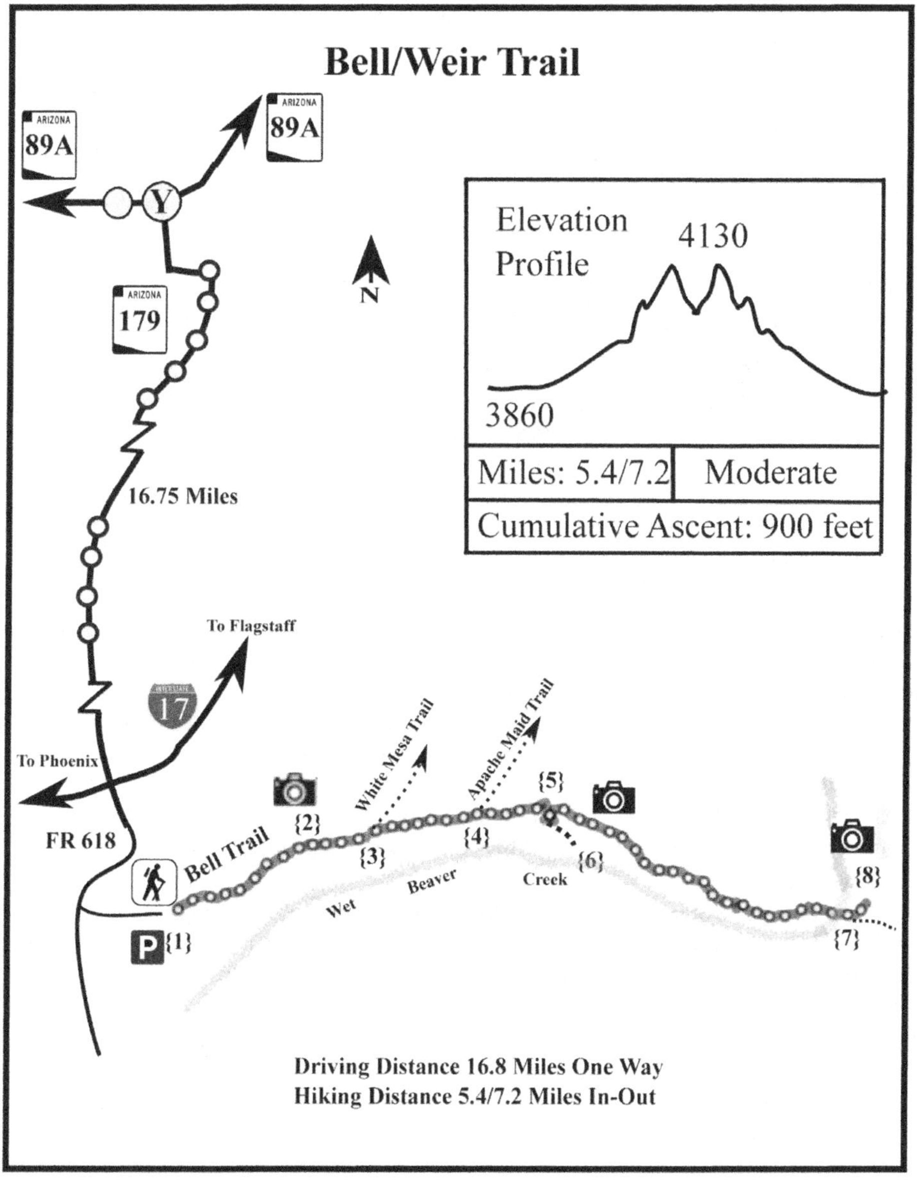

Bell/Weir Trail

Elevation Profile
4130
3860

Miles: 5.4/7.2 | Moderate
Cumulative Ascent: 900 feet

Driving Distance 16.8 Miles One Way
Hiking Distance 5.4/7.2 Miles In-Out

Boynton Canyon and Boynton Vortex ★

Summary: A favorite in-out hike to a famous Sedona vortex area then into a forested canyon with nice red rock views

Challenge Level: Easy for the vortex hike; Moderate for the canyon hike

Hiking Distance: About 0.6 miles each way or 1.2 miles round trip for the vortex; about 3.2 miles each way or 6.4 miles round trip for the canyon hike

Hiking Time: About 1 hour round trip for the vortex; about 3 1/2 hours round trip for the canyon hike

Trail Popularity: 🚶🚶🚶🚶

Trailhead Directions: From the "Y" roundabout (see page 7), drive west toward Cottonwood on SR 89A about 3 miles. Turn right onto Dry Creek Road. Stay on Dry Creek Road to a stop sign (about 3 miles) then turn left onto Boynton Pass Road. Proceed about 1.6 miles to a stop sign. Turn right, the trailhead parking is about 0.1 mile on the right {1}. (34°54.456'N; 111°50.928'W) There are toilets at the parking area.

Description: Boynton Canyon was named for John Boeington who was a horse rancher in the canyon around 1886. Boynton Canyon is a very popular trail. The nicest part of the trail is located beyond the Enchantment Resort. It has summer shade and good red rock views. It is also a well-known vortex site. After hiking about 0.25 mile from the parking area, you'll see a sign for the Boynton Vista Trail to the right {2}. Hike the Vista Trail for about 0.4 mile slightly uphill to two tall rock formations, both of which are considered vortexes {3}. You'll be hiking up about 225 feet to the vortexes. Kachina Woman is to the east; the Warrior is to the west. (Additional information on vortexes can be found on page 6.)

After visiting the vortexes, return to the Boynton Canyon Trail then continue to the north. The trail beside the Enchantment Resort is rocky and narrow, and is the most difficult part of the trail. Once you are past the Enchantment Resort, the trail widens and follows the canyon floor.

Just after you come to the end of the Enchantment Resort property, you can see evidence of prior habitation high up on the right {4}. Soon you'll enter a forest where the trail and views are excellent, although some of the views are blocked by the trees. You'll see some nice fall colors usually during the third or fourth week of October about 2.5 miles from the trailhead. The trail ends in a box canyon after a steep climb at the base of Secret Mountain {5}.

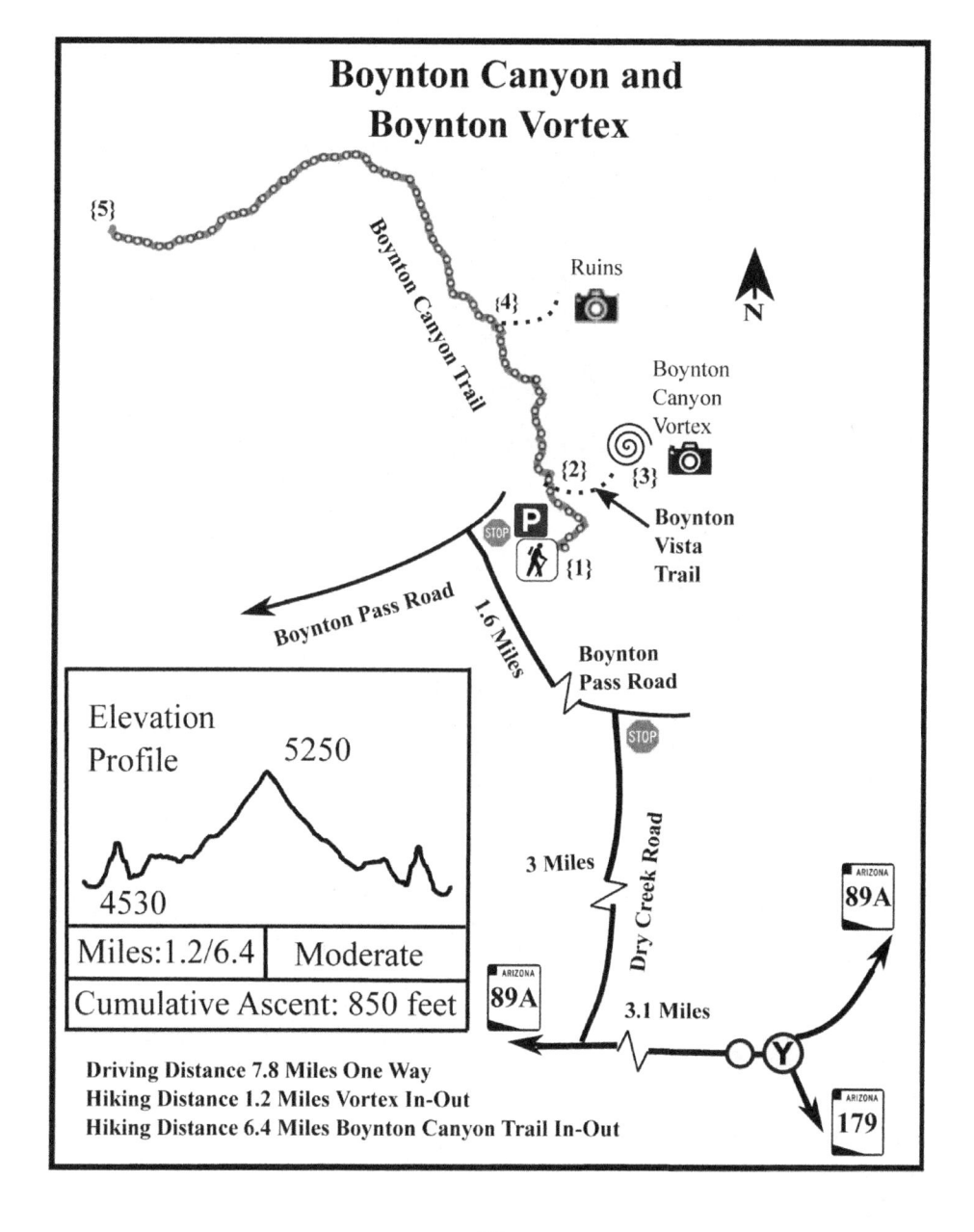

Color Photos: Scan the QR code below for additional color photos of this trail

Boynton Canyon and Boynton Vortex

{5}

Boynton Canyon Trail

{4} Ruins

Boynton Canyon Vortex

{2} {3}

Boynton Vista Trail

{1}

Boynton Pass Road

1.6 Miles

Boynton Pass Road

Elevation Profile
5250
4530

Miles: 1.2/6.4	Moderate
Cumulative Ascent: 850 feet	

3 Miles

Dry Creek Road

ARIZONA 89A

ARIZONA 89A

3.1 Miles

Y

ARIZONA 179

Driving Distance 7.8 Miles One Way
Hiking Distance 1.2 Miles Vortex In-Out
Hiking Distance 6.4 Miles Boynton Canyon Trail In-Out

Brins Mesa Trail

Summary: An in-out hike to the top of a beautiful mesa with red rock views all around or a two-vehicle hike

Challenge Level: Moderate

Hiking Distance: About 3.9 miles from the Jordan Road trailhead to the FR 152 trailhead or 7.8 miles round trip

Hiking Time: About ¾ hour to the mesa top; about 4 hours round trip between the two trailheads

Trail Popularity: 🚶🚶

Trailhead Directions: This trail has two trailheads, one accessed from Jordan Road and the second off Forest Road (FR) 152. To access the Jordan Road trailhead, from the "Y" roundabout (see page 7), drive north on SR 89A about 0.3 mile to the Jordan Road roundabout. Take the third exit onto Jordan Road then drive to the end. Turn left onto West Park Ridge. Drive 0.3 miles then proceed through the paved cul-de-sac, continuing on the dirt road for 0.5 mile to the main parking area {1}. (34°53.287'N; 111°46.098'W) This parking area also serves the Brins Mesa Overlook, Cibola, Jim Thompson and Jordan Trails. There are toilets at the parking area. Note: The dirt road is rough with potholes. A high clearance vehicle is recommended.

To access the second trailhead off Forest Road (FR) 152, from the "Y" roundabout, drive west on SR 89A toward Cottonwood about 3 miles. Turn right onto Dry Creek Road. Stay on Dry Creek Road for 2 miles then turn right onto FR 152. Proceed for 2.5 miles to the parking area on your right {4}. (34°55.008'N; 111°48.525'W)

Note: FR 152 is an extremely rough road beyond the 0.2 mile paved section; a high clearance vehicle and 4WD are strongly recommended.

Description: The trail begins on the west side of the parking area {1}. As you begin the hike up to Brins Mesa, you are rewarded with some outstanding views. You'll be hiking up 1.5 miles and about 550 feet to reach the edge of the mesa. The trail becomes much steeper as you approach it. Once you reach the edge of the mesa {2}, you'll enjoy views all around. Look to the right for the faint trail to the Brins Mesa Overlook (see Brins Mesa Overlook Trail). Continue straight ahead to hike to the second trailhead on FR 152, which is about another 2.4 miles away. After hiking about 1 mile, you'll intersect the Soldier Pass Trail {3}.

Hiking from the trailhead on FR 152 {4} is a pleasant, moderate uphill hike through trees. If possible, you may want to do this hike with two vehicles, one parked at each trailhead.

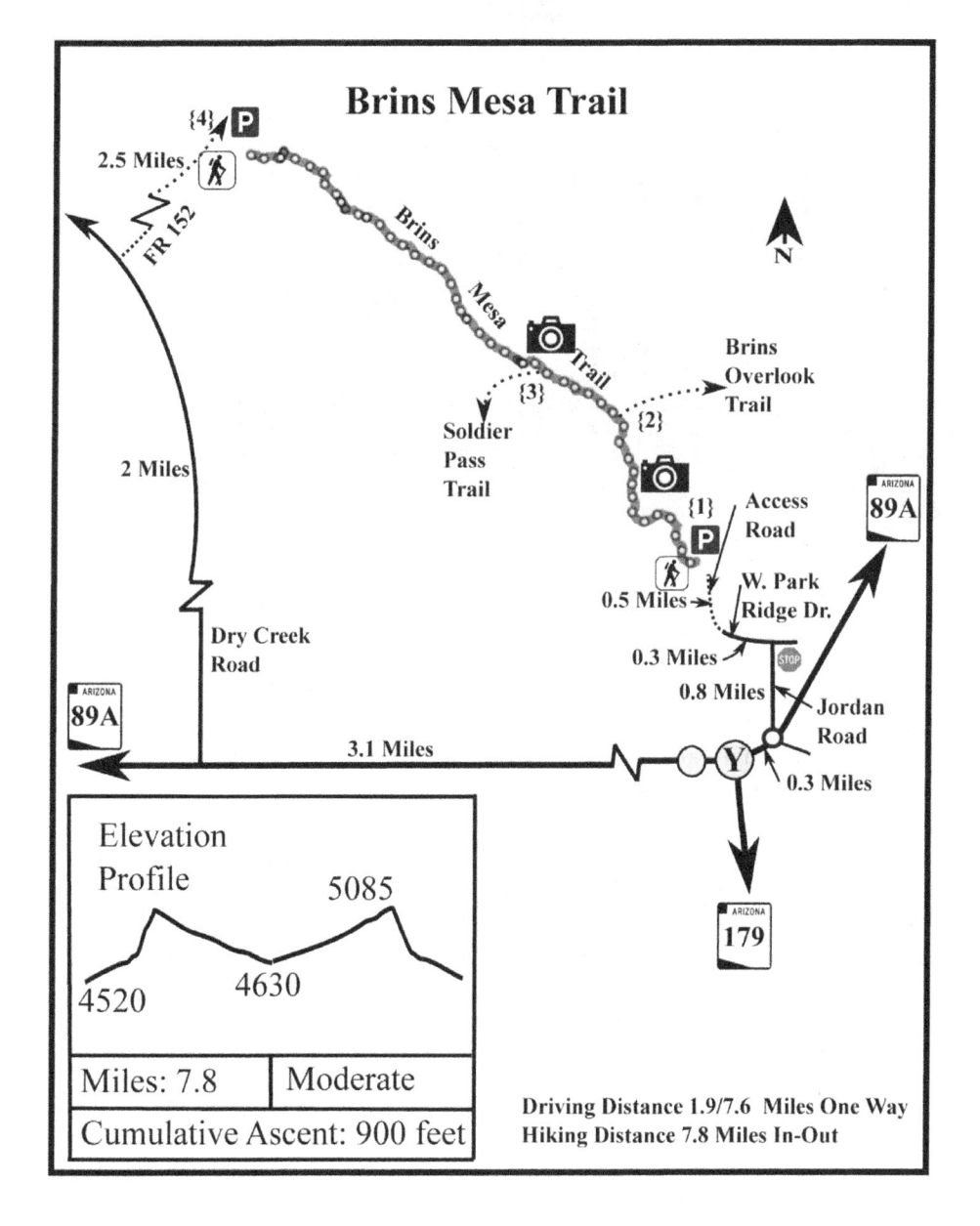

Color Photos: Scan the QR code below for additional color photos of this trail

Brins Mesa Trail

{4} P
2.5 Miles
FR 152
Brins Mesa Trail
{3}
Soldier Pass Trail
{2}
Brins Overlook Trail
{1}
Access Road
W. Park Ridge Dr.
0.5 Miles
0.3 Miles
0.8 Miles
Jordan Road
0.3 Miles
2 Miles
Dry Creek Road
ARIZONA 89A
ARIZONA 89A
3.1 Miles
ARIZONA 179
N

Elevation Profile
5085
4630
4520

Miles: 7.8	Moderate
Cumulative Ascent: 900 feet	

Driving Distance 1.9/7.6 Miles One Way
Hiking Distance 7.8 Miles In-Out

Brins Mesa Overlook Trail ★

Summary: A favorite hike up to a beautiful mesa then on to a knoll with red rock views all around.

Challenge Level: Moderate

Hiking Distance: About 1.5 miles each way to the top of Brins Mesa or 3 miles round trip; add 0.7 mile one way to the overlook or 4.4 miles round trip

Hiking Time: About 2 1/2 hours round trip

Trail Popularity:

Trailhead Directions: From the "Y" roundabout (see page 7), drive north on SR 89A about 0.3 mile to the Jordan Road roundabout. Take the third exit onto Jordan Road then drive to the end. Turn left onto West Park Ridge. Drive 0.3 miles then proceed through the paved cul-de-sac, continuing on the dirt road for 0.5 mile to the main parking area {1}. (34°53.287'N; 111°46.098'W) This parking area also serves the Brins Mesa, Cibola, Jim Thompson and Jordan Trails. There are toilets at the parking area. Note: The dirt road is rough with potholes. A high clearance vehicle is recommended.

Description: The trail begins on the west side of the parking area {1}. As you begin the hike up to Brins Mesa, you are rewarded with some outstanding views. You'll be hiking up 1.5 miles and about 550 feet to reach the edge of the mesa. The trail becomes much steeper as you approach it.

Immediately after you reach the mesa {2}, look for a faint trail to your right. You'll follow this trail for 0.2 mile then bear left at a fork in the trail {3}. If you go right, you'll shortly come to a scenic outcropping of red rock, which has a nice view {4}. As you continue along the left fork, the trail continues to gently rise then narrows as it follows the north side of Brins Mesa. You'll soon see the overlook ahead. A moderate amount of scrambling is needed to reach the top of the knoll, but the climb is well worth the effort. Once on top, there is a spectacular view overlooking Mormon Canyon {5}. Look high up on the rock face to the southeast. If you are lucky, that's where you may see Angel Falls flowing with the spring snow melt.

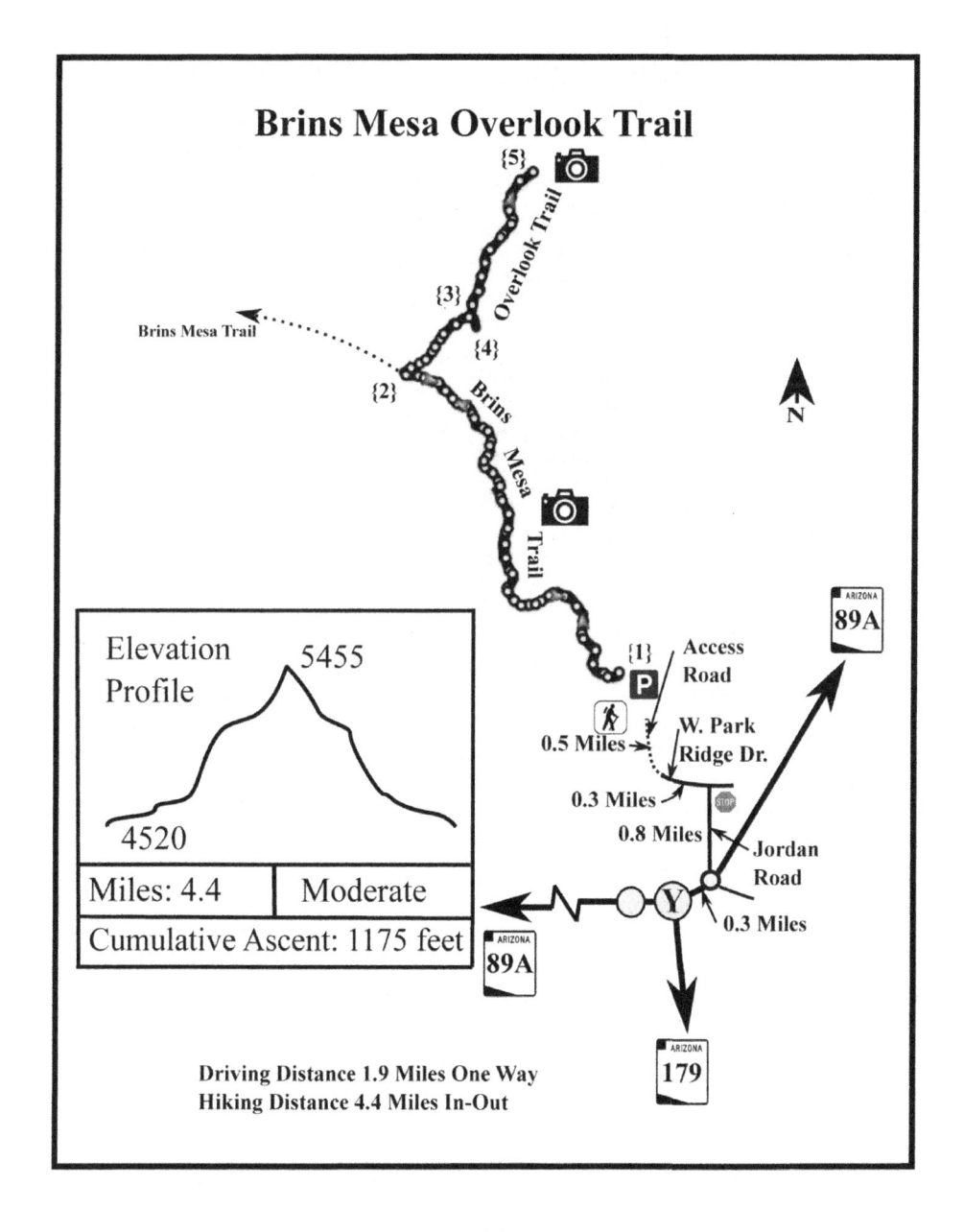

Color Photos: Scan the QR code below for additional color photos of this trail

Brins Mesa Overlook Trail

{5} Overlook Trail

{3}
{4}

Brins Mesa Trail
{2}

Brins Mesa Trail

{1} Access Road

W. Park Ridge Dr.
0.5 Miles
0.3 Miles
0.8 Miles

ARIZONA 89A

Jordan Road
0.3 Miles

ARIZONA 89A

ARIZONA 179

Elevation Profile
5455
4520

Miles: 4.4	Moderate
Cumulative Ascent: 1175 feet	

Driving Distance 1.9 Miles One Way
Hiking Distance 4.4 Miles In-Out

41

Brins Mesa/Soldier Pass Loop ★

Summary: A favorite loop hike to the top of a beautiful mesa then down past several Sedona landmarks with red rock views all around

Challenge Level: Moderate

Hiking Distance: About 5 miles loop

Hiking Time: About 3 hours round trip

Trail Popularity: 🚶🚶 🚶🚶

Trailhead Directions: From the "Y" roundabout (see page 7), drive north on SR 89A about 0.3 mile to the Jordan Road roundabout. Take the third exit onto Jordan Road then drive to the end. Turn left onto West Park Ridge. Drive 0.3 miles then proceed through the paved cul-de-sac, continuing on the dirt road for 0.5 mile to the main parking area{1}. (34°53.287'N; 111°46.098'W) This parking area also serves the Brins Mesa, Brins Mesa Overlook, Cibola, Jordan and Jim Thompson Trails. There are toilets at the parking area. Note: The dirt road is rough with potholes. A high clearance vehicle is recommended.

Description: You'll actually be hiking 4 trails to complete this loop hike. The Brins Mesa Trail begins on the west side of the parking area {1}. As you begin the hike up to Brins Mesa, you are rewarded with some outstanding views. At 0.6 mile, you'll have a view of Brins Mesa ahead {2}. At 1 mile, you'll cross a fairly large wash {3} then begin a rather steep ascent. Just beyond the wash there is a nice place to stop and take a rest {4}. You'll be hiking up about 550 feet to reach the edge of the mesa {5}. Once you reach the edge of the mesa {5}, you'll enjoy views all around. Continue straight ahead. The trail here is a gentle descent but is very rocky. After hiking about 1 mile, you'll intersect the Soldier Pass Trail {6}. Turn left here.

As you begin the Soldier Pass Trail, there is a nice place to stop and take a break at the 2.3 mile mark {7}. From here, the trail descends rather steeply. At 2.5 miles look to the left for a view of the Soldier Pass Arches {8}. You'll come to a social trail that leads to the arches after 2.8 miles {9} but, be advised, this trail is steep with drop offs so be extremely careful if you attempt to go to the arches. At 2.9 miles, the trail makes a left turn out of a wash {10}.

At 3.6 miles, you'll come to the Seven Sacred Pools, which usually have water in them, even when it hasn't rained for some time {11}. In another 0.3 mile, you'll come to the Devil's Kitchen, a very large sink hole {12}. Continue in an easterly direction then continue onto the Jordan Trail. At 4.3 miles, you'll intersect the Cibola Trail {13}. Continue on the Cibola Trail for another 0.7 mile to return to the parking area where you started.

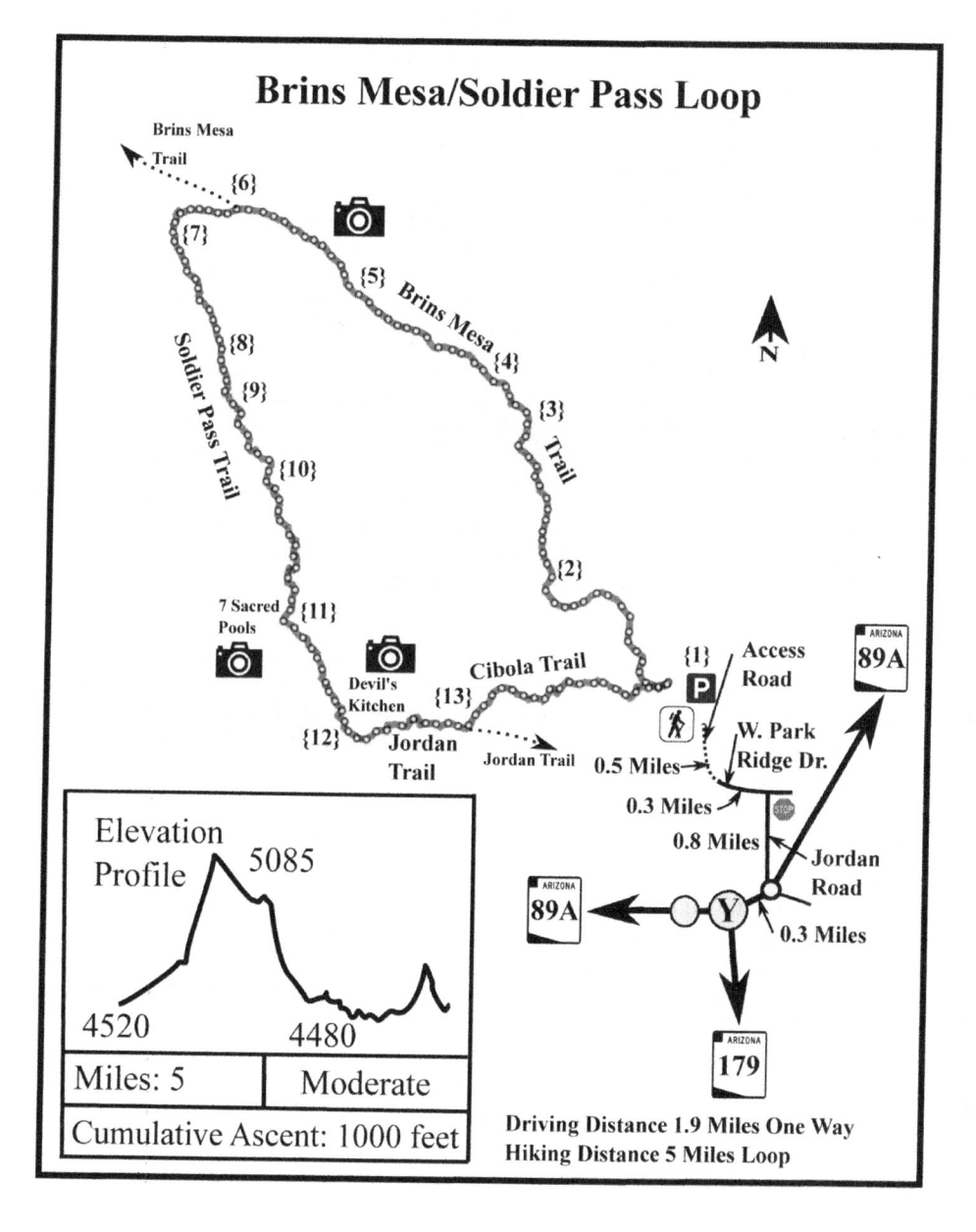

Color Photos: Scan the QR code below for additional color photos of this trail

Brins Mesa/Soldier Pass Loop

Brins Mesa Trail
{6}
{7}
{5} Brins Mesa
{8} {4}
{9}
{3}
Soldier Pass Trail
{10}
{2}
7 Sacred Pools {11}
Devil's Kitchen {13} Cibola Trail {1} Access Road
{12} Jordan Trail
Jordan Trail Jordan Trail 0.5 Miles W. Park Ridge Dr.
0.3 Miles
0.8 Miles
ARIZONA 89A
ARIZONA 89A
Jordan Road
Y
0.3 Miles
ARIZONA 179

Elevation Profile 5085
4520 4480

Miles: 5 | Moderate
Cumulative Ascent: 1000 feet

Driving Distance 1.9 Miles One Way
Hiking Distance 5 Miles Loop

43

Broken Arrow/Submarine Rock Loop ★

Summary: A favorite sunny, picturesque loop hike to the Devil's Dining Room, Submarine Rock and Chicken Point

Challenge Level: Moderate

Hiking Distance:
About 1.5 miles each way to Chicken Point or 3 miles round trip; about 4 miles round trip if you hike the loop to Submarine Rock then Chicken Point and return

Hiking Time: About 2 1/2 hours round trip

Trail Popularity:
🚶🚶🚶🚶

Trailhead Directions: From the "Y" roundabout (see page 7), drive south on SR 179 for 1.5 miles to the roundabout at Morgan Road. Take the third exit then proceed on Morgan Road. Drive about 0.6 mile to the trailhead parking on your left (the last part is a dirt road) {1}. (34°50.738'N; 111°45.424'W) This parking area also serves the Marg's Draw Trail. There is room for about 25 vehicles in the parking area.

Description: The trail is named for the movie, *Broken Arrow,* which was filmed in the area in 1950. From the parking area, go south across the jeep road to the trail. Initially, the trail essentially parallels the jeep road. About 0.2 mile from the parking area, you'll intersect the Hog Wash Trail and in another 75 feet, the Twin Buttes Trail. After hiking about 0.4 mile, watch for a fence on the right which surrounds a large sinkhole known as the Devil's Dining Room {2}. As you continue along the trail, after about another 0.4 mile you'll come to a sign and a fork in the trail {3}. Continue to the right on the Broken Arrow Trail for another 0.7 mile to Chicken Point or turn left to go to Submarine Rock.

Submarine rock is a very large rock formation with panoramic views all around. While you can scramble up on the north end, I prefer to hike around to the south end where it is easy to get on the top of Submarine Rock. To get to Chicken Point from the south end of Submarine Rock, look down and you'll see where the Pink Jeeps park. Go down to that parking area then follow the jeep road southwest to Chicken Point. Be sure to stay out of the way of the jeeps as you hike along this narrow road.

Chicken Point is named for thrill-seeking jeep drivers who once dared to drive close to the edge of the point (jeep access is no longer permitted on Chicken Point). If you look to the south, you'll see a chicken-shaped rock high up on the red rock cliff. Chicken Point is a nice place for a snack break as the views are outstanding {5}. You'll likely encounter some Pink Jeeps as the Broken Arrow tour brings many visitors to this beautiful area.

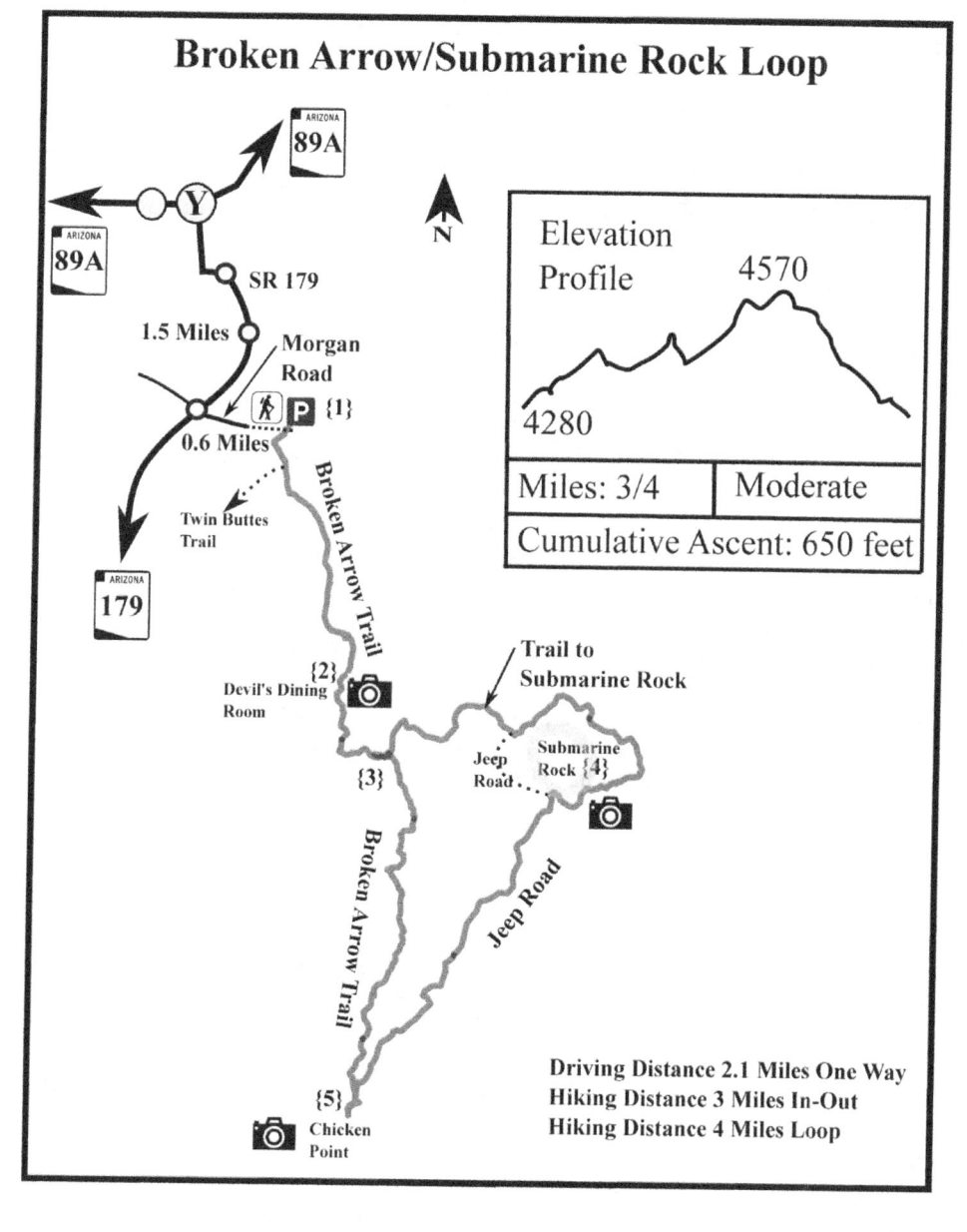

Color Photos: Scan the QR code below for additional color photos of this trail

Broken Arrow/Submarine Rock Loop

- ARIZONA 89A
- Y
- ARIZONA 89A
- SR 179
- 1.5 Miles
- Morgan Road
- P {1}
- 0.6 Miles
- Twin Buttes Trail
- ARIZONA 179
- Broken Arrow Trail
- {2} Devil's Dining Room
- Trail to Submarine Rock
- {3}
- Jeep Road
- Submarine Rock {4}
- Broken Arrow Trail
- Jeep Road
- {5} Chicken Point

Elevation Profile
4570
4280

| Miles: 3/4 | Moderate |

| Cumulative Ascent: 650 feet |

Driving Distance 2.1 Miles One Way
Hiking Distance 3 Miles In-Out
Hiking Distance 4 Miles Loop

Canyon of Fools/Mescal Loop

Summary: An in-out or loop hike through a unique landscape with great red rock views of Mescal Mountain and Boynton Canyon

Challenge Level: Moderate

Hiking Distance: About a 2.6 mile in-out hike or a 3 mile loop

Hiking Time: About 1 ½ hours round trip for the in-out hike; about 2 hours for the loop hike round trip

Trail Popularity:

Trailhead Directions:
From the "Y" roundabout (see page 7), drive west toward Cottonwood on SR 89A about 3 miles. Turn right onto Dry Creek Road. Stay on Dry Creek Road to a stop sign (about 3 miles) then turn left onto Boynton Pass Road. Proceed about 0.6 mile to a small unmarked parking area on the right {1}. (34°53.758'N; 111°50.206'W) There is room for about 4 vehicles here on the north side of Boynton Pass Road and room for about 4 vehicles on the south side (where the Dawa Trail begins). The trail begins on the north side of the road.

Description: I like this trail because for the first 0.4 mile, the terrain is so different from other trails. But you must be alert for mountain bikers around several blind corners. Shortly beyond the trail marker, turn right then follow a narrow canyon with high walls for about 0.4 mile. This is the "Fools" part of the canyon. You'll note that the mountain bikers sometimes take a path parallel to the trail so you'll be hiking a combination of the trail and biker path. As you continue north, you'll intersect the Yucca Trail after 0.5 mile and begin to have excellent views of Mescal Mountain ahead {2}. Make a sharp left turn (west) here to continue on the Canyon of Fools Trail. You'll soon be in a forest of junipers and pinyon pines and come to a nice spot for a break at 1.1 miles {3}. You'll intersect the Mescal Trail after 1.3 miles {4}. Return the same way for a 2.6 mile hike.

If you want to hike a loop, turn right at {4} then follow the Mescal Trail. This part of the Mescal Trail provides wonderful up-close views of Mescal Mountain. You'll find signs indicating Difficult and Extreme portions of the trail for the mountain bikers. I recommend you hike the Difficult path. After 0.7 mile, turn right onto the Yucca Trail {5}. You have great panoramic views of Mescal Mountain for the first 0.3 mile. Follow the Yucca Trail for 0.4 mile to the intersection with the Canyon of Fools Trail {2}. Turn left (south) here then follow the Canyon of Fools Trail back to the parking area for a 3 mile hike.

Note: Stay alert for mountain bikers in front of and behind you in the "Fools" part of the canyon because it is very narrow in places and there are several blind corners. Do not hike the Canyon of Fools Trail after a hard rain as the narrow canyon may be filled with fast moving water.

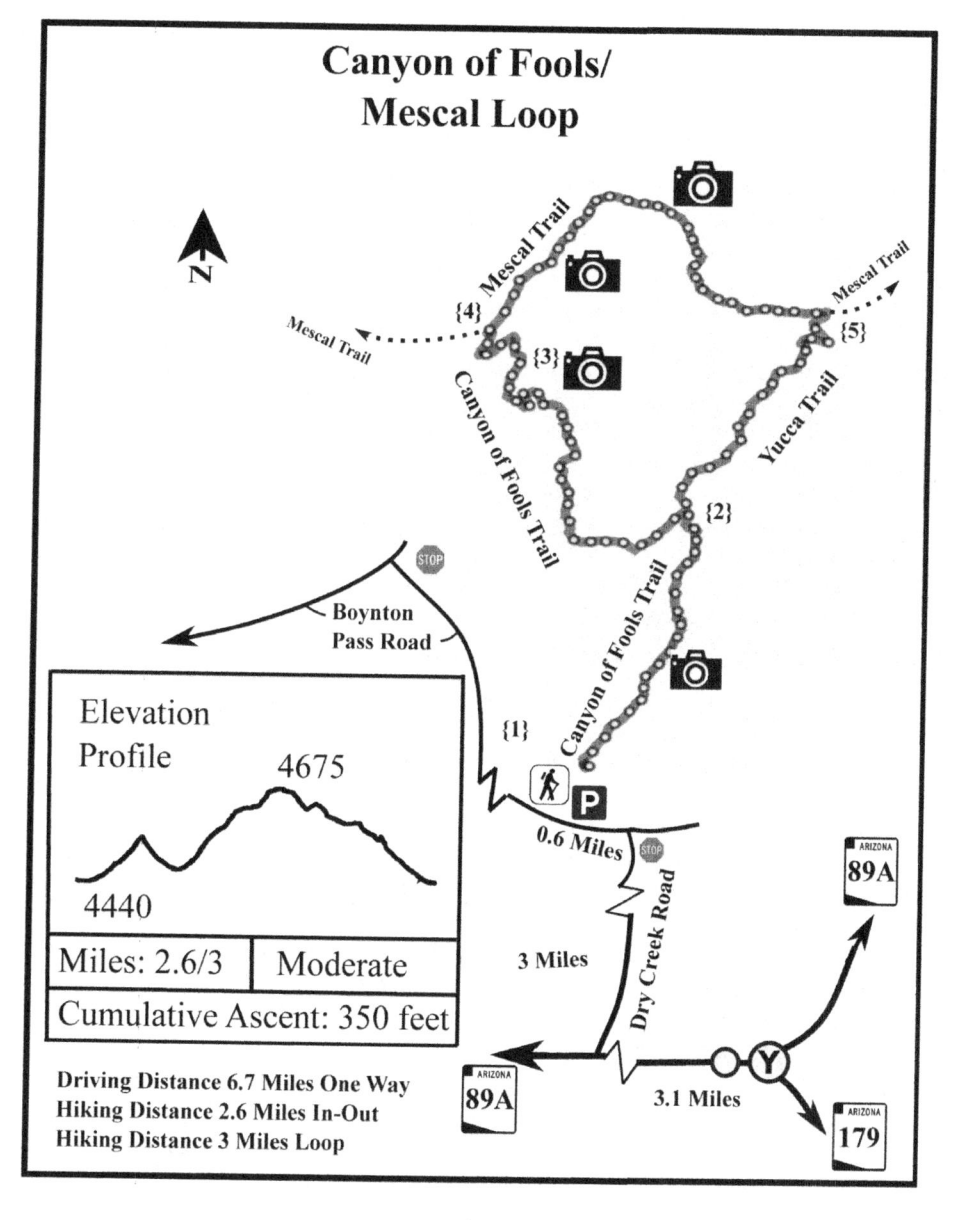

Color Photos: Scan the QR code below for additional color photos of this trail

Canyon of Fools/ Mescal Loop

Elevation Profile

4675

4440

| Miles: 2.6/3 | Moderate |

Cumulative Ascent: 350 feet

Driving Distance 6.7 Miles One Way
Hiking Distance 2.6 Miles In-Out
Hiking Distance 3 Miles Loop

47

Cathedral Rock Trail and Cathedral Vortex Trail ★

Summary: A favorite steep, sunny in-out hike to the saddle of Cathedral Rock for spectacular views all around and the location of one of Sedona's famous vortex sites

Challenge Level: Hard

Hiking Distance: About 0.75 miles each way or 1.5 miles round trip

Hiking Time: About 1 ½ hours round trip

Trail Popularity: 🚶🚶🚶

Trailhead Directions: From the "Y" roundabout (see page 7), drive south on SR 179 about 3.2 miles to the Back O' Beyond roundabout. Take the first exit then go west on the Back O' Beyond Road for about 0.75 mile. The main parking area with 18 spots and the overflow parking area with 22 spots are on your left {1}. (34°49.523'N; 111°47.303'W)

Parking is very limited and fills up fast at this popular trail. Arrive as early as you can. If you are hiking Thursday thru Sunday, you must take the shuttle because the parking area is closed. **(see Trailhead Shuttle Service page 5)** or park at a nearby trailhead (see Baldwin Loop or HT/Easy Breezy Loop) if the parking lot is full.

Description: The first part of the hike is relatively easy – the last part is a steep, strenuous hike. The trail begins on the west side of the main parking area on Back 'O Beyond Road. You'll start out crossing a dry creek bed. Continue climbing up until the trail intersects the Templeton Trail {2}. Turn right then go about 60 paces to the continuation of the Cathedral Rock Trail on your left {3}.

From here, the trail becomes very steep. Hiking boots or other footwear with good traction is recommended. Once you arrive at the saddle of Cathedral Rock {4}, you are at the location of one of four main vortex sites in Sedona. (Additional information on vortexes can be found on page 6.)

There are short trails along the south side of the east and west rock formations that lead to some good views, although the footing can be tricky.

Note: If heights, an extremely steep trail or tenuous footing bothers you, or the trail is wet or snowy (making it slippery), I do not recommend this trail.

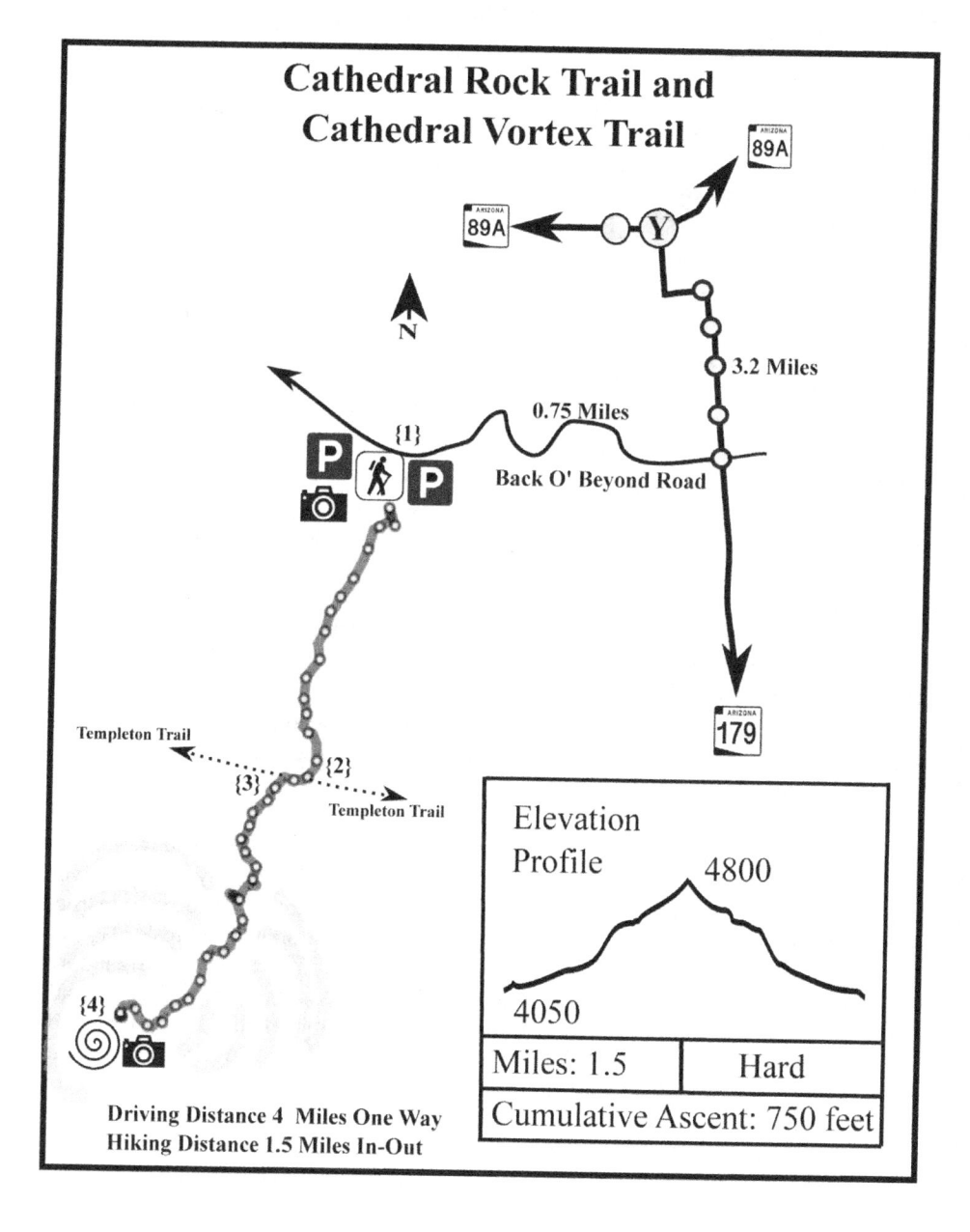

Color Photos: Scan the QR code below for additional color photos of this trail

Cathedral Rock Trail and Cathedral Vortex Trail

89A

89A

N

3.2 Miles

0.75 Miles

{1}

Back O' Beyond Road

179

Templeton Trail

{2}
{3}

Templeton Trail

{4}

Elevation Profile
4800
4050

| Miles: 1.5 | Hard |

Cumulative Ascent: 750 feet

Driving Distance 4 Miles One Way
Hiking Distance 1.5 Miles In-Out

49

Chimney Rock Lower Loop

Summary: A loop hike around the base of Chimney Rock and Little Sugarloaf with panoramic views

Challenge Level: Easy

Hiking Distance: About 3 miles loop, including overlook

Hiking Time: About 2 hours round trip

Trail Popularity: 🚶🚶🚶🚶

Trailhead Directions: From the "Y" roundabout (see page 7), drive west toward Cottonwood on SR 89A about 3 miles. Turn right onto Dry Creek Road then proceed for 0.5 mile. Turn right onto Thunder Mountain Road then drive 0.7 mile. The parking area is on your left {1}. (34°52.325'N; 111°48.735'W) The entrance gate opens each day at 8:00 am and closes at dusk. This parking area also serves the Chimney Rock Upper Loop and Thunder Mountain/Andante Loop.

Description: From the parking area, go west past the signboard for about 100 feet then turn right onto the Lower Chimney Trail. In 0.1 mile, you'll come to the intersection of the Thunder Mountain and Lower Chimney Trails {2}. Turn right here to continue on the Thunder Mountain Trail.

As you circle Chimney Rock, you'll soon see a large water tank on the right, and intersect a social trail after 0.4 mile {3}. Next you'll intersect the Andante Trail {4}. After 0.7 mile, the Thunder Mountain Trail goes off to the right {5}. Turn left here onto the Chimney Rock Pass Trail.

In 0.2 mile, look for a faint trail off to the right which leads to a scenic overlook {6}. You'll hike around the base of the first rock outcropping then scramble up on the second rock outcropping for the scenic view {7}; it's a 0.3 mile in-out scramble but worth it for the view.

About 125 feet past the trail to the overlook is another unmarked trail {8} to the left and another scramble, which leads to the base of the chimney of Chimney Rock. As you continue on, you'll intersect the Lizard Head Trail on the right {9} and an unmarked social trail {10} where you should bear left. You'll pass a nice spot for a break {11} and then at 1.4 miles, you'll intersect the Lower Chimney Rock Trail {12}. Turn right here. You'll shortly see a steep trail on the left, which leads to the summit on Little Sugarloaf. You'll have some nice views of Lizard Head Rock, Cockscomb and the 3 rock fingers of rock that make up Chimney Rock. The remainder of the trail is relatively flat. At about 2.6 miles, you pass through a fence {13}, then hike parallel with telephone poles for 0.1 mile. In another 0.25 mile, you'll intersect a connector trail and be just south of the parking area. Turn left here {14} to return to your vehicle.

Note: This trail is a favorite for local residents so you'll likely encounter people walking their dogs.

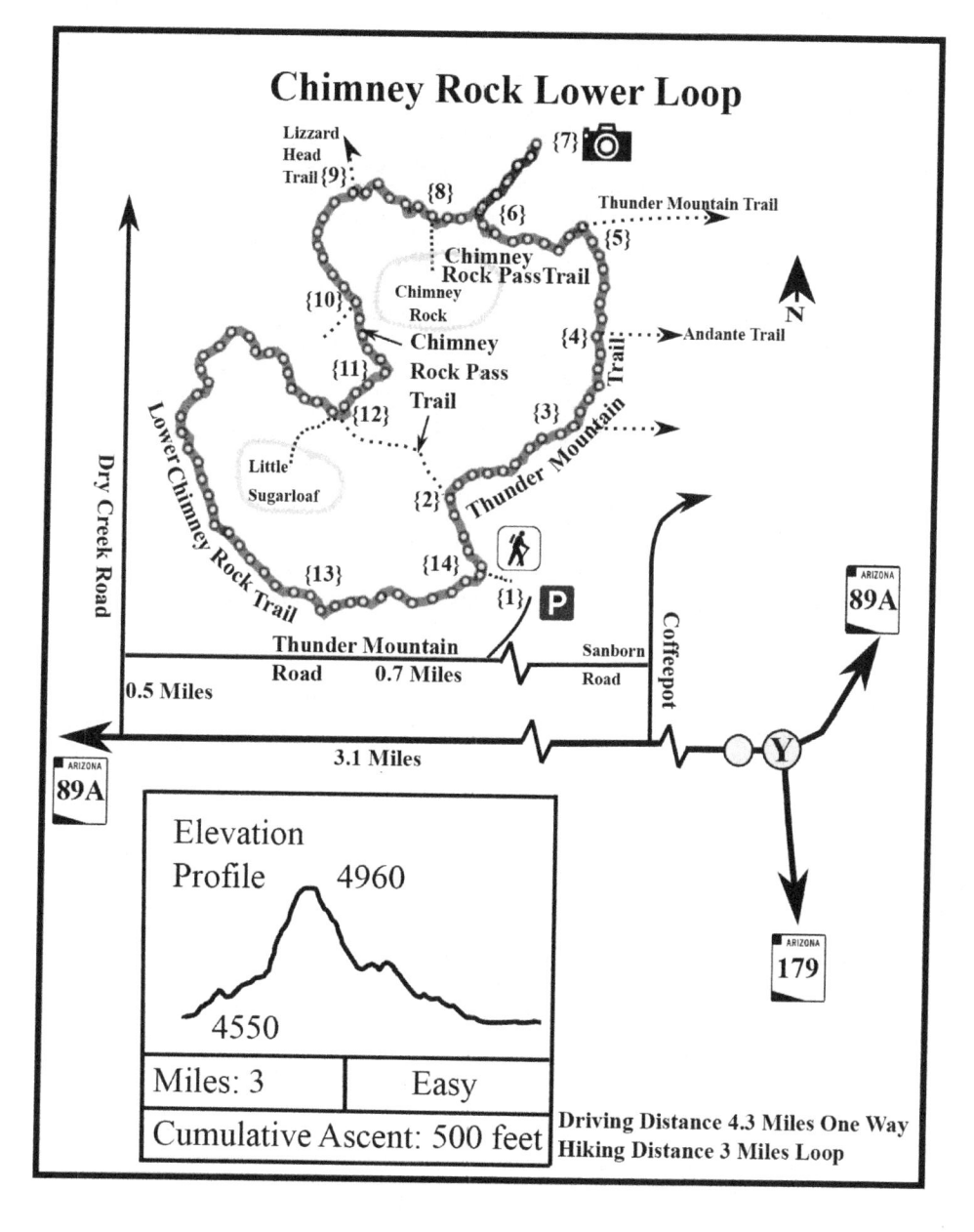

Color Photos: Scan the QR code below for additional color photos of this trail

Chimney Rock Lower Loop

- Lizzard Head Trail {9}
- {8}
- {7} 📷
- {6}
- Thunder Mountain Trail
- {5}
- Chimney Rock Pass Trail
- Chimney Rock
- {10}
- {4} → Andante Trail
- Chimney Rock Pass Trail
- {11}
- {12}
- {3}
- Thunder Mountain Trail
- Little Sugarloaf
- {2}
- Lower Chimney Rock Trail
- {13}
- {14}
- {1} 🅿
- Dry Creek Road
- Thunder Mountain Road 0.7 Miles
- Sanborn Road
- Coffeepot
- 0.5 Miles
- ARIZONA 89A
- 3.1 Miles
- Y
- ARIZONA 89A
- ARIZONA 179

Elevation Profile 4960
4550

Miles: 3	Easy
Cumulative Ascent: 500 feet	

Driving Distance 4.3 Miles One Way
Hiking Distance 3 Miles Loop

51

Chimney Rock Pass Loop ★

Summary: A favorite loop hike around the base of Chimney Rock with panoramic views

Challenge Level: Easy

Hiking Distance: About a 2 mile loop, including overlook

Hiking Time: About 1 1/2 hours round trip

Trail Popularity:
🚶🚶🚶🚶

Trailhead Directions: From the "Y" roundabout (see page 7), drive west toward Cottonwood on SR 89A about 3 miles. Turn right onto Dry Creek Road then proceed for 0.5 mile. Turn right onto Thunder Mountain Road then drive 0.7 mile. The parking area is on your left {1}. (34°52.325'N; 111°48.735'W) The entrance gate opens each day at 8:00 am and closes at dusk. This parking area also serves the Chimney Rock Lower Loop and Thunder Mountain/Andante Loop.

Description: From the parking area, go west past the signboard for about 100 feet then turn right onto the Lower Chimney Trail. In 0.1 mile, you'll come to the intersection of the Thunder Mountain and Lower Chimney Trails {2}.

For a morning hike, turn right here onto the Thunder Mountain Trail to hike in a counterclockwise direction because the views are better with the sun at your back. For an afternoon hike, continue straight ahead on the Lower Chimney Trail to hike in a clockwise direction.

As you circle Chimney Rock in the counterclockwise direction, you'll soon see a large water tank on the right, and intersect a social trail after 0.4 mile {3}. Next you'll intersect the Andante Trail {4}. After 0.7 mile, the Thunder Mountain Trail goes off to the right {5}. Turn left here onto the Chimney Rock Pass Trail.

In 0.2 mile, look for a faint trail off to the right which leads to a scenic overlook {6}. You'll hike around the base of the first rock outcropping then scramble up on the second rock outcropping for the scenic view {7}; it's a 0.3 mile in-out scramble but worth it for the view.

About 125 feet past the trail to the overlook is another unmarked trail {8} to the left and another scramble, which leads to the base of the chimney of Chimney Rock. As you continue on, you'll intersect the Lizard Head Trail on the right {9} and an unmarked social trail {10} where you should bear left. At 1.4 miles, you'll intersect a sign for the Lower Chimney Rock Trail and Summit, which is the summit on Little Sugarloaf {11}; stay left to complete the Chimney Rock Pass Loop.

Note: The signage on the trail shows Chimney Rock Trail and Chimney Rock Pass Trail at various places between {8} and {2}. Don't worry, you are on the correct trail. This trail is a favorite for local residents so you'll likely encounter people walking their dogs.

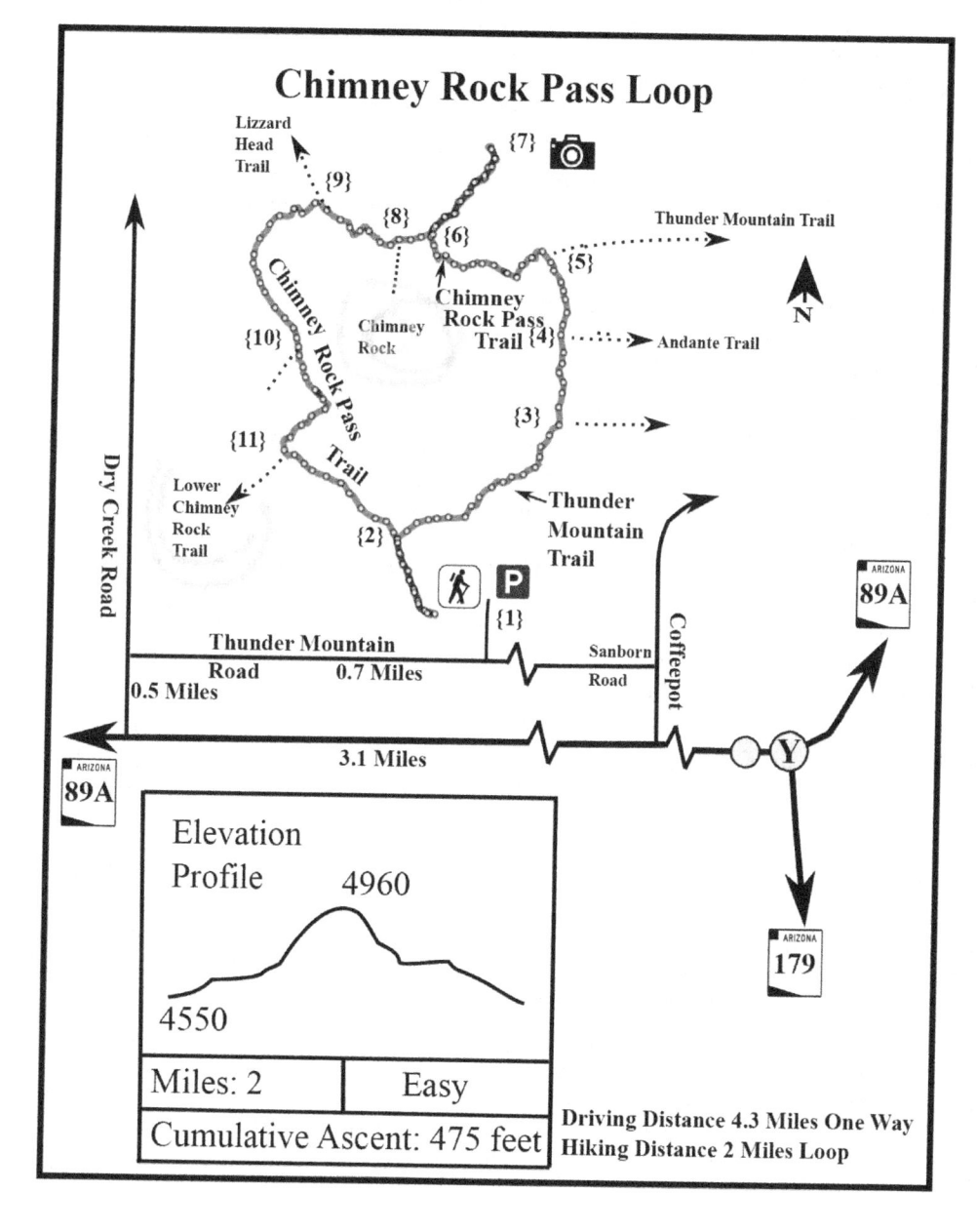

Color Photos: Scan the QR code below for additional color photos of this trail

Chimney Rock Pass Loop

- Lizzard Head Trail
- {9}
- {8}
- {7}
- {6} Chimney Rock Pass Trail {4}
- Thunder Mountain Trail
- {5}
- Chimney Rock
- {10}
- Andante Trail
- {3}
- {11}
- Lower Chimney Rock Trail
- {2}
- Thunder Mountain Trail
- {1}
- Dry Creek Road
- Thunder Mountain Road 0.5 Miles
- 0.7 Miles
- Sanborn Road
- Coffeepot
- 3.1 Miles
- ARIZONA 89A
- ARIZONA 89A
- ARIZONA 179
- N

Elevation Profile
4960
4550

Miles: 2	Easy
Cumulative Ascent: 475 feet	

Driving Distance 4.3 Miles One Way
Hiking Distance 2 Miles Loop

53

Chuckwagon In-Out Trail

Summary: A pleasant hike on a former mountain bike trail that parallels Forest Road 152 with partial shade, good red rock views all around and is an alternative way to get to the Devil's Bridge Trail

Challenge Level: Moderate

Hiking Distance: About 3.8 miles each way from the Dry Creek Vista parking area or 7.6 miles round trip; about 2.8 miles each way from the Mescal Trail parking area or 5.6 miles round trip

Hiking Time: About 4 hours round trip from the Dry Creek Vista parking area; about 3 hours round trip from the Mescal Day Use Trailhead parking area

Trail Popularity: 🚶🚶🚶

Trailhead Directions: There are two primary ways to access this trail. From the "Y" roundabout (see page 7), drive west toward Cottonwood on SR 89A about 3 miles. Turn right onto Dry Creek Road. Stay on Dry Creek Road for about 2 miles then turn right onto Forest Road (FR) 152. Drive 0.2 mile on the paved FR 152 to the Dry Creek Vista parking area on the left {1}. (34°53.425'N; 111°49.240'W) There are toilets and picnic tables here. Or, continue on Dry Creek Road for an additional 1 mile to a stop sign then turn right onto Long Canyon Road. Drive 0.3 mile to the Mescal Day Use Trailhead parking area {3} {4}. Parking is very limited at these parking areas. Rather than attempting to park at the parking lots, a better choice is to take the shuttle **(see Trailhead Shuttle Service page 5)** if the parking lots are full.

Description: From the Dry Creek Vista parking area {1}, the Chuckwagon Trail begins on the right of the interpretive signboard. After 0.7 mile, you'll come to a fork in the trail and a signpost {2}. The right fork leads to FR 152 and is a shorter way to Devil's Bridge (although you'll be hiking on the dusty FR 152 road). Stay left to continue on the Chuckwagon Trail. In 1.1 miles, you'll intersect the connector trail from the Mescal Day Use Trailhead parking area {6} on the left. If you begin at the Mescal Day Use Trailhead parking area {3} {4}, look for a sign that points south to the Chuckwagon Trail at the northeast end of parking area {3}. Hike this connector trail south 0.25 mile to the intersection with the Chuckwagon Trail {6} then turn left. You'll have some very nice panoramic views to the north {7}.

Hike northeast for 0.8 mile from {6} to a sign To Devils Bridge {8} which will lead you to Devil's Bridge {5} (see the Devil's Bridge Trail). There is a nice spot for a snack 0.15 mile past the turn to Devil's Bridge {9}. As you continue, you'll have views on both sides. After about 2 additional miles, you'll come to a fork in the trail {10}. I suggest you turn around here. The right fork leads to Brins Mesa trailhead after 0.5 mile. If you'd like to hike a loop see Chuckwagon Loop.

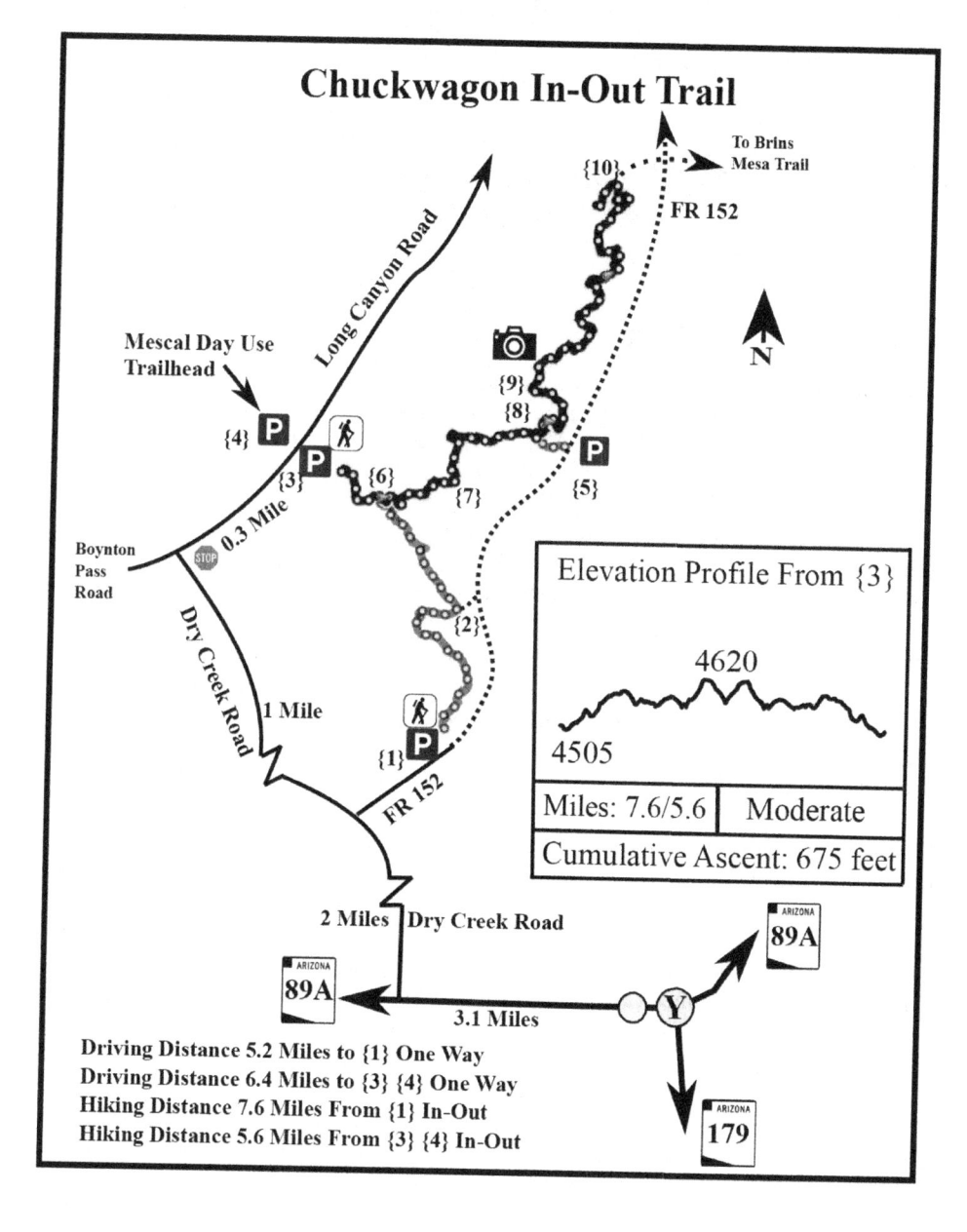

Color Photos: Scan the QR code below for additional color photos of this trail

Chuckwagon In-Out Trail

To Brins Mesa Trail
FR 152
Long Canyon Road
Mescal Day Use Trailhead
{4} {3} {6} {7} {5} {8} {9} {10}
0.3 Mile
Boynton Pass Road
Dry Creek Road
1 Mile
{2}
{1}
FR 152

Elevation Profile From {3}
4620
4505

| Miles: 7.6/5.6 | Moderate |

Cumulative Ascent: 675 feet

2 Miles Dry Creek Road
89A
89A
3.1 Miles
179

Driving Distance 5.2 Miles to {1} One Way
Driving Distance 6.4 Miles to {3} {4} One Way
Hiking Distance 7.6 Miles From {1} In-Out
Hiking Distance 5.6 Miles From {3} {4} In-Out

Chuckwagon Loop

Summary: A pleasant loop hike on a former mountain bike trail that parallels Forest Road 152 then goes to Long Canyon Road with partial shade, good red rock views all around and is an alternative way to get to the Devil's Bridge Trail

Challenge Level: Moderate

Hiking Distance: About 4.7 mile loop from the Mescal Day Use Trailhead parking area

Hiking Time: About 3 hours round trip from the Mescal Day Use Trailhead parking area

Trail Popularity: 🚶🚶🚶

Trailhead Directions: There are two primary ways to access this trail. From the "Y" roundabout (see page 7), drive west toward Cottonwood on SR 89A about 3 miles. Turn right onto Dry Creek Road. Stay on Dry Creek Road for about 2 miles then turn right onto Forest Road (FR) 152. Drive 0.2 mile on the paved FR 152 to the Dry Creek Vista parking area on the left {13}. (34°53.425'N; 111°49.240'W) There are toilets and picnic tables here. Or, continue on Dry Creek Road for an additional 1 mile to a stop sign then turn right onto Long Canyon Road. Drive 0.3 mile to the Mescal Day Use Trailhead parking area {1} {2}. Parking is very limited at these parking areas. Rather than attempting to park at the parking lots, a better choice is to take the shuttle **(see Trailhead Shuttle Service page 5)** if the parking lots are full.

Description: I suggest hiking this loop from the Mescal Day Use Trailhead parking area {1} {2}. Look for a sign that points south to the Chuckwagon Trail at the northeast end of parking area {2}. Hike this connector trail south 0.25 mile to the intersection with the Chuckwagon Trail {3} then turn left. You'll soon have some very nice panoramic views to the north {4}.

Hike northeast for 0.8 mile from {4} to a sign To Devils Bridge {5} which will lead you to the Devil's Bridge parking area {6} (see the Devil's Bridge Trail). There is a nice spot for a snack 0.15 mile past the turn to Devil's Bridge {7}. As you continue, you'll have views on both sides. The trail continues with a series of ups and downs, but nothing too steep. After about 2 additional miles, you'll come to a fork in the trail {8}. The right fork leads to Brins Mesa trailhead after 0.5 mile. The Chuckwagon Trail continues to the left.

You'll cross a shallow wash then a deeper wash after 0.2 mile {9}. There is a nice spot to stop after another 0.6 mile {10}. The trail takes two sharp turns then is relatively flat for the next 0.6 mile until you come to Long Canyon Road {11}. Cross the road and continue just past the interpretive signboard then turn left onto the connector trail. Follow the connector trail to the intersection with the Mescal Trail {12} Turn left here then follow the Mescal Trail back to the parking areas {1} {2}.

Note: You'll likely encounter mountain bikers as this is a favorite bike trail. Also, for a longer hike start at the Dry Creek parking area {13}. This will add 2.2 miles to the hike for a total of 6.9 miles.

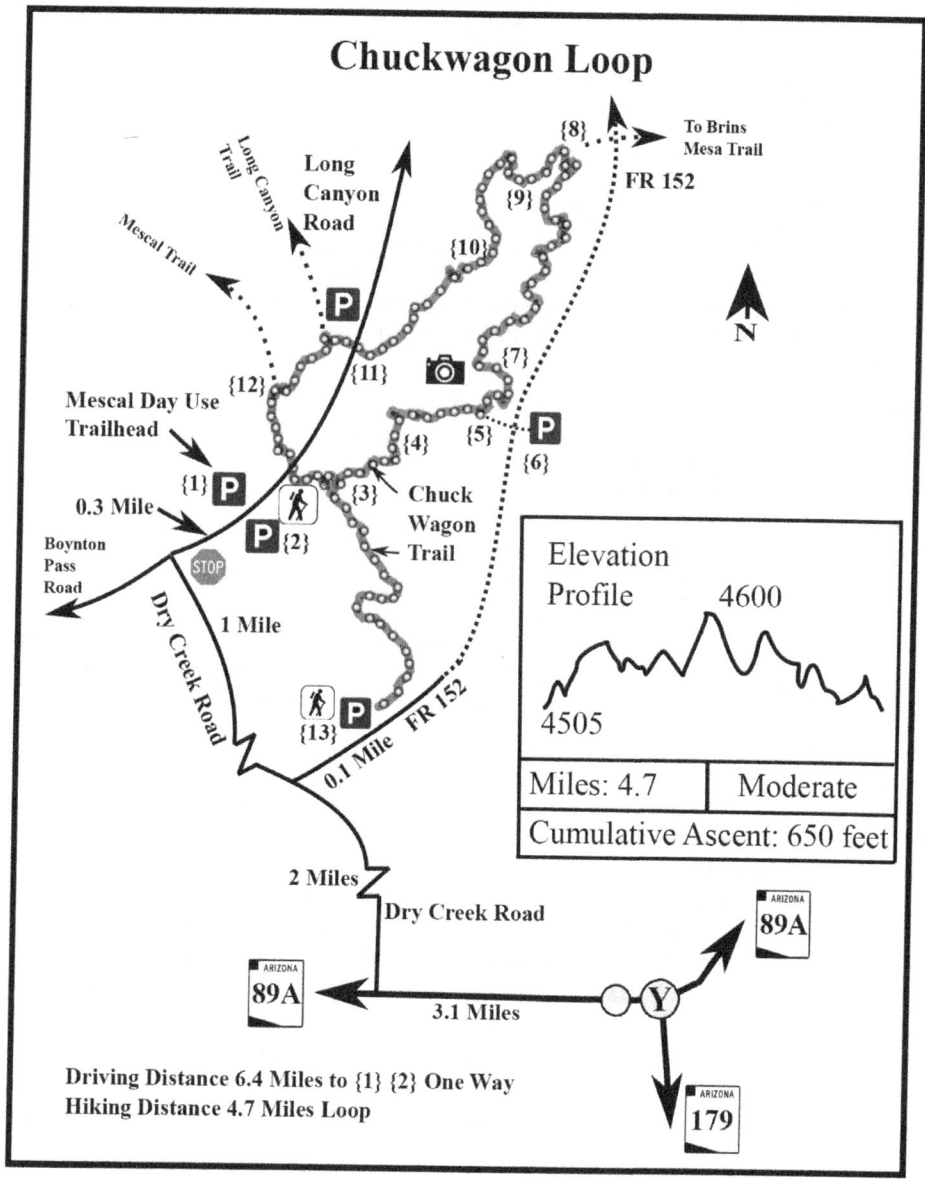

Color Photos: Scan the QR code below for additional color photos of this trail

Chuckwagon Loop

Elevation Profile
4600
4505

Miles: 4.7	Moderate
Cumulative Ascent: 650 feet	

Driving Distance 6.4 Miles to {1} {2} One Way
Hiking Distance 4.7 Miles Loop

57

Cibola Pass/Jordan Loop

Summary:
This close-to-town, loop hike provides some spectacular red rock views with the option to visit the Devil's Kitchen sinkhole and the Seven Sacred Pools

Challenge Level:
Easy to Moderate

Hiking Distance:
About 0.75 mile each way or 1.5 miles round trip; about a 2.2 mile loop if you hike the Cibola Pass Trail then return on the Jordan Trail; about 3.6 miles loop if you hike the Cibola Pass Trail to the Jordan Trail to the Soldier Pass Trail to the Seven Sacred Pools returning via the Jordan Trail

Hiking Time: About 1 ½ hour round trip for the Cibola Pass/Jordan loop; about 2 ½ hours round trip to the Seven Sacred Pools and return

Trail Popularity: 🚶🚶🚶

Trailhead Directions: From the "Y" roundabout (see page 7), drive north on SR 89A about 0.3 mile to the Jordan Road roundabout. Take the third exit onto Jordan Road then drive to the end. Turn left onto West Park Ridge. Drive 0.3 miles then proceed through the paved cul-de-sac, continuing on the dirt road for 0.5 mile to the main parking area {1}. (34°53.287'N; 111°46.098'W) This parking area also serves the Brins Mesa, Brins Mesa Overlook, Jim Thompson and Jordan Trails. There are toilets at the parking area. Note: The dirt road is rough with potholes. A high clearance vehicle is recommended.

Description: Begin hiking the trail on the west side of the parking area near the toilets. Go through the opening in the cable fence. The Cibola Pass Trail branches left from the Brins Mesa Trail after about 400 feet {2}. The trail is quite steep in places. As you proceed, you'll have some very nice red rock views including the Cibola Mitten rock formation. At about 0.4 mile, you'll approach two fence posts on the left side {3}. If you go straight for a short distance, you'll have some great views. Return to the fence posts then continue on the trail. You'll intersect the Jordan Trail after hiking 0.75 mile {4}. Turn around here to return to the parking area via the Cibola Trail for a 1.5 mile hike Or turn south and follow the Jordan Trail back to the parking area for a 2.2 mile loop.

Or proceed west on the Jordan Trail for 0.4 mile to the Soldier Pass Trail. Turn right onto the Soldier Pass Trail, which leads to Devil's Kitchen (a very large sink hole) {5}. Continue on the Soldier Pass Trail for 0.4 mile and you'll arrive at the Seven Sacred Pools {6}. You'll have hiked about 3.6 miles for the entire hike from the Seven Sacred Pools when you return to the parking area via the Jordan Trail.

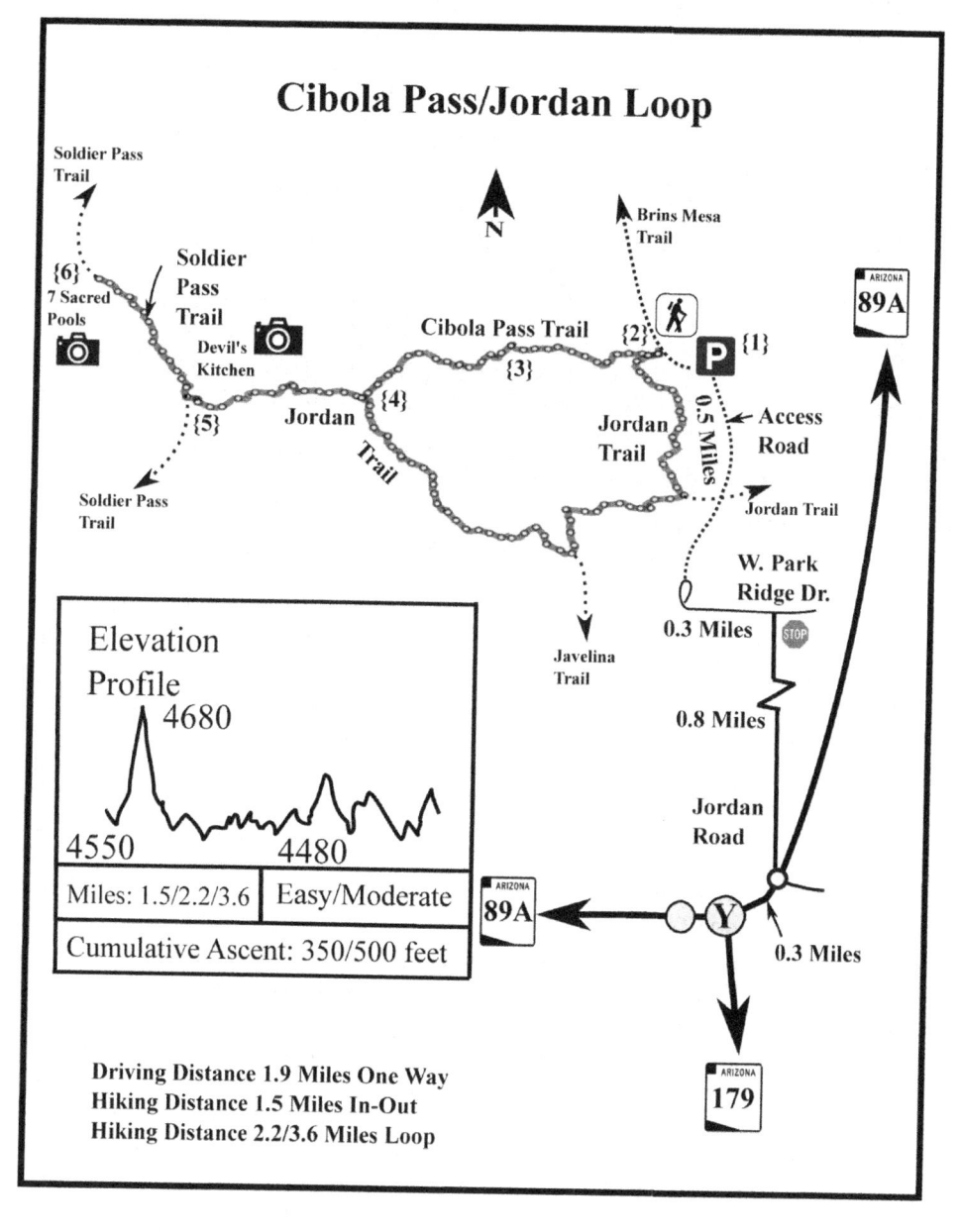

Color Photos: Scan the QR code below for additional color photos of this trail

Cibola Pass/Jordan Loop

Soldier Pass Trail

{6} 7 Sacred Pools

Soldier Pass Trail

Devil's Kitchen

Cibola Pass Trail {2}

Brins Mesa Trail

ARIZONA 89A

{1} P

{3}

0.5 Miles

{5}

{4} Jordan Trail

Jordan Trail

Access Road

Soldier Pass Trail

Jordan Trail

W. Park Ridge Dr.

0.3 Miles

Javelina Trail

0.8 Miles

Jordan Road

Elevation Profile
4680
4550
4480

Miles: 1.5/2.2/3.6	Easy/Moderate
Cumulative Ascent: 350/500 feet	

ARIZONA 89A

Y

0.3 Miles

ARIZONA 179

Driving Distance 1.9 Miles One Way
Hiking Distance 1.5 Miles In-Out
Hiking Distance 2.2/3.6 Miles Loop

Cockscomb/Aerie Loop

Summary:
A loop hike circling Doe Mountain with excellent views of Doe Mountain, Bear Mountain, Fay Canyon and Boynton Canyon

Challenge Level:
Moderate

Hiking Distance:
About 5.4 miles around Doe Mountain using the Cockscomb and Aerie Trails to make a loop hike

Hiking Time: About 3 hours round trip

Trail Popularity:

Trailhead Directions: From the "Y" roundabout (see page 7), drive west toward Cottonwood on SR 89A about 3 miles. Turn right onto Dry Creek Road. Stay on Dry Creek Road to a stop sign (about 3 miles) then turn left onto Boynton Pass Road. Proceed about 1.6 miles to a stop sign. Turn left then continue on Boynton Pass Road. Drive about 2.5 miles then turn left onto Aerie Road, which is about 0.5 mile past the Doe Mountain/Bear Mountain parking area on the left side of Boynton Pass Road. Follow Aerie Road then take the right fork to the parking area {1}. (34°53.139'N; 111°52.194'W) This parking area also serves the Aerie Trail.

Description: You'll begin by hiking the Cockscomb Trail and return via the Aerie Trail to complete the loop. The trail begins near the signboard at the west end of the parking lot. About 100 feet south of the parking area is a trail sign. Go straight then follow the Cockscomb Trail to hike a counter clockwise loop around the south, east, north then west side of Doe Mountain. The best views are along the north and west side of Doe Mountain on the Aerie Trail.

Follow the Cockscomb Trail until you come to a fence after 0.9 mile, then you'll see a social trail on the right after 1.1 miles. Turn left here. You'll cross Aerie Road after 1.2 miles then intersect the Rupp Trail after 1.6 miles {2}.

You'll come to a nice scenic spot after 2 miles {3} then intersect the Dawa Trail after 2.6 miles {4} and the Aerie Trail after another 0.8 mile {5}. If you continue straight on the Cockscomb Trail, you'll come to the Fay Canyon parking area. Turn left (southwest) to follow the Aerie Trail across the west side of Doe Mountain to complete the loop.

At 4.6 miles, you'll cross the trail leading up to Doe Mountain {6}. The Aerie Trail takes a slight jog here at the intersection with the Doe Mountain Trail but it is well-marked. Continue on the Aerie Trail back to the parking area {1} on your 5.4 mile loop hike.

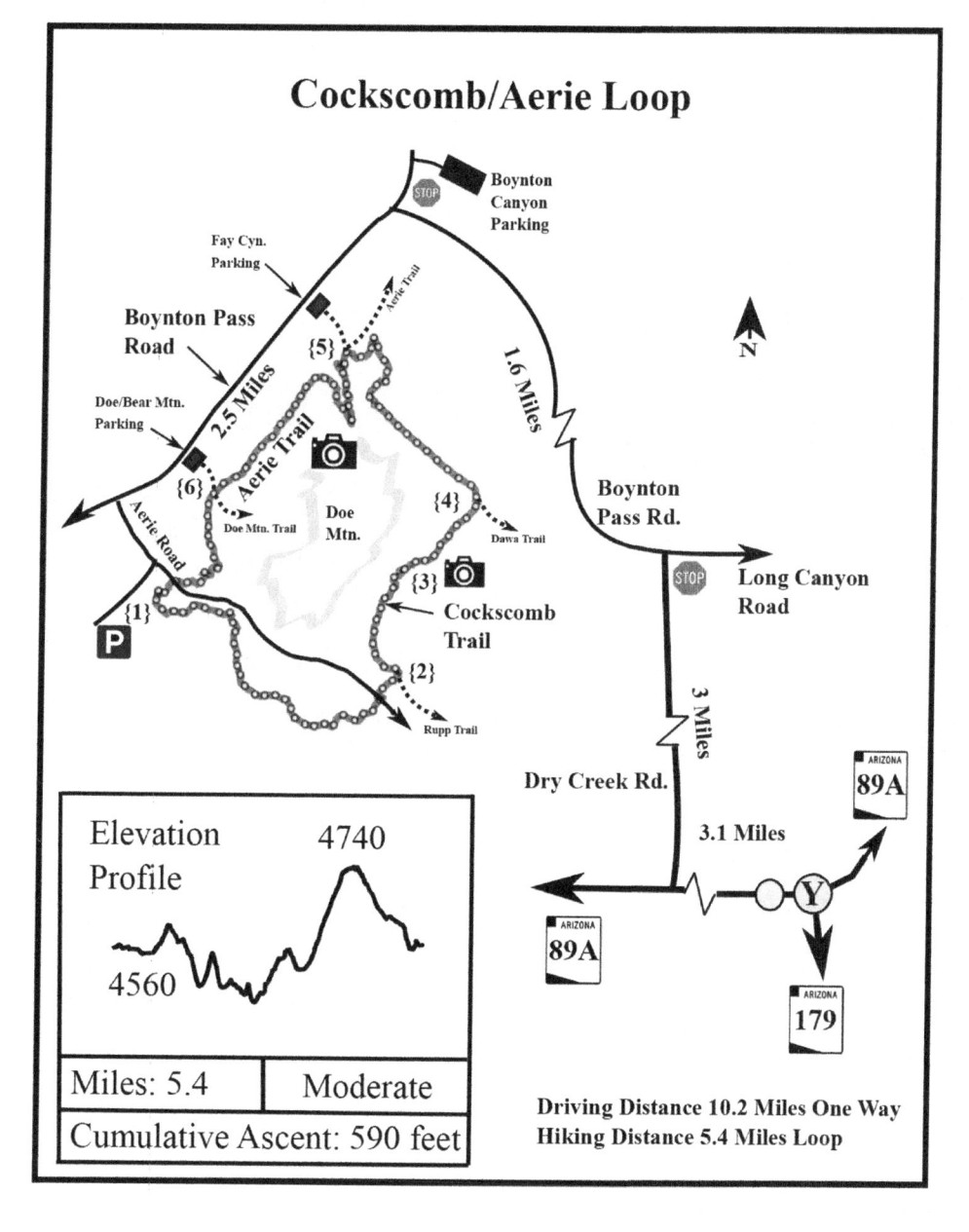

Color Photos: Scan the QR code below for additional color photos of this trail

Cockscomb/Aerie Loop

Boynton Canyon Parking

Fay Cyn. Parking

Boynton Pass Road

Doe/Bear Mtn. Parking

Aerie Trail

2.5 Miles

1.6 Miles

{5}

{6}

{4}

{3}

{2}

{1}

Doe Mtn. Trail

Doe Mtn.

Dawa Trail

Cockscomb Trail

Rupp Trail

Aerie Road

Boynton Pass Rd.

Long Canyon Road

3 Miles

Dry Creek Rd.

3.1 Miles

ARIZONA 89A

ARIZONA 89A

ARIZONA 179

N

Elevation Profile
4740
4560

Miles: 5.4 | Moderate
Cumulative Ascent: 590 feet

Driving Distance 10.2 Miles One Way
Hiking Distance 5.4 Miles Loop

Coffeepot Trail

Summary: An in-town, in-out hike that takes you to the base of Coffeepot Rock

Challenge Level: Easy

Hiking Distance: About 1.2 miles each way or 2.4 miles round trip

Hiking Time: About 1 ½ hours round trip

Trail Popularity:

Trailhead Directions: From the "Y" roundabout (see page 7), drive west toward Cottonwood on SR 89A for just under 2 miles then turn right onto Coffeepot Drive. Drive about 0.5 miles then turn left at the stop sign onto Sanborn. Continue to the second street then turn right onto Little Elf. Little Elf ends at Buena Vista so turn right onto Buena Vista then turn left into the parking area {1}. (34°52.458'N; 111°47.793'W) This parking area also serves the Teacup, Thunder Mountain and Sugarloaf Trails. It has only 14 spots so can fill quickly.

Description: Follow the Sugarloaf-Teacup Trail for 0.4 mile to a signpost. Turn right at the signpost {2} to continue on the Teacup Trail. You'll soon come to a sign for the Sugarloaf Loop Trail {3}. Continue on the Teacup Trail for another 0.15 mile then, at a vertical sign showing the Teacup Trail continuing straight ahead, turn left {4} onto an unmarked trail called the Coffeepot Trail, which will lead you to the base of Coffeepot Rock.

There are many social trails in this area so be sure to follow the cairns until you turn onto the Coffeepot Trail. There aren't any cairns along the Coffeepot Trail, but it is easy to follow. You'll hike on rock ledges under Coffeepot Rock until you come to Shark Rock {5}, which looks like the open mouth of a giant shark. Continue on until the ledges eventually become too narrow and steep to go any farther {6}. Return the way you came for a 2.4 mile hike.

There is little shade on this trail making this a hot summer hike. This is a favorite hike for locals so you'll likely encounter folks walking their dogs.

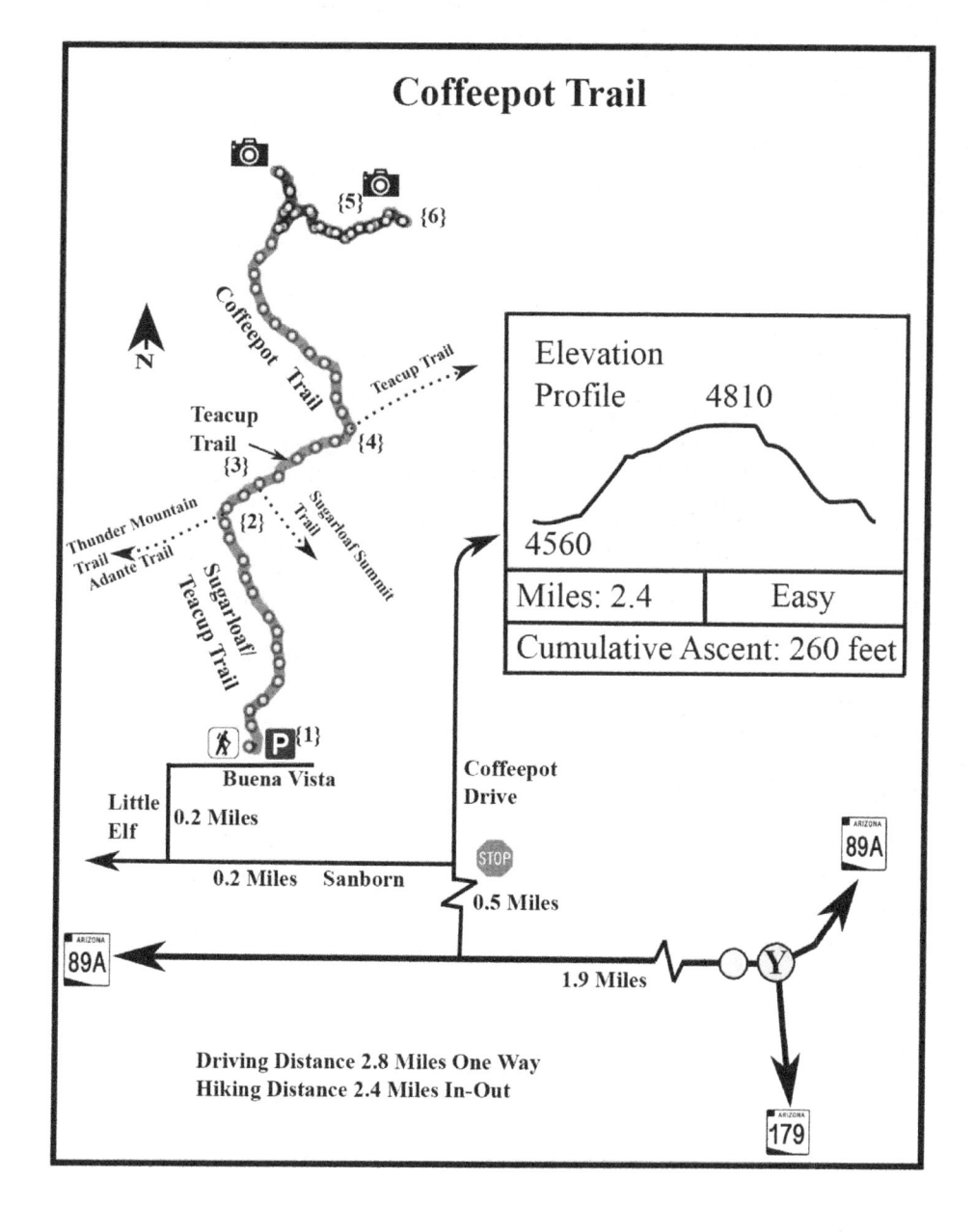

Color Photos: Scan the QR code below for additional color photos of this trail

Coffeepot Trail

Elevation Profile 4810

4560

| Miles: 2.4 | Easy |

Cumulative Ascent: 260 feet

Coffeepot Trail
Teacup Trail
Teacup Trail
Thunder Mountain Trail
Adante Trail
Sugarloaf Summit Trail
Sugarloaf/Teacup Trail
Buena Vista
Little Elf
0.2 Miles
0.2 Miles Sanborn
Coffeepot Drive
0.5 Miles
89A
1.9 Miles
89A
179

Driving Distance 2.8 Miles One Way
Hiking Distance 2.4 Miles In-Out

Cookstove to Harding Springs Trails

Summary: A two-vehicle hike up the side of Oak Creek Canyon through a pine forest and down again

Challenge Level: Hard

Hiking Distance: About 2.9 miles

Hiking Time: About 3 hours roundtrip

Trail Popularity:

Trailhead Directions: This is a two-vehicle hike. Park one vehicle at Cave Springs and one at the artesian well at Pine Flats. From the "Y" roundabout (see page 7), drive north on SR 89A about 11.7 miles (mile marker 385.6) then turn left toward the Cave Springs campground. Park your first vehicle in the parking area on the right, just off SR 89A {13}. (35°00.039'N; 111°44.253'W) Continue north on SR 89A about 1.3 miles (mile marker 386.9) to the Pine Flats campground. Park the other vehicle on the west side of SR 89A near the well {1}, but don't block access to the well. (35°00.877'N; 111°44.256'W)

Description: Once you park the second vehicle, cross SR 89A to the sign for the Cookstove Trail, which is directly across from the well then hike up the east side of Oak Creek Canyon. The trail is very steep and there are places where erosion has taken place making footing tricky. You'll be climbing about 750 feet to a flat mesa {2}. Turn right then hike south following the edge of Oak Creek Canyon. You'll turn away from Oak Creek Canyon to skirt a side canyon then make a series of turns {3}{4}{5}. You'll cross several washes and hike along an old road then rejoin the trail and intersect the Harding Springs Trail {6}{7}{8}{9}{10}.

Before starting down the steep Harding Springs Trail (to your other vehicle), continue about 450 feet south along the canyon rim to a nice overlook area {11}.

The unmarked, unmaintained trail is difficult to follow at times, and is not a straight line between the top of the Cookstove Trail and the Harding Springs Trail. Also, you'll be climbing over some fallen trees. I strongly recommend using a portable GPS unit to hike between the trails across the mesa (go to https://greatsedonahikes.com/gps/gps.html). This is a shady hike in the summer, with good foliage colors in the fall. Because of potential slippery conditions, do not attempt this hike if the trail is wet or snow-covered.

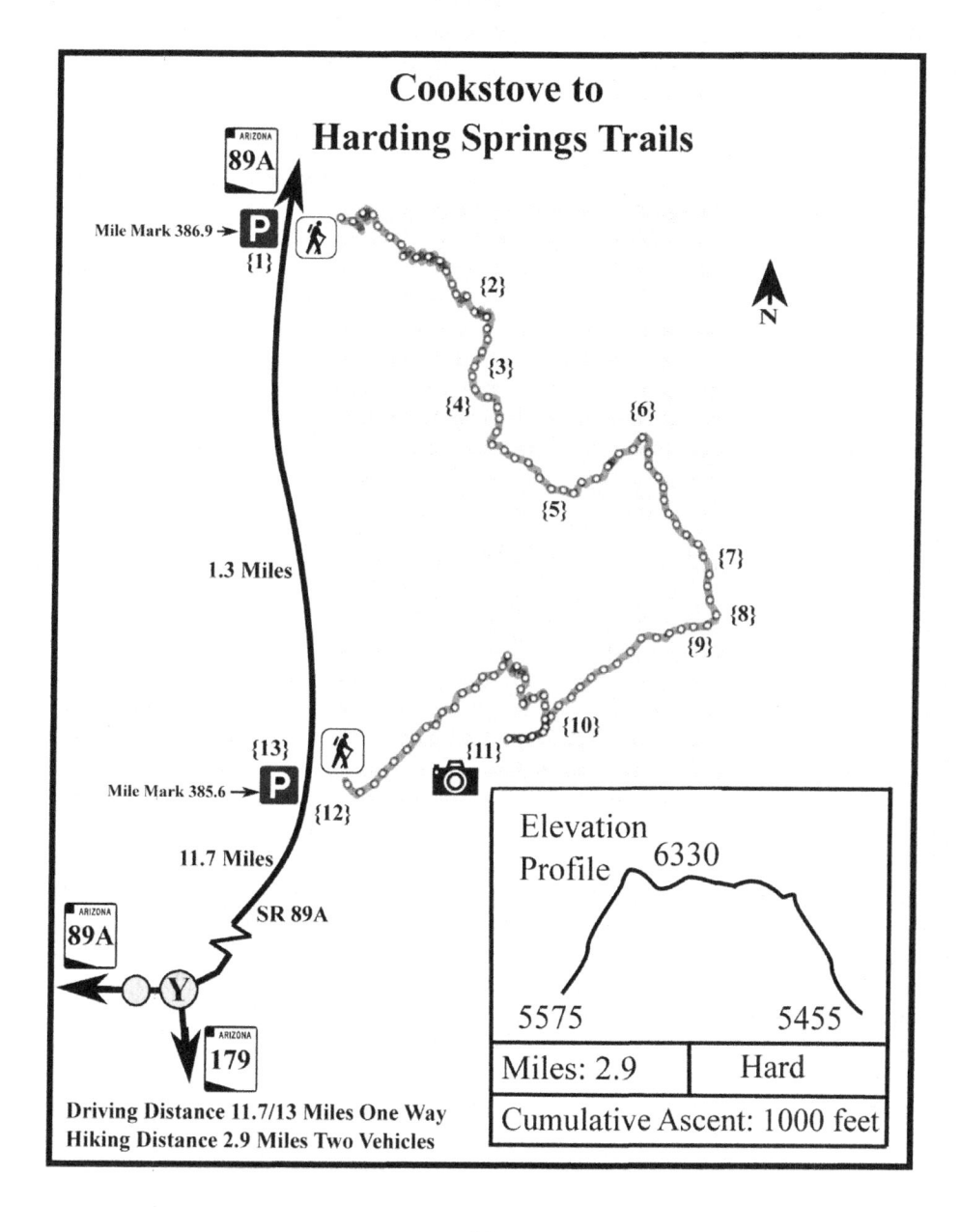

Color Photos: Scan the QR code below for additional color photos of this trail

Cookstove to Harding Springs Trails

Mile Mark 386.9 — {1}

{2} {3} {4} {5} {6} {7} {8} {9} {10} {11}

1.3 Miles

{13} Mile Mark 385.6 {12}

11.7 Miles
SR 89A

Elevation Profile 6330
5575   5455

Miles: 2.9	Hard

Cumulative Ascent: 1000 feet

Driving Distance 11.7/13 Miles One Way
Hiking Distance 2.9 Miles Two Vehicles

Courthouse Butte Alternate Loop

Summary: A pleasant loop hike circling Courthouse Butte

Challenge Level: Moderate

Hiking Distance: About 4.5 miles loop

Hiking Time: About 2 ½ hours round trip

Trail Popularity: 🚶🚶 🚶🚶 🚶🚶

Trailhead Directions: From the "Y" roundabout (see page 7), drive south on SR 179 for about 6 miles. After you drive about 3.2 miles, just past the Back O' Beyond roundabout, SR 179 becomes a divided highway. Continue driving south. About 1.8 miles beyond the Back O' Beyond roundabout, southbound SR 179 adds a passing lane on the left. Continue past the Court House Vista parking area for another mile and turn left into the Bell Rock Vista parking area {1}. (34°47.501'N; 111°45.699'W) There are toilets at the parking area.

Description: This trail is similar to the Courthouse Butte Loop Trail except you'll be hiking a connector trail between Bell Rock and Courthouse Butte. It combines panoramic and close-up views of these two famous rock formations as well as distant views of Rabbit Ears, the Chapel of the Holy Cross and Cathedral Rock. The trail is fairly open, so it provides limited shade making it a hot summer hike.

I like to hike this loop in the clockwise direction. From the Bell Rock Vista parking area {1}, hike past the interpretive signboard then follow the well defined trail. The trail starts out wide and is defined by fences on both sides. You'll soon see a sign Bell Rock Path↑ then intersect a trail and sign, Big Park Loop →. Turn right here then follow this trail a short distance then turn left at the trail and sign, To Courthouse Butte Loop. Follow this trail for 0.4 mile to the intersection with the Courthouse Butte Loop Trail {2}. Here, turn left then follow the Courthouse Butte Loop Trail for 0.1 mile to the Rector Connector Trail {3}.

Turn right then follow the Rector Connector for 0.6 mile where you'll intersect the Bell Rock Climb Trail {4}. Turn right and carefully descend the Bell Rock Climb Trail. You'll soon intersect the Bell Rock Pathway {5}. Make a right turn onto the Bell Rock Pathway then follow the signs to the Courthouse Butte Loop Trail. After 0.2 mile, you'll intersect the Courthouse Butte Loop Trail then after another 0.2 mile the Llama Trail {6}. Continue on the Courthouse Butte Loop Trail. A good stopping point for a snack break is near Muffin Rock {7}, which some call UFO Rock.

The Courthouse Butte Loop Trail is joined by the Big Park Loop Trail {8} then you'll intersect the Middle Trail {9} then 0.25 mile later a sign pointing to the Big Park Loop Trail {2}. Turn left at {2} then follow the trail back to the parking lot {1}.

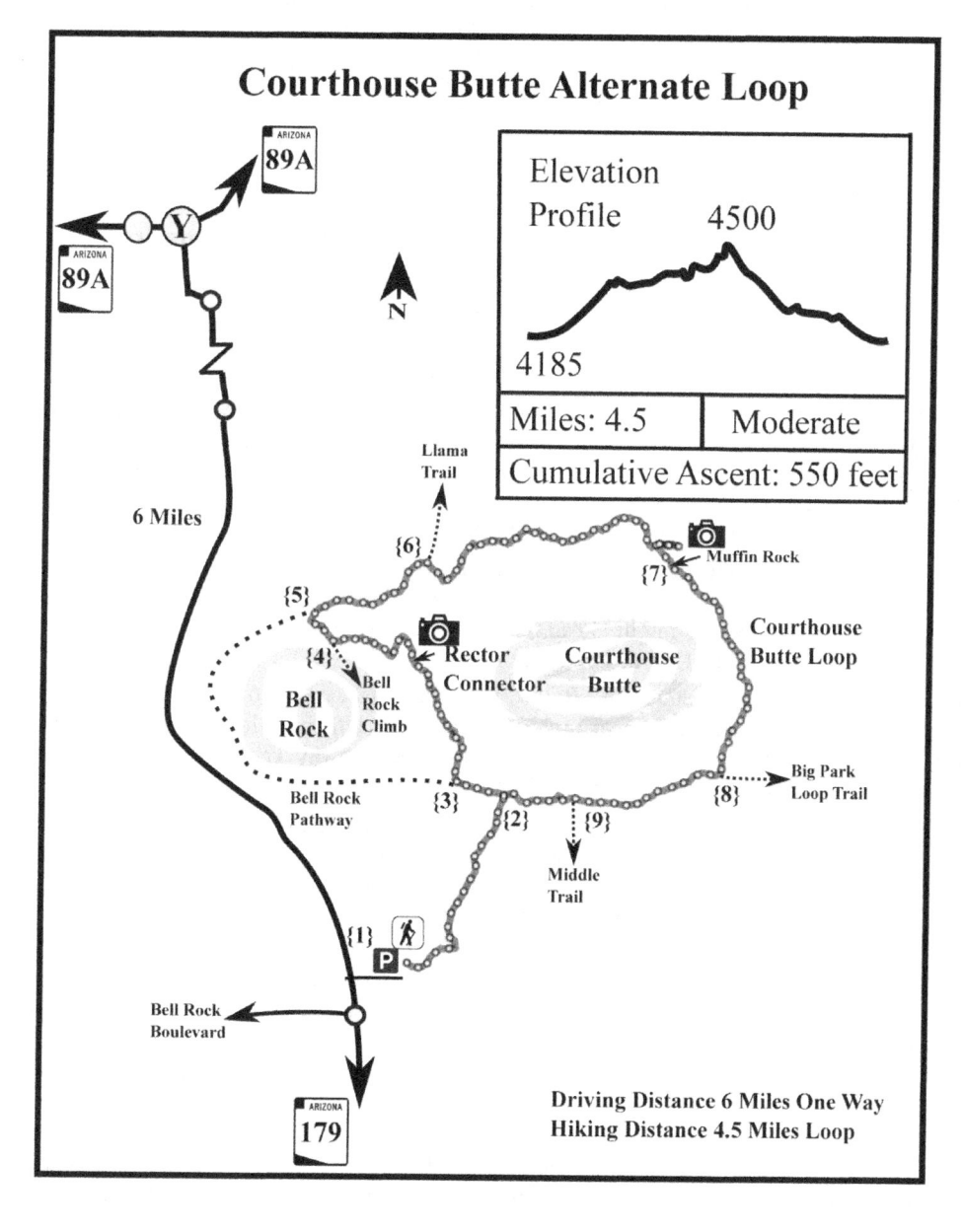

Color Photos: Scan the QR code below for additional color photos of this trail

Courthouse Butte Alternate Loop

Elevation Profile
4500
4185

Miles: 4.5	Moderate
Cumulative Ascent: 550 feet	

89A
89A
6 Miles

Llama Trail
{6}
{5}
{4} Rector Connector
Bell Rock Climb
Bell Rock
Courthouse Butte
Muffin Rock
{7}
Courthouse Butte Loop
{8} Big Park Loop Trail
Bell Rock Pathway {3} {2} {9}
Middle Trail
{1}
P
Bell Rock Boulevard
179

Driving Distance 6 Miles One Way
Hiking Distance 4.5 Miles Loop

67

Courthouse Butte Loop

Summary: A pleasant loop hike circling Bell Rock and Courthouse Butte

Challenge Level: Moderate

Hiking Distance: About 4.2 miles loop

Hiking Time: About 2 ½ hours round trip

Trail Popularity:

Trailhead Directions: There are two parking areas you can use for this hike. There are toilets at both the parking areas. From the "Y" roundabout (see page 7), drive south on SR 179 for about 5 miles to the first parking area. After you drive about 3.2 miles, just past the Back O' Beyond roundabout, SR 179 becomes a divided highway. Continue driving south. About 1.8 miles beyond the Back O' Beyond roundabout, southbound SR 179 adds a passing lane on the left. From the passing lane, turn left at the sign for the Court House Vista parking area {1}. (34°48.350'N; 111°46.009'W)

Before you turn, you'll see Bell Rock ahead of you on the left side of SR 179. The trail starts on the southeast side of the parking area. After you park, walk past the interpretive signboard then proceed straight ahead on the Bell Rock Trail. Follow it for 0.1 mile to the intersection with the Courthouse Butte Loop Trail {2}.

If you continue driving south on SR 179, in 1 mile you'll come to the Bell Rock Vista parking area south of Bell Rock on your left. Turn left into the parking area {8}. (34°47.501'N; 111°45.699'W) Follow the Bell Rock Pathway Trail north for about 0.5 mile until you intersect the Courthouse Butte Loop Trail {7}.

Description: These trails circling Courthouse Butte and Bell Rock combine panoramic and close-up views of these two famous rock formations as well as distant views of Rabbit Ears, the Chapel of the Holy Cross and Cathedral Rock. The trail is fairly open, so it provides limited shade making it a hot summer hike.

I like to hike this loop in the clockwise direction from the Bell Rock Vista parking area {8}, although either direction provides great views. From the Bell Rock Vista parking area, the trail starts out wide and is defined by fences on both sides. Follow the Bell Rock Pathway around the west side of Bell Rock then follow the signs for Courthouse Butte Loop between {2} and {3}. You'll intersect several trails as you hike including the Llama Trail {3} and Big Park Loop Trail {5} {6}. A good stopping point for a snack break is near Muffin Rock, which some call UFO Rock {4}. The Courthouse Butte Loop Trail and the Big Park Loop Trail are combined between {5} and {6}. For a shortcut back to the parking lot, turn left at {6} where you'll see a sign pointing to the Big Park Loop Trail.

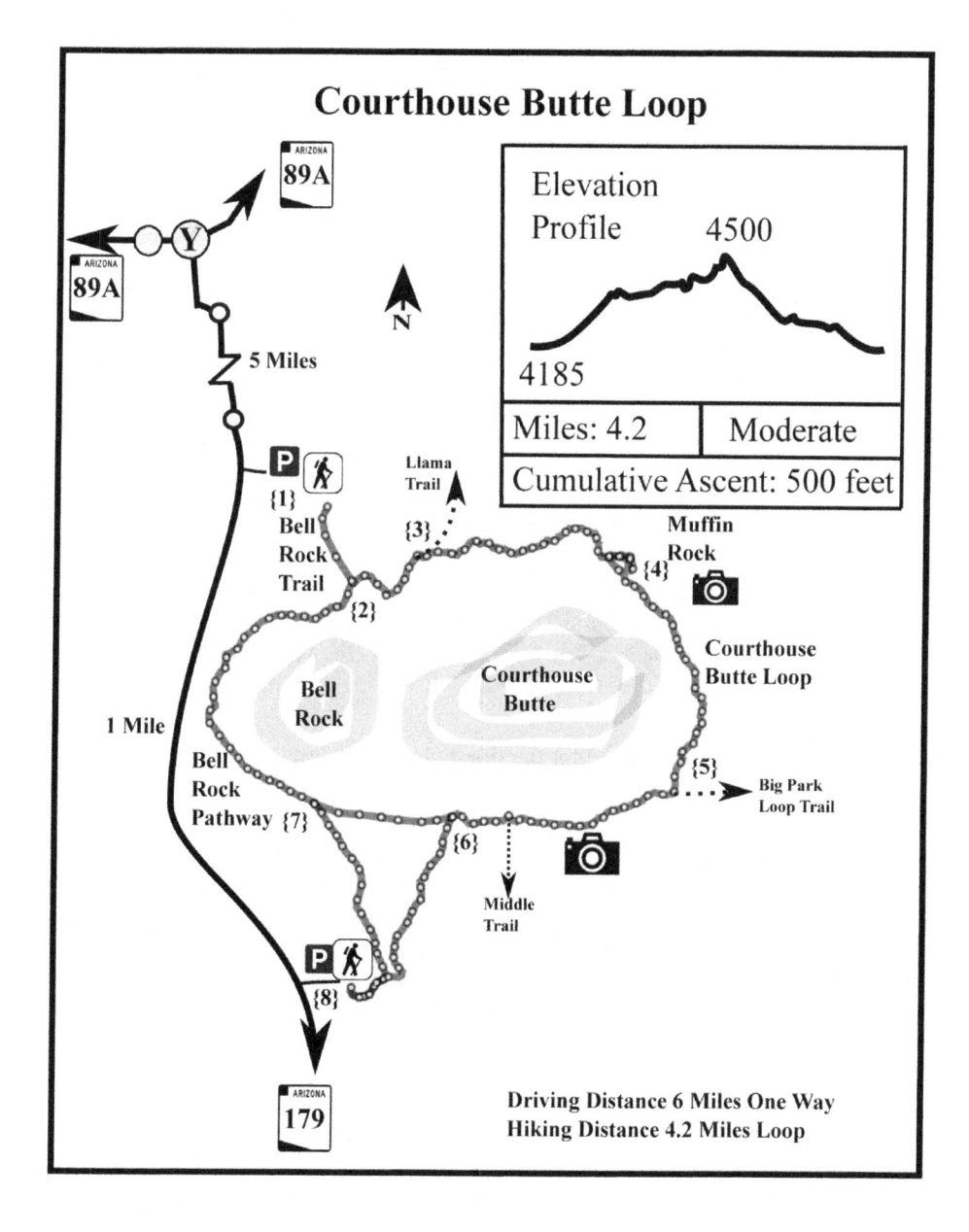

Color Photos: Scan the QR code below for additional color photos of this trail

Courthouse Butte Loop

Elevation Profile
4500
4185

Miles: 4.2 | Moderate
Cumulative Ascent: 500 feet

{1} Bell Rock Trail
{2}
{3} Llama Trail
{4} Muffin Rock
{5} Big Park Loop Trail
{6} Middle Trail
{7} Bell Rock Pathway
{8}

Bell Rock
Courthouse Butte
Courthouse Butte Loop

5 Miles
1 Mile
89A
179

Driving Distance 6 Miles One Way
Hiking Distance 4.2 Miles Loop

69

Cow Pies Trail

Summary: An in-out stroll over slick rock with nice views all around

Challenge Level: Easy

Hiking Distance: About 1 mile each way or 2 miles round trip

Hiking Time: About 1 ½ hour round trip

Trail Popularity:

Trailhead Directions: From the "Y" roundabout (see page 7), drive south on SR 179 about 0.3 mile to the Schnebly Hill Road roundabout. Take the second exit then proceed 3.7 miles on Schnebly Hill Road. The trailhead parking is on your right {1}. (34°52.318'N; 111°42.779'W) This parking area also serves the Hangover/Munds Wagon Loop. The trailhead is across the road from the parking area.

Note: Schnebly Hill Road is paved for the first mile but the last 2.7 miles is an unpaved road and can be very rough; a high clearance vehicle and 4WD are strongly recommended.

Description: The name Cow Pies is likely because the four huge circular sandstone mounds resemble very large cow droppings. Soon you'll pass by an area dotted with small black rocks, which are pieces of lava. Some believe this to be another powerful vortex area {2}. (Additional information on vortexes can be found on page 6.) Continue along the trail for 0.3 mile then make a left turn {3} when you arrive at a large area of flat rock (known as slick rock) to go to the cow pies. If you go straight, you'll be hiking the Hangover Trail (see Hangover/Munds Wagon Loop).

As you continue to the left, you'll hike up on the cow pies, which border Bear Wallow. You'll have to do a bit of scrambling in some areas to ascend the cow pies. There isn't a defined trail so you'll be free to explore the cow pies. There are a number of areas that provide good views {4} {5}. Because the red rocks can be very slippery when wet, do not attempt this hike if the rocks are wet or there is snow or ice present.

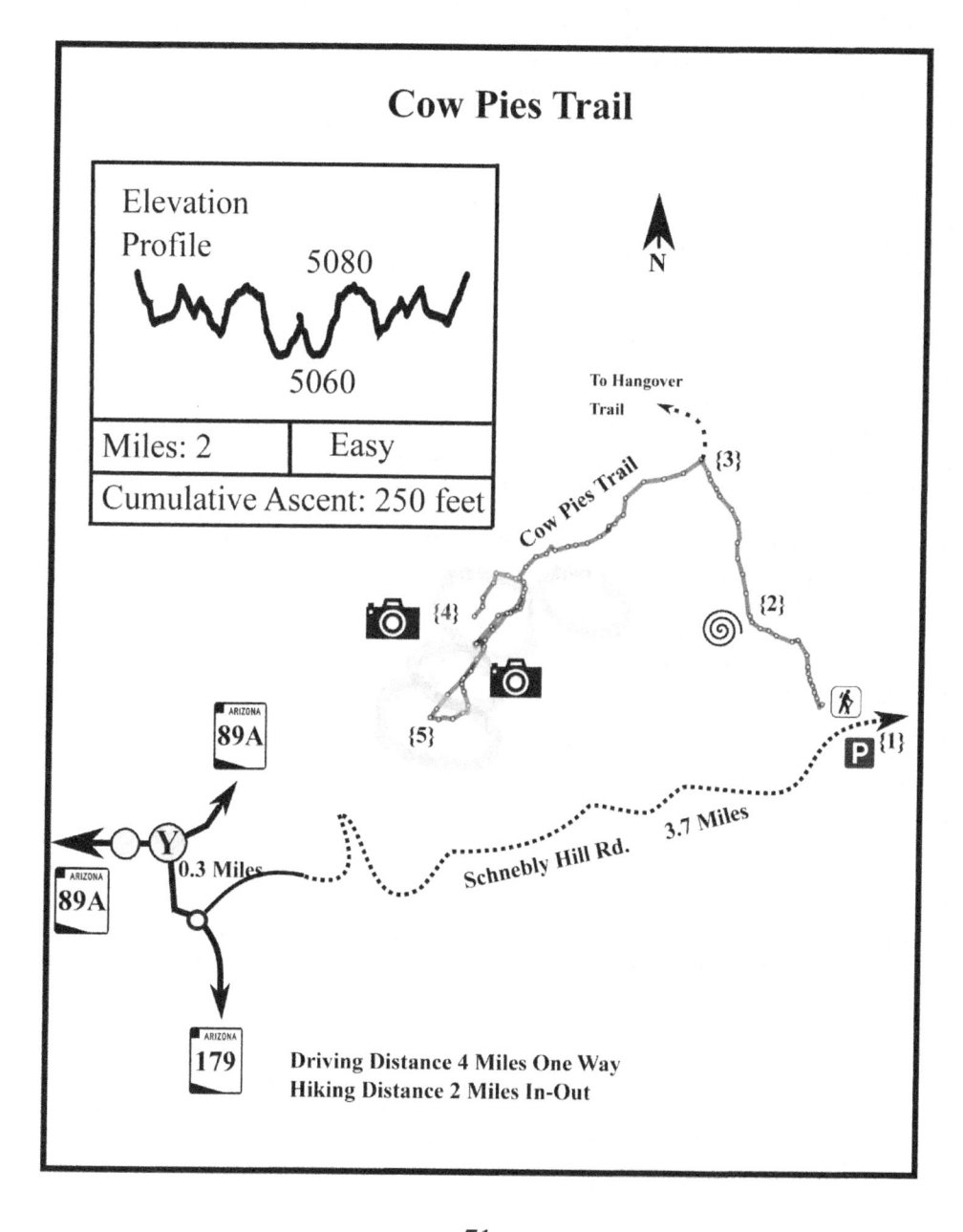

Color Photos: Scan the QR code below for additional color photos of this trail

Cow Pies Trail

Elevation Profile
5080
5060

Miles: 2 | Easy
Cumulative Ascent: 250 feet

N

To Hangover Trail

Cow Pies Trail

{3}
{2}
{4}
{5}
{1}

ARIZONA 89A
ARIZONA 89A
ARIZONA 179

0.3 Miles
Schnebly Hill Rd.
3.7 Miles

Driving Distance 4 Miles One Way
Hiking Distance 2 Miles In-Out

Devil's Bridge Trail ★

Summary: A favorite in-out climb with steep stairs up to the largest natural stone arch in the Sedona area
Challenge Level: Moderate
Hiking Distance: About 3.1 miles each way from the Dry Creek Vista parking area or 6.2 miles round trip; about 1 mile each way From the Devil's Bridge (DB) parking area or 2 miles round trip; about 2.2 miles each way from the Mescal Day Use Trailhead parking area or 4.4 miles round trip;
Hiking Time: About 3 ½ hours round trip from the Dry Creek Vista parking area; about 1½ hour round trip from the DB parking area; about 2 ½ hours round trip from the Mescal Day Use Trailhead parking area
Trail Popularity: 🚶🚶 🚶🚶 🚶🚶 🚶🚶
Trailhead Directions: From the "Y" roundabout (see page 7), drive west toward Cottonwood on SR 89A about 3 miles. Turn right onto Dry Creek Road. Stay on Dry Creek Road for about 2 miles then turn right onto Forest Road (FR) 152. Drive for 0.2 mile and park at the Dry Creek Vista parking area on the left {1}. (34°53.425'N; 111°49.240'W) If you have a high clearance vehicle, proceed for another 1.1 miles on the unpaved, very rough FR 152 to the DB parking area on your right {2}. (34°54.172'N; 111°48.833'W) Or rather than turn onto FR 152, a third alternative is to continue on Dry Creek Road another 1 mile to a stop sign then turn right onto Long Canyon Road. Drive 0.3 mile to the Mescal Day Use Trailhead parking area on the left {3} (34°54.100'N; 111°49.667'W) or right {4}. Parking is very limited at these parking areas. Rather than attempting to park at the parking lots, a better choice is to take the shuttle **(see Trailhead Shuttle Service page 5)**.
Note: FR 152 is an extremely rough road beyond the 0.2 mile paved section; a high clearance vehicle and 4WD are strongly recommended.
Description: From the Dry Creek Vista parking area {1}, go to the signboard where you'll see a small sign pointing to the right for the Chuckwagon (CW) Trail. Follow the CW Trail and after 0.7 mile, you'll come to a fork and a signpost {5}. The right fork leads to FR 152. I recommend that you continue on the CW Trail otherwise you'll be hiking on the dusty FR 152 road. You'll pass the intersection of the trail to the Mescal Day Use Trailhead parking area {3} {4} after 1.1 miles {6}. Continue on the CW Trail for a total of 2.1 miles then turn right onto the connector trail {7} to the Devil's Bridge parking area across FR 152 {2}.

For most folks, I recommend starting from the Mescal Day Use Trailhead parking area {3} {4}. Look for a sign that points south to the Chuckwagon Trail at the northeast end of parking area {4} and hike for 0.2 mile then turn left onto the CW Trail {6}. Hike for 0.8 mile to the turn to Devil's Bridge {7}.

Devil's Bridge is a large natural stone arch that you can walk on. It is reachable with a moderate amount of climbing (up some 400 feet); the view of the arch and from the arch are well worth the climb. The trail splits about 15 feet past a large rock next to the trail {8}. Go straight then right to reach the top of the arch; take the left fork to go beneath the arch. If you take the trail to the top of the arch {9}, you'll be hiking up some steep natural stone steps (with no hand rails) so watch your footing. If you have a fear of heights, you may want to be extra careful on this hike, or only take the left trail to view the arch from beneath. Devil's Bridge gets very busy on weekends and holidays.

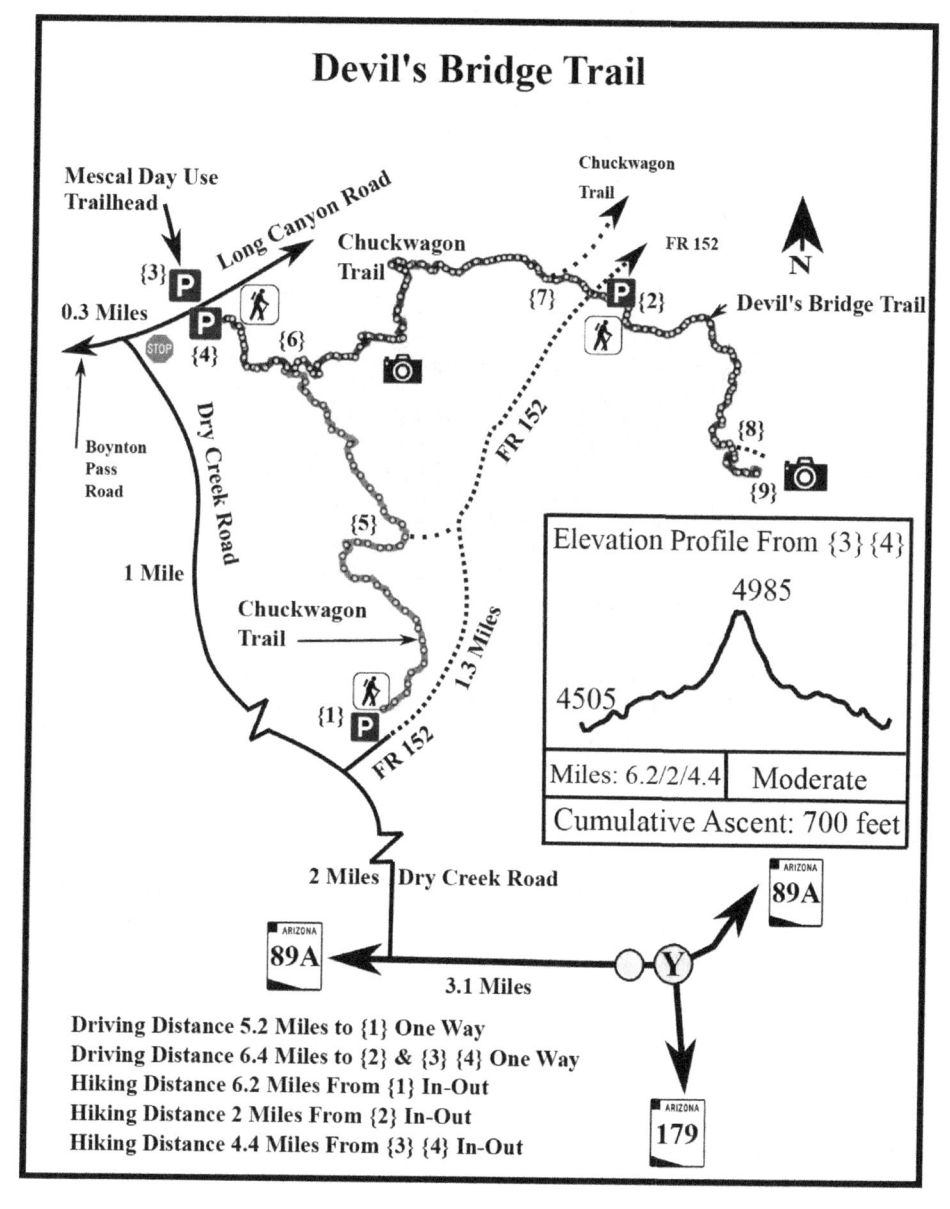

Color Photos: Scan the QR code below for additional color photos of this trail

Devil's Bridge Trail

Mescal Day Use Trailhead
Long Canyon Road
Chuckwagon Trail
FR 152
Devil's Bridge Trail
0.3 Miles
{3} P
{4} P
{6}
{7}
{2} P
{8}
{9}
Boynton Pass Road
Dry Creek Road
1 Mile
{5}
Chuckwagon Trail
1.3 Miles
{1} P
FR 152

Elevation Profile From {3} {4}
4985
4505
Miles: 6.2/2/4.4 | Moderate
Cumulative Ascent: 700 feet

2 Miles Dry Creek Road
3.1 Miles
ARIZONA 89A
ARIZONA 89A
ARIZONA 179

Driving Distance 5.2 Miles to {1} One Way
Driving Distance 6.4 Miles to {2} & {3} {4} One Way
Hiking Distance 6.2 Miles From {1} In-Out
Hiking Distance 2 Miles From {2} In-Out
Hiking Distance 4.4 Miles From {3} {4} In-Out

Doe Mountain Trail ★

Summary: A favorite climb up to the top of Doe Mountain with panoramic red rock views all around

Challenge Level: Moderate

Hiking Distance: About 2.6 miles loop

Hiking Time: About 2 hours round trip

Trail Popularity: 🚶🚶🚶

Trailhead Directions: From the "Y" roundabout (see page 7), drive west toward Cottonwood on SR 89A about 3 miles. Turn right onto Dry Creek Road. Stay on Dry Creek Road to a stop sign (about 3 miles) then turn left onto Boynton Pass Road. Proceed about 1.6 miles to a stop sign. Turn left, continuing on Boynton Pass Road. The trailhead parking is the second one on the left side, about 1.8 miles from the stop sign {1}. (34°53.596'N; 111°51.945'W) The trailhead is at the south side of the parking area. This parking area also serves the Bear Mountain Trail. There are toilets at the parking area.

Description: From the parking area, hike southeast toward Doe Mountain and you'll soon intersect the Aerie Trail {2}. The trail has several switchbacks and is narrow in places. Just before you reach the rim, you'll hike up a narrow slot in the rocks. Once through the slot and on the mesa, turn around and look down at the parking area. Pay attention to where you came up {3} by observing your location relative to the parking area below because it can be hard to find the way back down after hiking around the top of Doe Mountain.

Although the top of Doe Mountain is crisscrossed with social trails, the preferred way is to proceed straight across to the southern side of Doe Mountain then proceed in a clockwise direction around then back to the trail down to the parking area. Another popular way is to go to the left then skirt the outer edge of the mountain for some great views {4} {5} {6} {7}. You may be bushwhacking a bit, so be sure to wear hiking boots to protect your ankles from the cactus and brush you'll be stepping over. The spectacular views are all around.

Note: The unmarked, unmaintained trail is difficult to follow at times. I strongly recommend using a portable GPS unit to hike around the top of Doe Mountain and back to the trail to the parking area (go to https://greatsedonahikes.com/gps/gps.html).

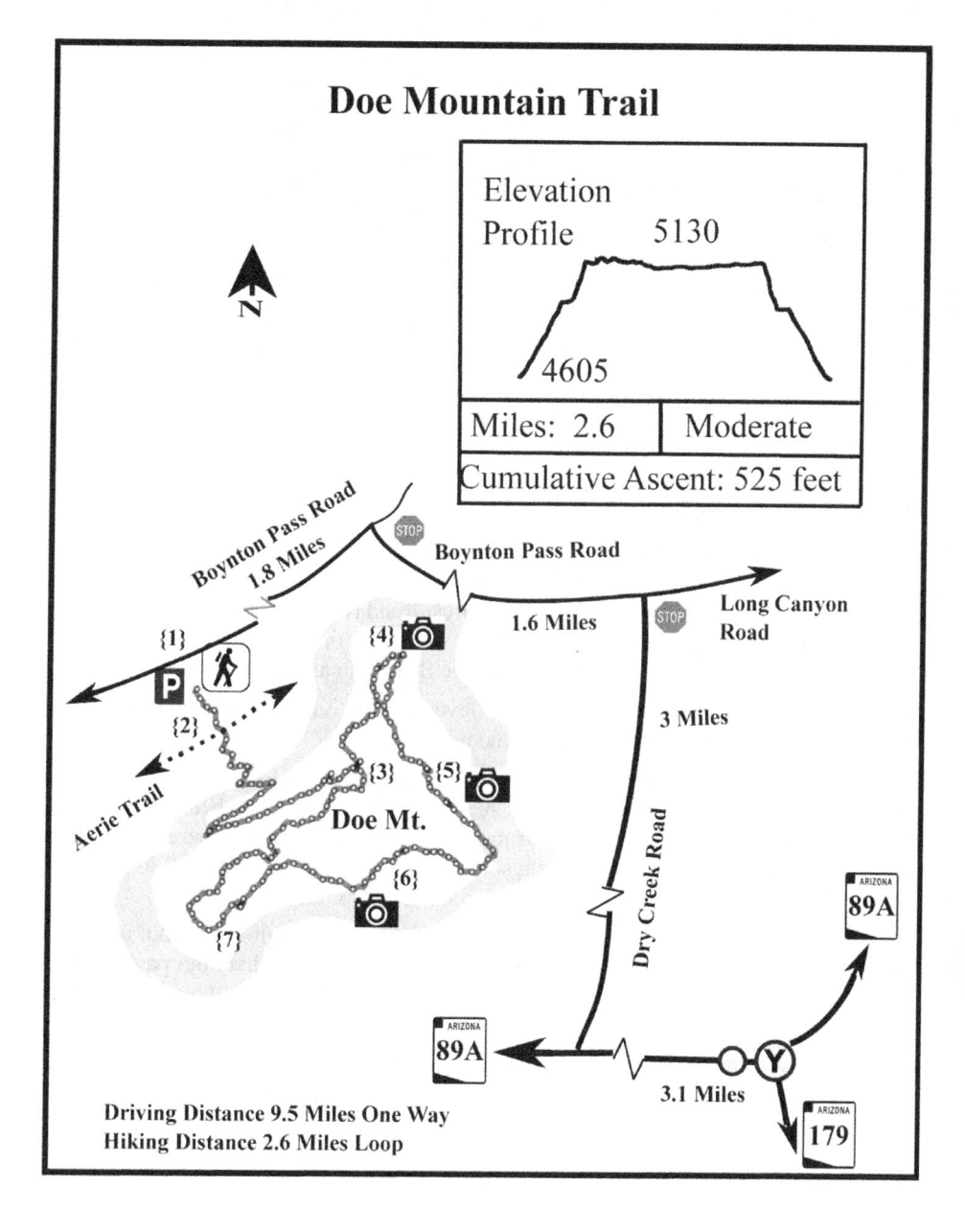

Color Photos: Scan the QR code below for additional color photos of this trail

Doe Mountain Trail

Elevation Profile 5130
4605

Miles: 2.6 | Moderate
Cumulative Ascent: 525 feet

Boynton Pass Road 1.8 Miles

Boynton Pass Road 1.6 Miles

Long Canyon Road

3 Miles

Aerie Trail

Doe Mt.

{1} {2} {3} {4} {5} {6} {7}

Dry Creek Road

3.1 Miles

ARIZONA 89A
ARIZONA 89A
ARIZONA 179

Driving Distance 9.5 Miles One Way
Hiking Distance 2.6 Miles Loop

75

Dry Creek Trail

Summary: An in-out hike that follows the path of Dry Creek through a forest

Challenge Level: Easy to Moderate, depending on length of hike

Hiking Distance: About 2.25 miles each way or 4.5 miles round trip

Hiking Time: About 2 ½ hours round trip

Trail Popularity:

Trailhead Directions: From the "Y" roundabout (see page 7), drive west toward Cottonwood on SR 89A about 3 miles. Turn right onto Dry Creek Road. Stay on Dry Creek Road for 2 miles then turn right onto Forest Road (FR) 152. Proceed to the end of FR 152 (about 4.5 miles) to the parking area on the left {1}. (34°56.236'N; 111°47.678'W) The parking area also serves the Bear Sign and Vultee Arch Trails.

Note: FR 152 is an extremely rough road beyond the 0.2 mile paved section; a high clearance vehicle and 4WD are strongly recommended.

Description: This trail, which is at the northern edge of the Red Rock-Secret Mountain Wilderness, follows the path cut by Dry Creek and crosses the creek bed about a dozen times. Because it is located at the end of the very rough FR 152, it isn't used very much and has become hard to follow in certain spots. I recommend you use a GPS loaded with the trail data (go to https://greatsedonahikes.com/gps/gps.html).

You'll be hiking in a northerly direction and intersect the Bear Sign Trail about 0.75 mile from the parking area {2}. The Dry Creek Trail is easy to follow here but pay attention when you cross the creek bed because the continuation of the trail on the other side isn't always obvious.

As you continue, the canyon cut by Dry Creek gets narrower and you are treated to nice views of towering red rock formations, although some of the views are blocked by the stands of cypress and pines {3}. You'll come to a nice place for a snack after about 1.6 miles {4}. You can hike another 0.75 mile further up the creek bed if you like {5} but the trail becomes more difficult to follow {6}.

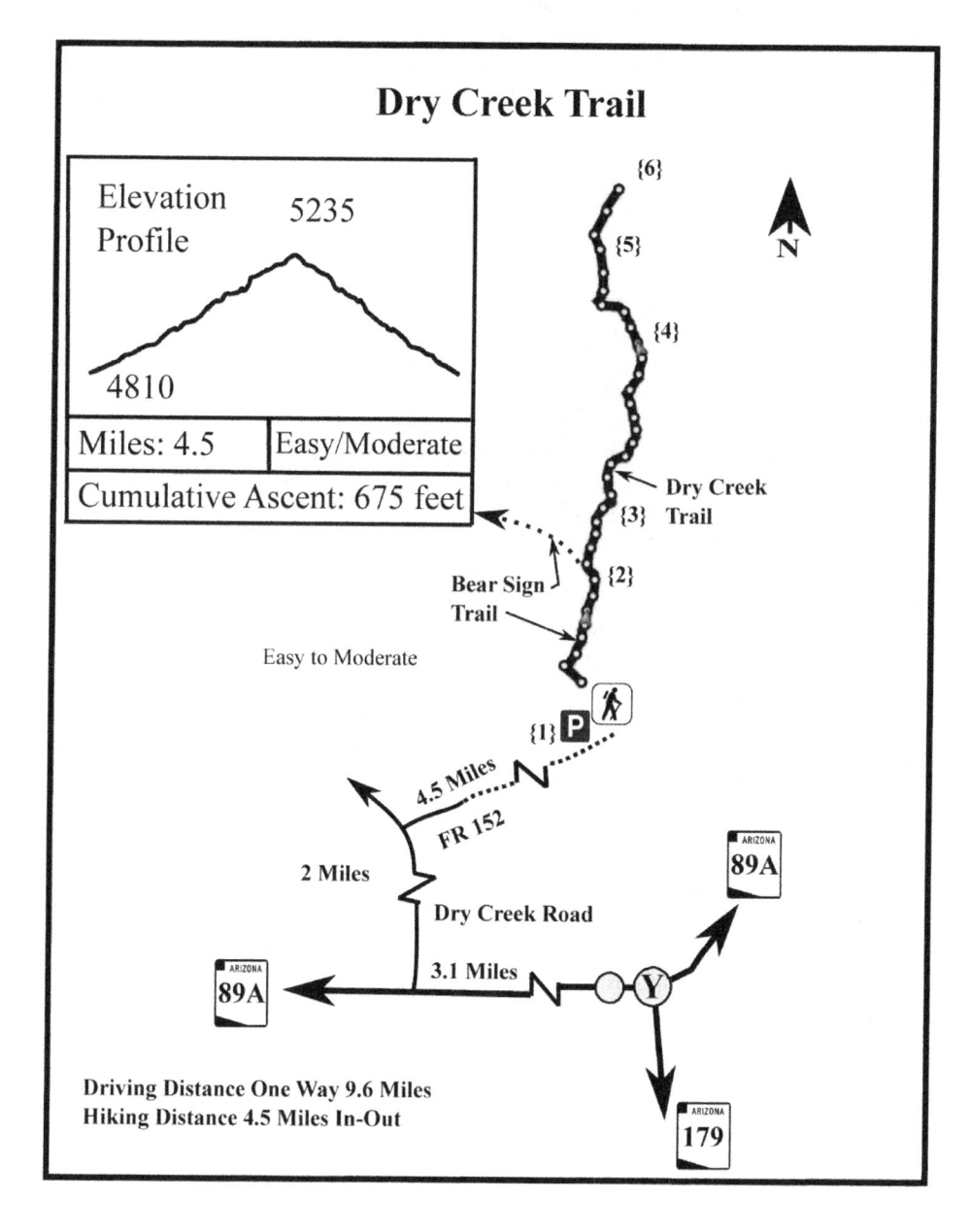

Color Photos: Scan the QR code below for additional color photos of this trail

Dry Creek Trail

Elevation Profile 5235
4810

Miles: 4.5 | Easy/Moderate
Cumulative Ascent: 675 feet

Easy to Moderate

{1} {2} {3} {4} {5} {6}

Dry Creek Trail

Bear Sign Trail

4.5 Miles
FR 152
2 Miles
Dry Creek Road
3.1 Miles

89A · 89A · 179

Driving Distance One Way 9.6 Miles
Hiking Distance 4.5 Miles In-Out

77

Fay Canyon Trail ★

Summary: A favorite short, pleasant in-out stroll through a canyon with good red rock views and an optional side trip to view a natural arch

Challenge Level:
Easy for the Fay Canyon Trail; Moderate if you climb up to Fay Canyon Arch

Hiking Distance:
About 1.2 miles each way to the rock slide or 2.4 miles round trip. Add 0.5 mile round trip if you hike to Fay Canyon Arch or 2.9 miles round trip.

Hiking Time:
About 1 ½ hours round trip

Trail Popularity:
🚶 🚶 🚶 🚶

Trailhead Directions:
From the "Y" roundabout (see page 7), drive west toward Cottonwood on SR 89A about 3 miles. Turn right onto Dry Creek Road. Stay on Dry Creek Road to a stop sign (about 3 miles) then turn left onto Boynton Pass Road. Proceed about 1.6 miles to a stop sign. Turn left, continuing on Boynton Pass Road. Park at the first parking area on the left side, about 0.8 miles from the stop sign {1}. (34°54.101'N; 111°51.450'W) The trailhead is across the road from the west end of the parking area. There are toilets at the parking area.

Description: Fay Canyon is one of my favorite trails for non-hiker guests because it is short, relatively level, and very scenic, although some of the views are blocked by trees. The trail essentially ends at a massive rock slide {4}.

For those wanting a greater challenge, there is a side trail {2} located on the east side of the main trail about 0.6 mile from the main parking area that leads to a natural stone arch {3}. (See photo above) The arch is somewhat obscured by the trees. You'll have to scramble up about 225 feet on this unmarked trail if you want to go to the arch, which is located up next to the cliff face {3}. This will add about 0.5 mile to the hike. This side trail is narrow and steep with cactus along the edges and loose rock so watch your footing. There is a narrow slot up under the arch where the rocks have separated and you can slip into the opening. Some people suggest that the area under the arch is a powerful vortex spot. (Additional information on vortexes can be found on page 6.)

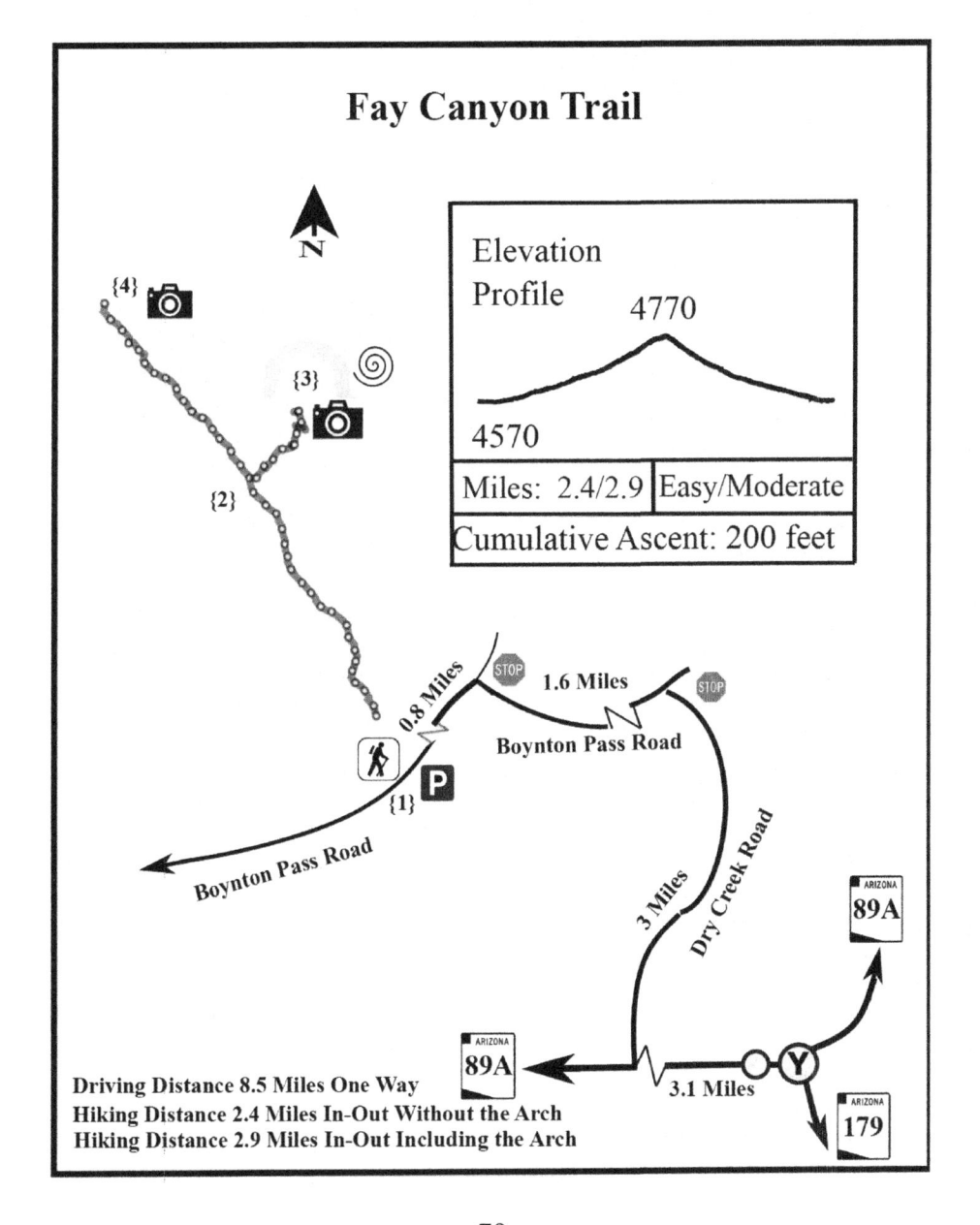

Color Photos: Scan the QR code below for additional color photos of this trail

Fay Canyon Trail

Elevation Profile
4770
4570

Miles: 2.4/2.9	Easy/Moderate
Cumulative Ascent: 200 feet	

0.8 Miles
1.6 Miles
Boynton Pass Road
{1}
Boynton Pass Road
3 Miles
Dry Creek Road
ARIZONA 89A
ARIZONA 89A
3.1 Miles
ARIZONA 179

Driving Distance 8.5 Miles One Way
Hiking Distance 2.4 Miles In-Out Without the Arch
Hiking Distance 2.9 Miles In-Out Including the Arch

Hangover/Munds Wagon Loop

Summary: A scenic loop or in-out hike around some large rock formations
Challenge Level: Moderate for the in-out hike, hard for the loop hike
Hiking Distance: About 3.2 miles in-out, 5.1 miles for the loop hike
Hiking Time: About 2 ½ hours in-out; 3 1/2 hours loop hike
Trail Popularity: 🚶🚶
Trailhead Directions: From the "Y" roundabout (see page 7), drive south on SR 179 about 0.3 mile to the Schnebly Hill Roundabout. Take the second exit then proceed 3.7 miles on Schnebly Hill Road. The trailhead parking is on your right {1}. (34°52.318'N; 111°42.779'W) This parking area also serves the Cow Pies Trail.

Note: Schnebly Hill is paved for the first mile but the last 2.7 miles is an unpaved road and can be very rough; a high clearance vehicle and 4WD are strongly recommended.

Description: This loop hike provides outstanding views but the trail is extremely difficult in places. You'll be hiking the Cow Pies Trail for the first 0.3 mile. Soon you'll pass by an area dotted with small black rocks, which are pieces of lava {2}. Some believe this to be another powerful vortex area. (Additional information on vortexes can be found on page 6.)

Instead of turning left to go to Cow Pies {3}, continue straight ahead to the base of Mitten Ridge. The trail turns left {4.} You'll soon come to a sign for the Hangover Trail {5}. As you continue west along the ridge, you'll have to pay attention to follow the trail in some parts. The trail is very narrow with steep drop-offs in places. You'll be hiking on some narrow ledges so watch your footing. Watch for a sharp left turn about 0.2 mile beyond the social trail {6}. When you arrive at the saddle, which is at the west end of Mitten Ridge, you'll have a nice view of Midgley Bridge and Wilson Mountain to the north {7}. Return to the parking area from here for a 3.2 mile round trip hike.

To hike the loop, go to the east end of the saddle where you'll see the continuation of the Hangover Trail. You'll be hiking along a narrow trail with large drop-offs. The trail is off-camber and steep in many places so be extra careful. You'll come to several interesting hollows in another 0.2 mile {8}. As you continue, you are rewarded with outstanding views of Sedona but be sure to watch your footing.

After a total of 4 miles, you'll intersect the Munds Wagon Trail {9}. Make a left turn here then follow the Munds Wagon Trail. After another 0.5 mile, there is a social trail on your right that leads up to Schnebly Hill Road. Don't make the turn, but continue straight ahead then slightly to the left to stay on the main trail {10}. You'll cross Schnebly Hill Road after another 0.5 mile {11} then soon make a left turn {12} back to the parking area {1} for a 5.1 mile loop hike.

Note: Do not attempt this trail if it is wet or there is snow or ice on the trail. Be sure you have hiking boots with good traction. Do not attempt if you have a fear of heights or of narrow, steep trails with large drop-offs. Be aware of mountain bikers.

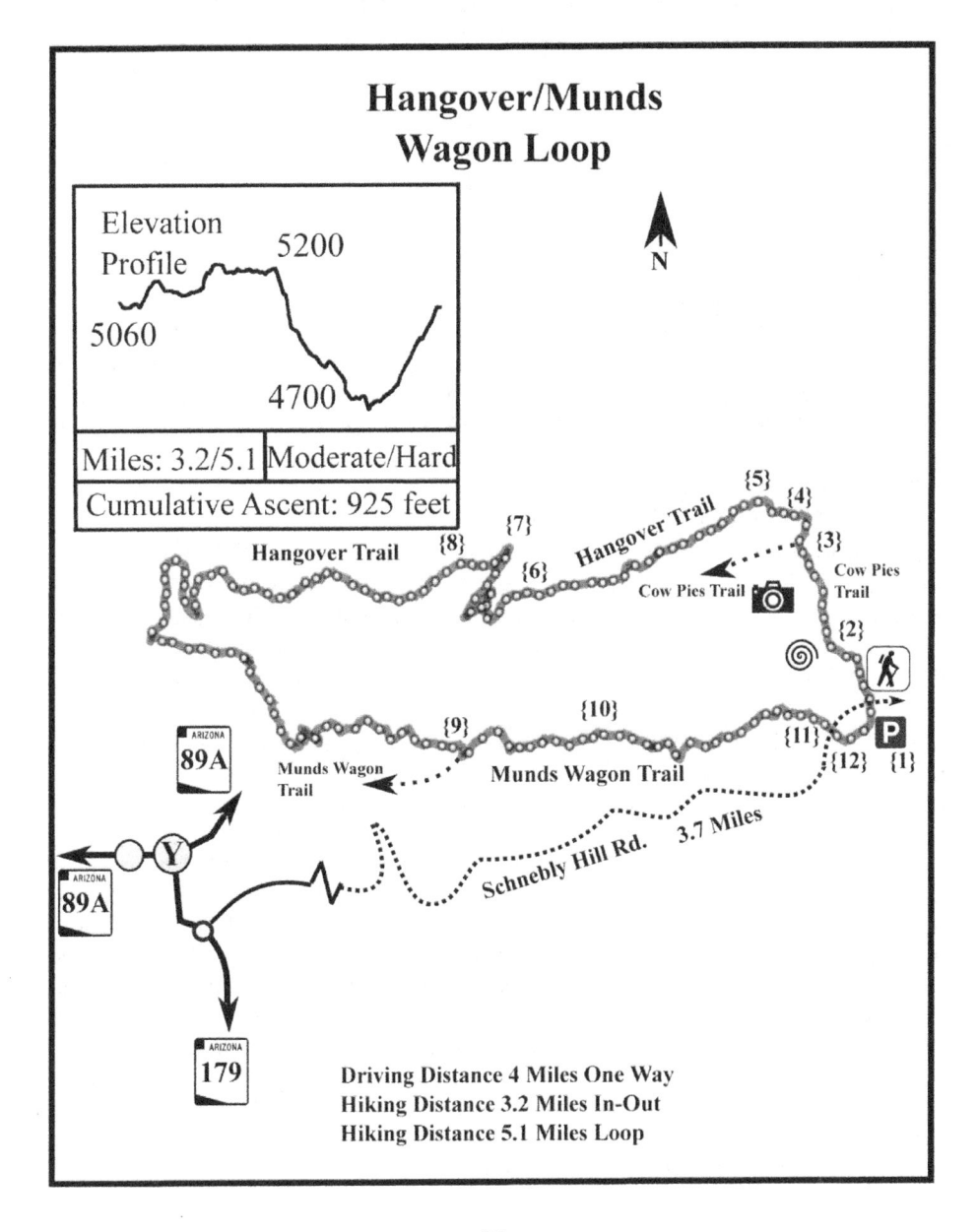

Color Photos: Scan the QR code below for additional color photos of this trail

Hangover/Munds Wagon Loop

Elevation Profile
5200
5060
4700

Miles: 3.2/5.1 | Moderate/Hard
Cumulative Ascent: 925 feet

Hangover Trail
Cow Pies Trail
Munds Wagon Trail
Schnebly Hill Rd. 3.7 Miles

89A
179

Driving Distance 4 Miles One Way
Hiking Distance 3.2 Miles In-Out
Hiking Distance 5.1 Miles Loop

HiLine Trail ★

Summary: A favorite in-out or two-vehicle hike on a narrow trail that skirts the face of a red rock formation offering panoramic views of Sedona's red rocks.

Challenge Level: Moderate

Hiking Distance: 2 miles each way to a great view of Cathedral Rock or 4 miles round trip; about 3.6 miles each way to the Baldwin Loop Trail or 7.2 miles round trip; 4.7 miles as a two-vehicle hike from the Yavapai Vista parking area to the Turkey Creek parking area

Hiking Time: About 2 hours to the great view of Cathedral Rock round trip; about 4 hours to the Baldwin Trail and return; about 3 hours as a two vehicle hike to the Turkey Creek parking area from the Yavapai Vista parking area

Trail Popularity:

Trailhead Directions: From the "Y" roundabout (see page 7), drive south on SR 179 about 4.8 miles to mile marker 308.5 then turn right into the Yavapai Vista parking area {1}. (34°48.442'N: 111°46.174'W) (Note: The Yavapai Vista parking area is accessible only from southbound SR 179.) For a two-vehicle hike, park the second vehicle at the Turkey Creek Trail parking area {14}, located 4 miles west on Verde Valley School Road (see Baldwin Loop). (34°48.762'N; 111°48.589'W)

Description: Hike past the interpretive signboard and around the metal railing then continue straight ahead. At the intersection of the Kaibab and Yavapai Vista Trails {2}, continue on the Kaibab Trail for 0.2 mile then turn left onto the Slim Shady Trail {3}. There are no signs for the HiLine Trail at this point. Continue on Slim Shady for about 0.2 mile where you will see a sign and the beginning of the HiLine Trail on your right {4}.

The HiLine Trail is used by many mountain bikers so you may encounter them on this narrow trail. The trail has a number of narrow spots {5} so watch your footing. You'll have nice views of Courthouse Butte, Bell Rock, Lee Mountain, Rabbit Ears, and get your first view of Cathedral Rock after 1.2 miles from the parking area {6}. As you continue, the views of Cathedral Rock get better and better {7}. A good place to stop is 2 miles from the parking area {8}. I suggest you turn around here for a 4 mile round trip hike, but if you wish to hike further, make a right turn to begin the descent. You'll intersect the Transept Trail and after 0.4 mile the trail turns west at a cairn {9} You'll be crossing large expanses of slick rock for the next 0.6 mile. At 3 miles from the parking area, the trail begins a steep, slippery descent so watch your footing {10}. Shortly after the descent you'll be in a wash and as you continue you'll intersect the Baldwin Loop Trail in another 0.6 mile {11}. Turn around here for a 7.2 mile round trip hike, or, for a two vehicle hike, turn left onto the Baldwin Trail, follow it for 0.6 mile then turn left (south) at the sign {12} for the trail to the Turkey Creek parking area {14}. In 400 feet, bear right {13} for a shortcut back to the Turkey Creek parking area {14}.

Note: This trail is narrow and uneven with large drop-offs – do not attempt it if there is snow or ice on the trail.

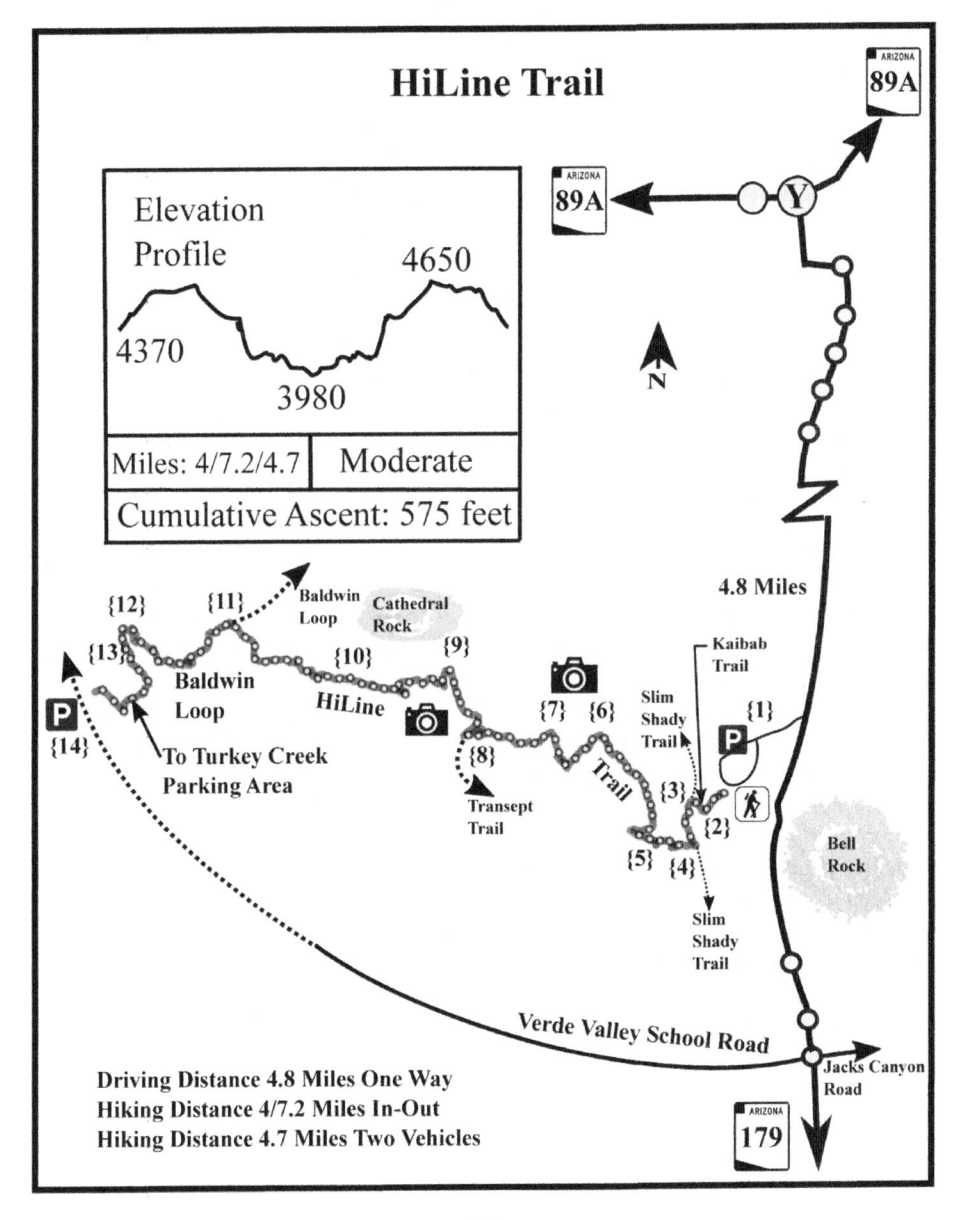

Color Photos: Scan the QR code below for additional color photos of this trail

HiLine Trail

Elevation Profile
4650
4370
3980

Miles: 4/7.2/4.7 — Moderate
Cumulative Ascent: 575 feet

Driving Distance 4.8 Miles One Way
Hiking Distance 4/7.2 Miles In-Out
Hiking Distance 4.7 Miles Two Vehicles

83

Honanki and Palatki Heritage Sites

Summary: A visit to two separate Sinagua pueblo ruins and rock art

Challenge Level: Easy

Hiking Distance: Honanki: About 0.25 mile each way or 0.5 mile round trip. **Palatki:** About 0.3 mile each way to the ruins or 0.6 mile round trip; add another 0.3 mile each way to the rock art or 1.2 miles round trip.

Hiking Time: About ¼ hour to and from each site but plan on at least an hour to view the ruins and rock art

Trail Popularity: Honanki 🥾🥾; Palatki 🥾🥾🥾🥾

Trailhead Directions: From the "Y" roundabout (see page 7), drive west toward Cottonwood on SR 89A about 3 miles. Turn right onto Dry Creek Road {1}. Stay on Dry Creek Road to a stop sign (about 3 miles) then turn left onto Boynton Pass Road {2}. Proceed about 1.6 miles to a stop sign. Turn left, continuing on Boynton Pass Road {3}. The road is paved for the first 2 miles then becomes gravel. Drive 4 miles to a stop sign then turn right onto Forest Road (FR) 525 {4}. After about 0.1 mile, you'll come to a fork {5}. The left fork leads to the Honanki parking area in 4.5 miles {7}. (34°56.193'N; 111°56.078'W) On the way you'll pass a fork which leads to the Bradshaw Overlook {6}. The right fork leads to the Palatki parking area in 1.8 miles {8}. (34°54.891'N; 111°54.136'W)

Note: These unpaved roads can be very rough so a high clearance vehicle is recommended. Pets are not allowed beyond the parking areas at either site.

Description: The Sinagua, ancestors of the Hopi, lived at Honanki and Palatki from about AD 1100 to 1300. Here they raised their families, made tools from stone, leather and wood, and hunted deer and rabbit.

Honanki: The Pink Jeep Company manages the Honanki (meaning bear house) site. There usually is a person at the entrance booth but there are no volunteers or rangers stationed here. You are on your own to wander through the site. There is a metal rail fence to keep unauthorized folks out but you are very close to the structures. You may encounter people touring the site who are on jeep tours at the time you are there. The Pink Jeep Company asks that you not interfere with the tours.

Palatki: Palatki (meaning red house) includes cliff dwellings, petroglyphs (etched markings) and pictographs (painted symbols). You must make a reservation for a 1 hour site tour at https://www.recreation.gov (search for Palatki) or calling (877) 444-6777. There is $1 reservation fee per person plus the cost of a Red Rock Pass (or equivalent).

After you park at Palatki, walk to the Visitor Center and check in. Each trail is about 0.3 mile long. The trail to the cliff dwellings has about 60 rock steps and is steeper than the 15 step trail to the rock art. There are rangers and volunteers on duty to give the site's history and answer questions.

Color Photos: Scan the Honanki QR Code

Scan the Palatki QR Code

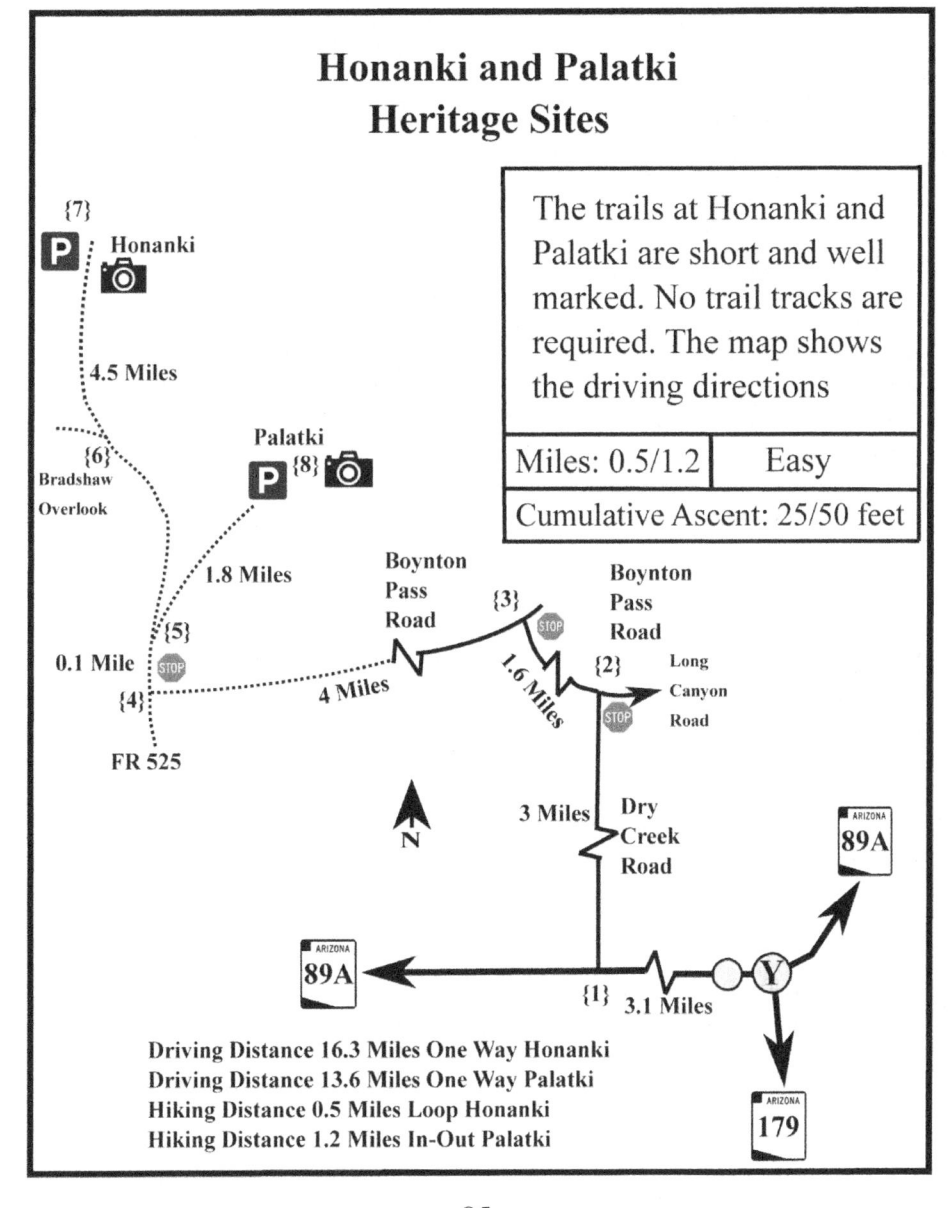

Honanki and Palatki Heritage Sites

{7} Honanki 🅿️ 📷

4.5 Miles

{6} Bradshaw Overlook

Palatki {8} 🅿️ 📷

1.8 Miles

{5}

0.1 Mile 🛑

{4}

FR 525

4 Miles

Boynton Pass Road

{3} 🛑

1.6 Miles

Boynton Pass Road

🛑 {2} Long Canyon Road

N

3 Miles Dry Creek Road

ARIZONA 89A

ARIZONA 89A ← {1} 3.1 Miles Y

ARIZONA 179

The trails at Honanki and Palatki are short and well marked. No trail tracks are required. The map shows the driving directions

| Miles: 0.5/1.2 | Easy |

Cumulative Ascent: 25/50 feet

Driving Distance 16.3 Miles One Way Honanki
Driving Distance 13.6 Miles One Way Palatki
Hiking Distance 0.5 Miles Loop Honanki
Hiking Distance 1.2 Miles In-Out Palatki

HS Canyon Trail

Summary: A pleasant in-out hike through a narrow, forested canyon

Challenge Level: Moderate

Hiking Distance: About 2.1 miles each way or 4.2 miles round trip

Hiking Time: About 2 ½ hours round trip

Trail Popularity: 🚶

Trailhead Directions: From the "Y" roundabout (see page 7), drive west toward Cottonwood on SR 89A about 3 miles. Turn right onto Dry Creek Road. Stay on Dry Creek Road for 2 miles then turn right onto Forest Road (FR) 152. Proceed on FR 152 for 3.4 miles to the Secret Canyon parking area on your left {1}. (34°55.797'N; 111°48.391'W)

Note: FR 152 is an extremely rough road beyond the 0.2 mile paved section; a high clearance vehicle and 4WD are strongly recommended.

Description: To reach the HS Canyon Trail, you begin hiking the Secret Canyon Trail. You'll cross a wash after 0.6 mile {2}. Look to the right because after a rain there usually is a nice small pool of water. Proceed another 0.1 mile and you'll see the HS Canyon Trail #50 sign on your left {3}.

The HS Canyon Trail gently rises about 625 feet providing good red rock views, although the forest of alligator junipers, oak and pinyon pines obscures many of them. You'll find a lot of manzanita along the trail. At higher elevations on the trail, more manzanita trees appear among the manzanita bushes. You'll come to a nice spot for a photo after 1 mile {4}. As you proceed, the trail becomes somewhat overgrown – a result of its relative inaccessibility because of the poor condition of FR 152.

The name (HS Trail) reportedly comes from the early riders finding lots of horse s**t on this trail. When the Forest Service officially named the trail, they kept the initials (HS) but named it after Henry Schuerman, an early Sedona resident. The HS Canyon Trail is a good hike in the summer as there is plenty of shade. The trail ends next to Maroon Mountain {5}.

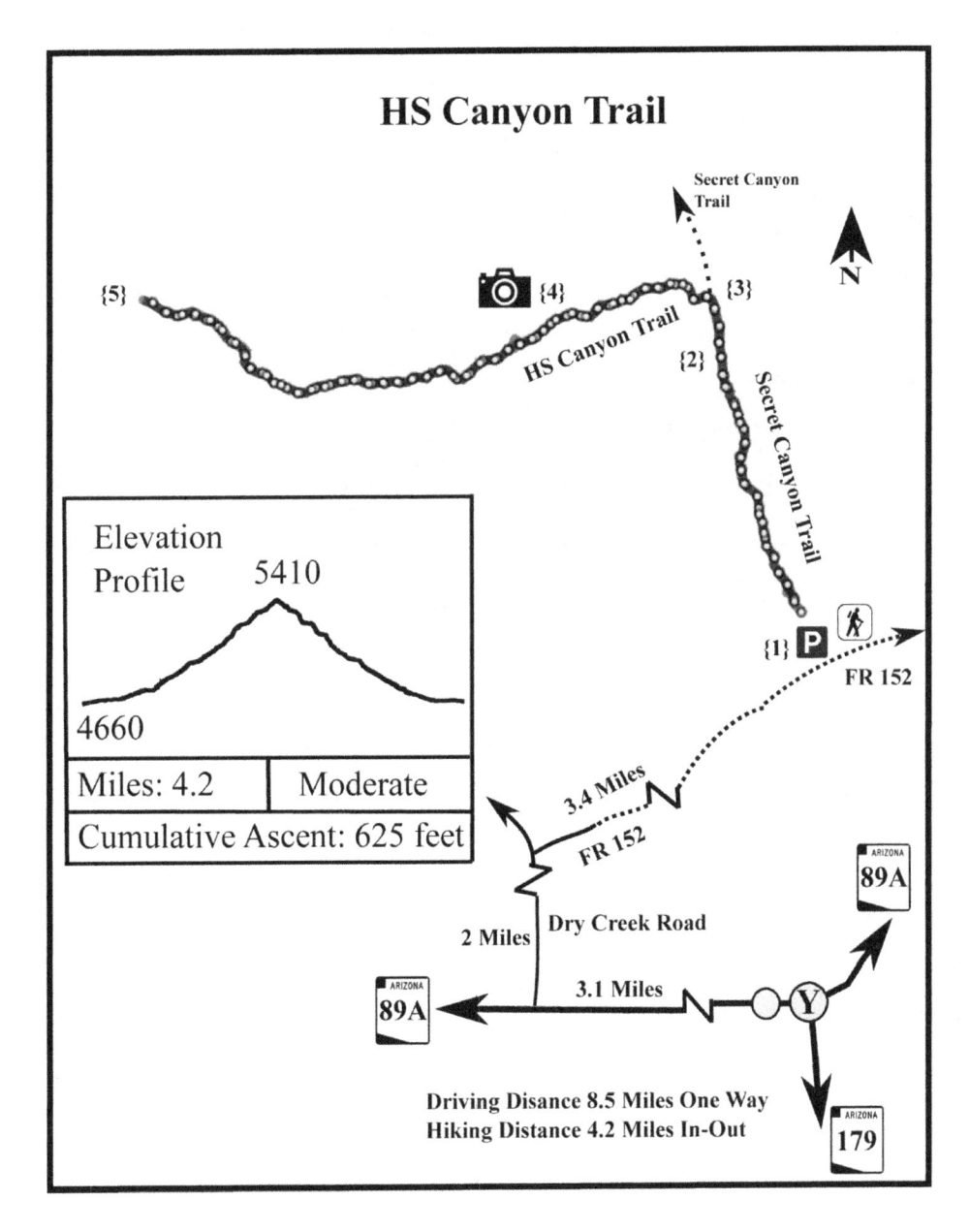

Color Photos: Scan the QR code below for additional color photos of this trail

HS Canyon Trail

Secret Canyon Trail

{5} {4} {3}

HS Canyon Trail

{2}

Secret Canyon Trail

{1} P

FR 152

Elevation Profile
5410

4660

Miles: 4.2	Moderate
Cumulative Ascent: 625 feet	

3.4 Miles

FR 152

2 Miles Dry Creek Road

ARIZONA 89A

3.1 Miles Y

ARIZONA 89A

ARIZONA 179

Driving Disance 8.5 Miles One Way
Hiking Distance 4.2 Miles In-Out

HT/Easy Breezy Loop

Summary:
A partially shaded in-out or loop hike to the base of Cathedral Rock

Challenge Level:
Moderate

Hiking Distance:
About 2.6 miles each way to the intersection of the Cathedral Rock Trail or 5.2 miles round trip; 5.1 miles as a loop hike

Hiking Time: About 3 ½ hours round trip

Trail Popularity:

Trailhead Directions: From the "Y" roundabout (see page 7), drive south on SR 179 about 3.5 miles. Just past the Back O' Beyond roundabout, you'll see a Scenic View sign and a hiking sign on the right side of SR 179 and a left turn lane on the left. Turn left here then proceed to the parking area {1}. (34°49.433'N; 111°46.555'W) This parking area also serves the Bell Rock Pathway and Little Horse Trails. There are toilets at the parking area. Parking is limited at this popular trail. Rather than attempting to park at the trailhead, a better choice is to take the shuttle **(see Trailhead Shuttle Service page 5)** if the parking area is full.

Description: You'll be hiking three trails to get to the base of Cathedral Rock. This is an alternate way of getting to Cathedral Rock if the Back O' Beyond parking area is full. You'll begin by hiking south on the Bell Rock Pathway. After 0.3 mile, you'll intersect the beginning of the Little Horse Trail {2}. Continue south for another 0.2 mile, then cross the footbridge. The HT Trail begins on your right {3}. As you hike along the HT Trail, you'll pass under both the northbound and southbound lanes of SR 179. There are pinyon pines in this area so you are partially shaded. You are following the wash you crossed on the footbridge. After 1.4 miles, you'll intersect the Easy Breezy Trail {4}. Continue on the HT Trail for another 0.3 mile then turn right onto the Templeton Trail {5}.

As you approach Cathedral Rock, the landscape changes to a desert environment so you'll see ocotillo plants, which likely will have their red blooms displayed in mid to late April. You'll intersect the west end of the Easy Breezy Trail at the 2.7 mile mark {6} and after another 0.1 mile, the Cathedral Rock Trail coming up from the parking area on the Back O' Beyond Road {7}. From here you can scramble up to the saddle of Cathedral Rock (see Cathedral Rock Trail).

For a loop hike, on the return trip turn onto the Easy Breezy Trail {6}. Follow it to the intersection with the HT Trail {4}. Turn left here to return to the parking area.

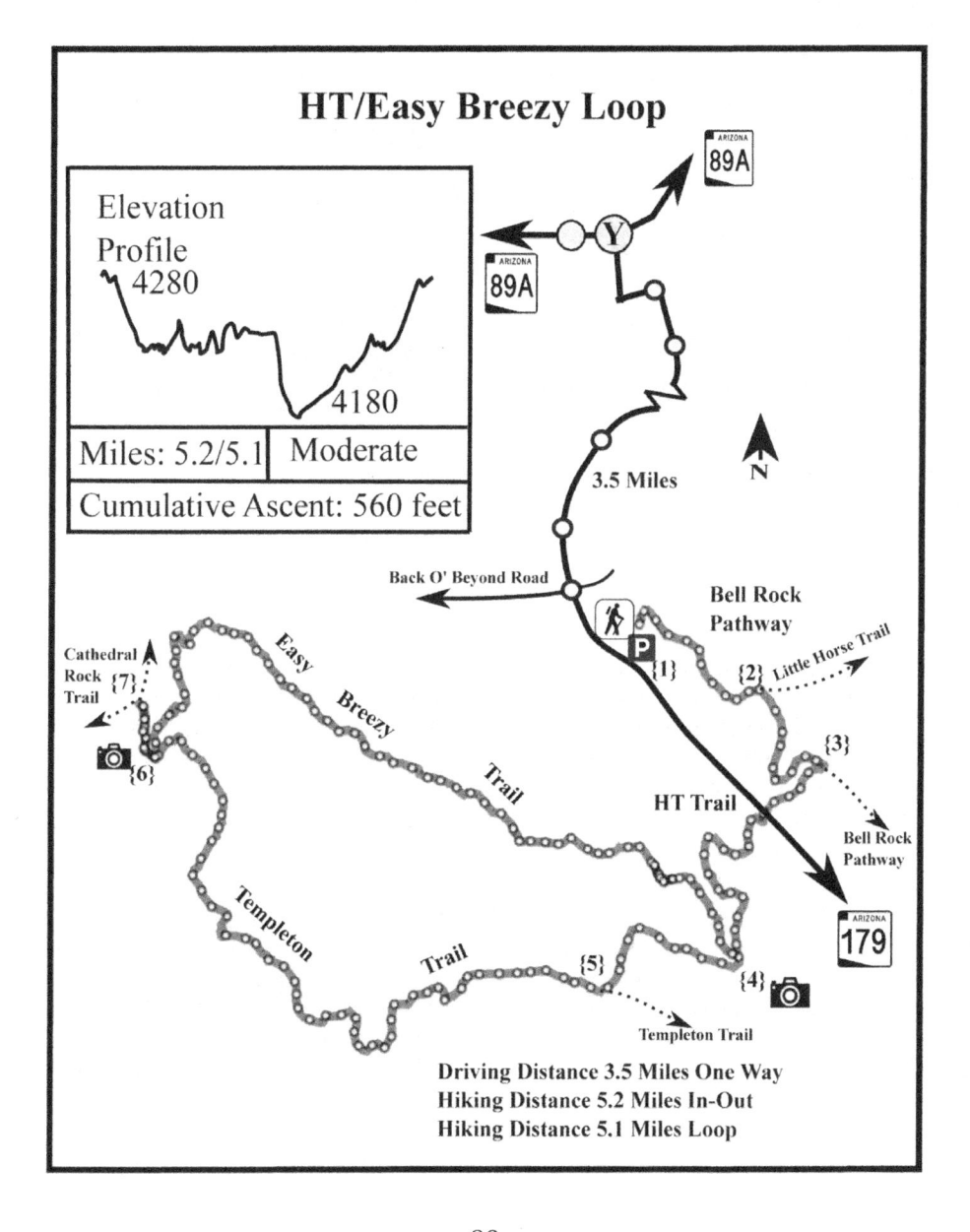

Color Photos: Scan the QR code below for additional color photos of this trail

HT/Easy Breezy Loop

Elevation Profile
4280
4180

Miles: 5.2/5.1 | Moderate
Cumulative Ascent: 560 feet

3.5 Miles

Back O' Beyond Road

Bell Rock Pathway

Little Horse Trail

{1} {2} {3}

Cathedral Rock Trail {7}

{6}

Easy Breezy Trail

HT Trail

Bell Rock Pathway

Templeton Trail

{5} {4}

Templeton Trail

Driving Distance 3.5 Miles One Way
Hiking Distance 5.2 Miles In-Out
Hiking Distance 5.1 Miles Loop

89

Huckaby Trail

Summary: An in-out or two-vehicle hike to the banks of Oak Creek with a great view of Midgley Bridge

Challenge Level: Moderate

Hiking Distance: About 2.5 miles each way or 5 miles round trip; or 3 miles as a two-vehicle hike

Hiking Time: About 3 hours round trip as an in-out hike; about 2 hours as a two vehicle hike

Trail Popularity:

Trailhead Directions: From the "Y" roundabout (see page 7), drive south on SR 179 about 0.3 mile to the Schnebly Hill roundabout then take the second exit. Proceed on the paved Schnebly Hill Road for 1 mile then turn left into the parking area {1}. (34°52.000'N; 111°44.925'W) This parking area also serves the Munds Wagon Trail. There are toilets at the parking area. If you are doing a two-vehicle hike, park the other vehicle at the Midgley Bridge parking area (see Wilson Canyon Trail).

Description: The Huckaby Trail begins on the west side of the parking area. You'll soon intersect the Marg's Draw Trail on the left {2}. Huckaby then turns north and crosses Bear Wallow Wash. The trail rises and falls as you approach Oak Creek Canyon. After about 0.7 mile, look for an overlook on the left {3} with a bench for a nice view of Uptown Sedona and Wilson Mountain. After about 1.6 miles, you'll have your first view of Midgley Bridge {4}. Look around for the views of Lucy, Snoopy, Cathedral Rock and many other named rock formations.

As you approach Oak Creek, the trail descends quite steeply {5}. At the 2 mile mark, you'll be down in the flood plain along Oak Creek where shade is provided by the riparian trees. Watch for poison ivy along the trail. Unless the water is low and you want to cross to the other side of Oak Creek by doing some rock-hopping {7}, end the hike where you have an awesome view of Midgley Bridge, just north of Uptown Sedona {6}. If you continue across Oak Creek, you'll hike up about 150 feet then turn west to reach Midgley Bridge. You can make this hike a two-vehicle hike – one vehicle parked at the Schnebly Hill Road parking area {1} and the other parked at Midgley Bridge {8}. Just make sure you can cross Oak Creek.

Note: There is no shade for the first 2 miles of this trail so it is a hot summer hike until you descend down to Oak Creek.

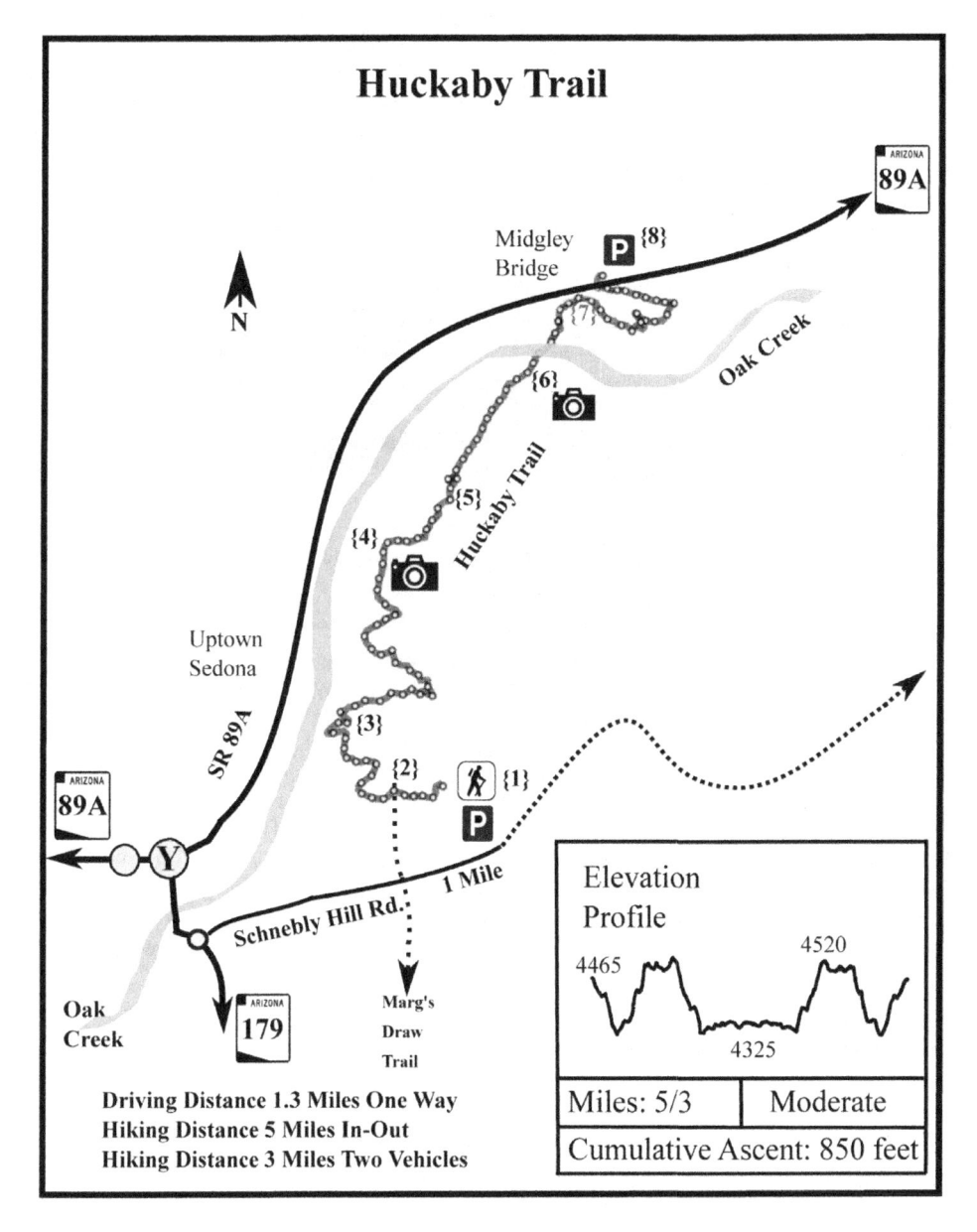

Color Photos: Scan the QR code below for additional color photos of this trail

Huckaby Trail

Elevation Profile
4465
4520
4325

Miles: 5/3	Moderate
Cumulative Ascent: 850 feet	

Driving Distance 1.3 Miles One Way
Hiking Distance 5 Miles In-Out
Hiking Distance 3 Miles Two Vehicles

Jim Thompson Trail

Summary: An in-out hike around the south edge of Steamboat Rock overlooking Midgley Bridge

Challenge Level: Moderate

Hiking Distance: About 2.7 miles each way or 5.4 miles round trip

Hiking Time: About 3 hours round trip

Trail Popularity: 🚶🚶

Trailhead Directions: From the "Y" roundabout (see page 7), drive north on SR 89A about 0.3 mile to the Jordan Road roundabout. Take the third exit onto Jordan Road then drive to the end. Turn left onto West Park Ridge. Drive 0.3 mile then proceed through the paved cul-de-sac, continuing on the dirt road for 0.5 mile to the main parking area {1}. (34°53.287'N; 111°46.098'W) This parking area also serves the Brins Mesa, Cibola and Jordan Trails. There are toilets at the parking area. Note: The dirt road is rough with potholes. A high clearance vehicle is recommended.

Description: Built by Jim Thompson in the 1880s as a road to a homestead at Indian Gardens, the trail begins on the northeast side of the parking area {2}. You'll begin by hiking north then quickly turn right and begin hiking south. After hiking 0.4 mile, you'll intersect the end of the Jordan Trail {3}. In another 0.3 mile, you'll come to an old gate frame. You'll be hiking in an easterly direction along Jim Thompson's old wagon road toward the base of Steamboat Rock.

There are excellent views to the north. The views to the south include Cathedral Rock and Uptown Sedona. Because you are looking into the sun, photographs to the south can be a challenge. I usually stop after about 2.5 miles where you can see Midgley Bridge and look across Oak Creek Canyon {4}. If you continue on for about 0.25 mile, you'll intersect the Wilson Canyon Trail {5} after descending about 125 feet.

Note: There is only partial shade for about the first 0.5 mile and no shade after that so it can be a hot hike in the summer.

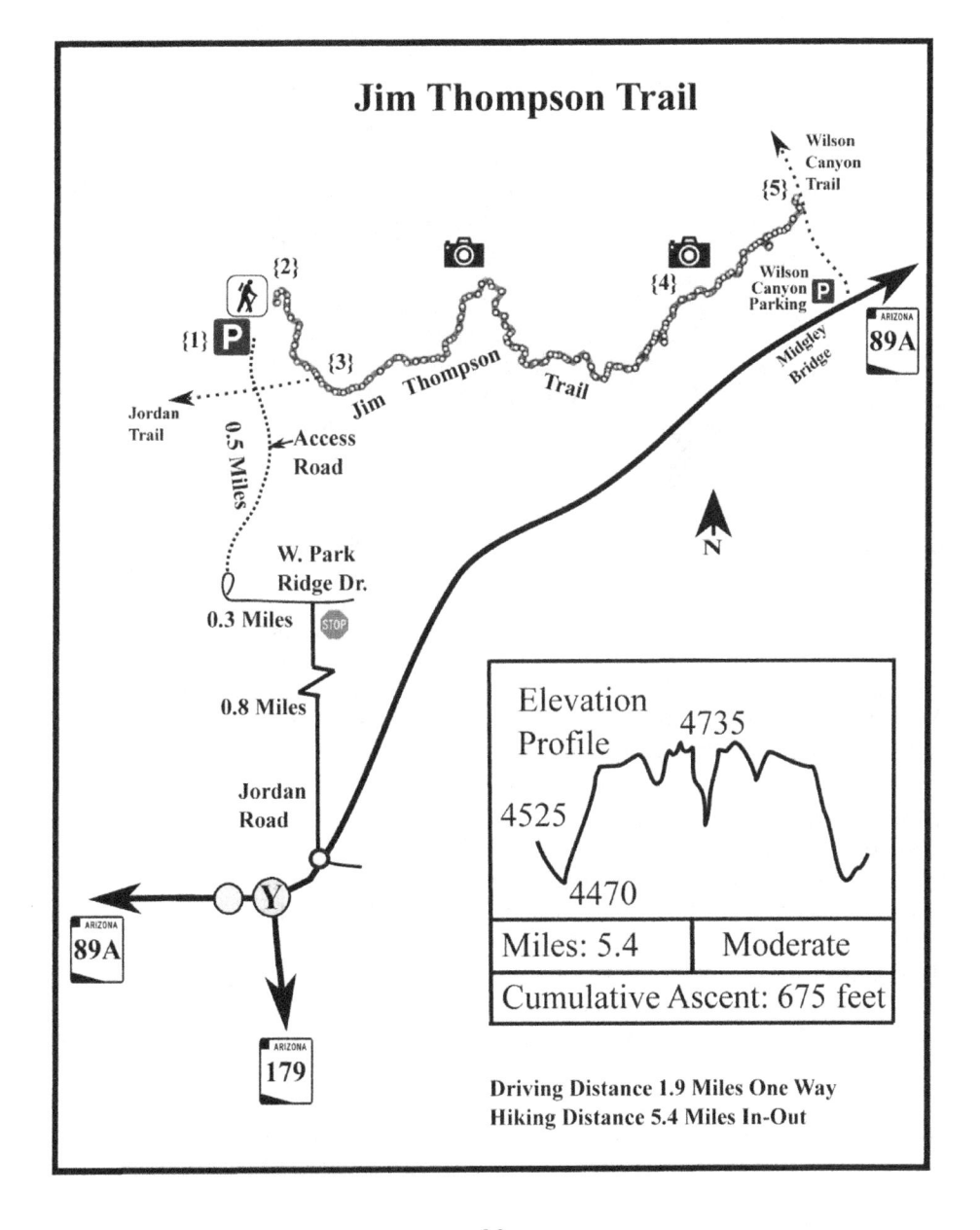

Color Photos: Scan the QR code below for additional color photos of this trail

Jim Thompson Trail

{1} {2} {3} {4} {5}

Wilson Canyon Trail
Wilson Canyon Parking
Midgley Bridge
89A

Jim Thompson Trail

Jordan Trail
0.5 Miles
Access Road

W. Park Ridge Dr.
0.3 Miles
0.8 Miles
Jordan Road

89A
Y
179

N

Elevation Profile 4735 4525 4470	
Miles: 5.4	Moderate
Cumulative Ascent: 675 feet	

Driving Distance 1.9 Miles One Way
Hiking Distance 5.4 Miles In-Out

Jordan Trail

Summary: An in-out partially shaded hike near town that ends at the Soldier Pass Trail

Challenge Level: Easy to Moderate

Hiking Distance: About 1.6 miles each way or 3.2 miles round trip

Hiking Time: About 2 hours round trip

Trail Popularity: 🚶🚶🚶

Trailhead Directions: From the "Y" roundabout (see page 7), drive north on SR 89A about 0.3 mile to the Jordan Road roundabout. Take the third exit onto Jordan Road then drive to the end. Turn left onto West Park Ridge. Drive then proceed through the paved cul-de-sac. The road becomes dirt and you'll shortly come to a small parking area and an extension of the Jordan Trail on the left {2}. I recommend you continue on another 0.4 mile to the main parking area {1}. (34°53.287'N; 111°46.098'W) This parking area also serves the Brins Mesa, Cibola and Jim Thompson Trails. There are toilets at the main parking area. The trailhead at the main parking area is on the west side, near the toilets. Note: The dirt road is rough with potholes. A high clearance vehicle is recommended.

Description: From the main parking area {1}, you'll hike a short distance to the west, then turn south. After 0.4 mile, you'll intersect a sign for the Jordan Trail {3}. Turn right (west) then begin hiking the main trail somewhat uphill as you hike along an old road. If you turn left (east), you'll cross the road then intersect the Jim Thompson Trail after 0.2 mile.

The views gradually improve as you continue the hike. You'll intersect the Javelina Trail after another 0.3 mile {4}, intersect the Ant Hill Trail and then intersect the Cibola Trail at the 1.4 mile mark {5}. Continue on the Jordan Trail until you intersect the Soldier Pass Trail at Devil's Kitchen, which is the largest sinkhole in the Sedona area {6}.

If you want to continue a little further, hike north on the Soldier Pass Trail for 0.4 mile to the Seven Sacred Pools {7}. You can retrace your route or hike back on the Cibola Trail to the parking area. The Jordan Trail is popular with mountain bikers so you may encounter them on the trail.

Color Photos: Scan the QR code below for additional color photos of this trail

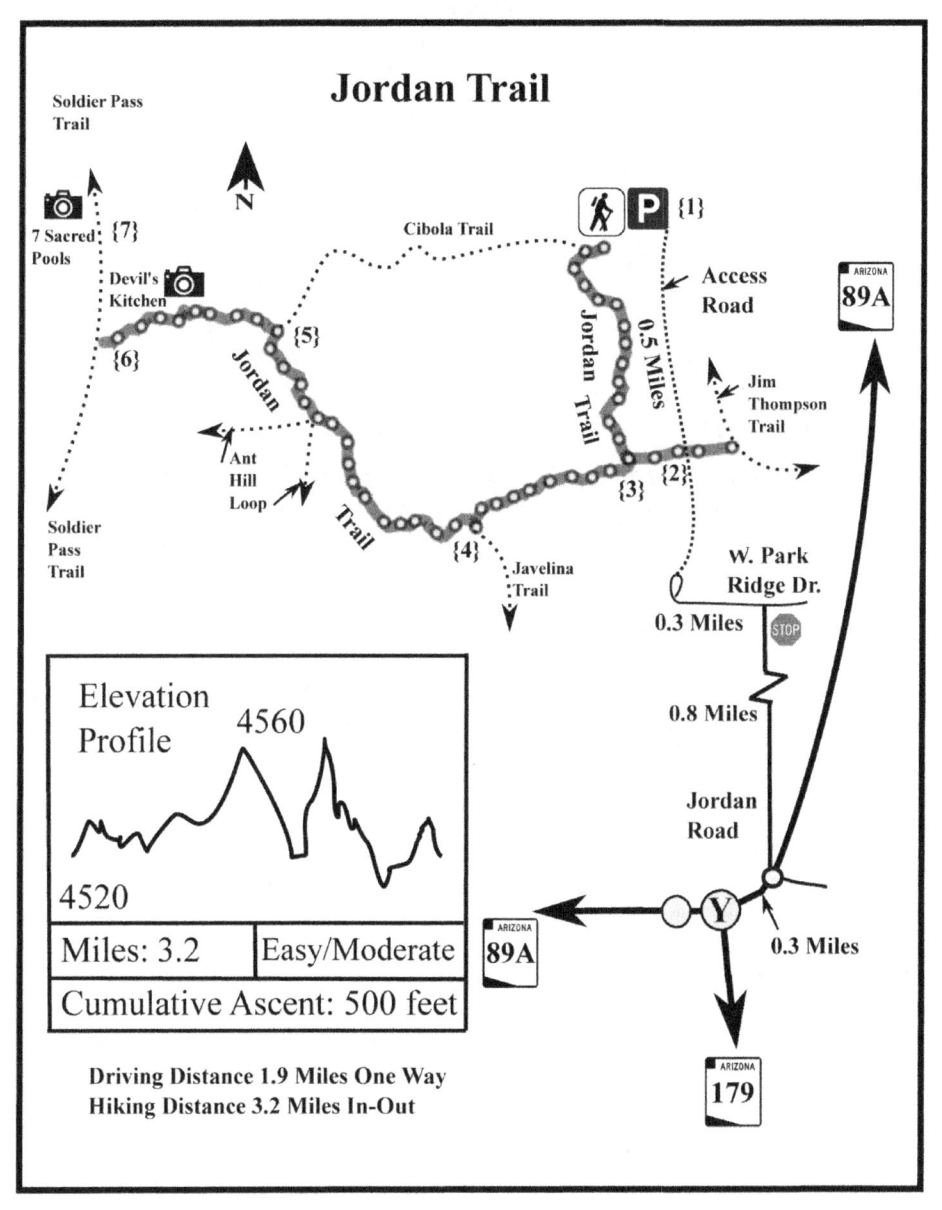

Jordan Trail

- Soldier Pass Trail
- 7 Sacred Pools {7}
- Devil's Kitchen
- {6}
- {5}
- Jordan Trail
- Ant Hill Loop
- Cibola Trail
- {1}
- Access Road
- 0.5 Miles
- Jordan Trail
- Jim Thompson Trail
- {3} {2}
- {4}
- Javelina Trail
- Soldier Pass Trail
- ARIZONA 89A
- W. Park Ridge Dr.
- 0.3 Miles
- 0.8 Miles
- Jordan Road
- ARIZONA 89A
- Y
- 0.3 Miles
- ARIZONA 179

Elevation Profile
4560
4520

Miles: 3.2	Easy/Moderate
Cumulative Ascent: 500 feet	

Driving Distance 1.9 Miles One Way
Hiking Distance 3.2 Miles In-Out

95

Kelly Canyon Trail

Summary:
A pleasant, shaded in-out hike in a ponderosa pine forest with interesting rocks and cliffs

Challenge Level:
Easy to Moderate

Hiking Distance:
About 3 miles each way or 6 miles round trip

Hiking Time:
About 3 hours round trip

Trail Popularity:

Trailhead Directions: From the "Y" roundabout (see page 7), drive north on SR 89A about 17.5 miles. When you reach mile marker 391, watch for a brown sign with the numbers 237 on it. In about 0.3 mile, turn right onto Forest Road (FR) 237 {1}, located 1.5 miles beyond the Oak Creek Vista. Follow the dirt road about 1 mile. Just past the Designated Dispersed Campsites 401-426 sign on the right, you'll be alongside a rustic fence on the right and you'll see a yellow sign with a left arrow ahead. (35°03.517'N; 111°43.140'W) Park along the fence off the road (to let traffic get by your vehicle) then walk up to the yellow sign {2}. Climb over the fence then walk down the faint road. Continue in the same direction for about 500 feet until you go over the bank and down into Pumphouse Wash {3}. Be careful and watch your footing as you hike down as it is steep with loose rocks. Continue east then hike through the opening in the rocks ahead of you for another 500 feet to the beginning of the trail (see photo above) {4}.

Description: This trail takes you across Pumphouse Wash then up Kelly Canyon which is thickly forested and shady. It is a very peaceful and beautiful hike, although you won't find red rock views here. You'll be climbing over several downed trees. There are interesting rock formations as you travel along with many wildflowers in the summer. At 0.8 mile, you'll make a left turn then scramble down about 30 feet into the wash {5} to follow the trail. As you continue, you'll be climbing over and around trees that have fallen across the trail. The trail is seldom used but you shouldn't have trouble following it. Bear left at the fork located about 1.25 miles in {6}. You'll come to a downed tree after another 0.3 mile {7}. You'll intersect several social trails along the way {8} {9}. After hiking a total of 3 miles, you'll intersect FR 237 {9}.

The ambient temperature you encounter on this trail will be about 10 degrees cooler than in Sedona because of the elevation (about 6400 feet) and the shade provided by the trees. It is a pleasant summer hike, but watch for poison ivy, especially in the wash beyond {5}.

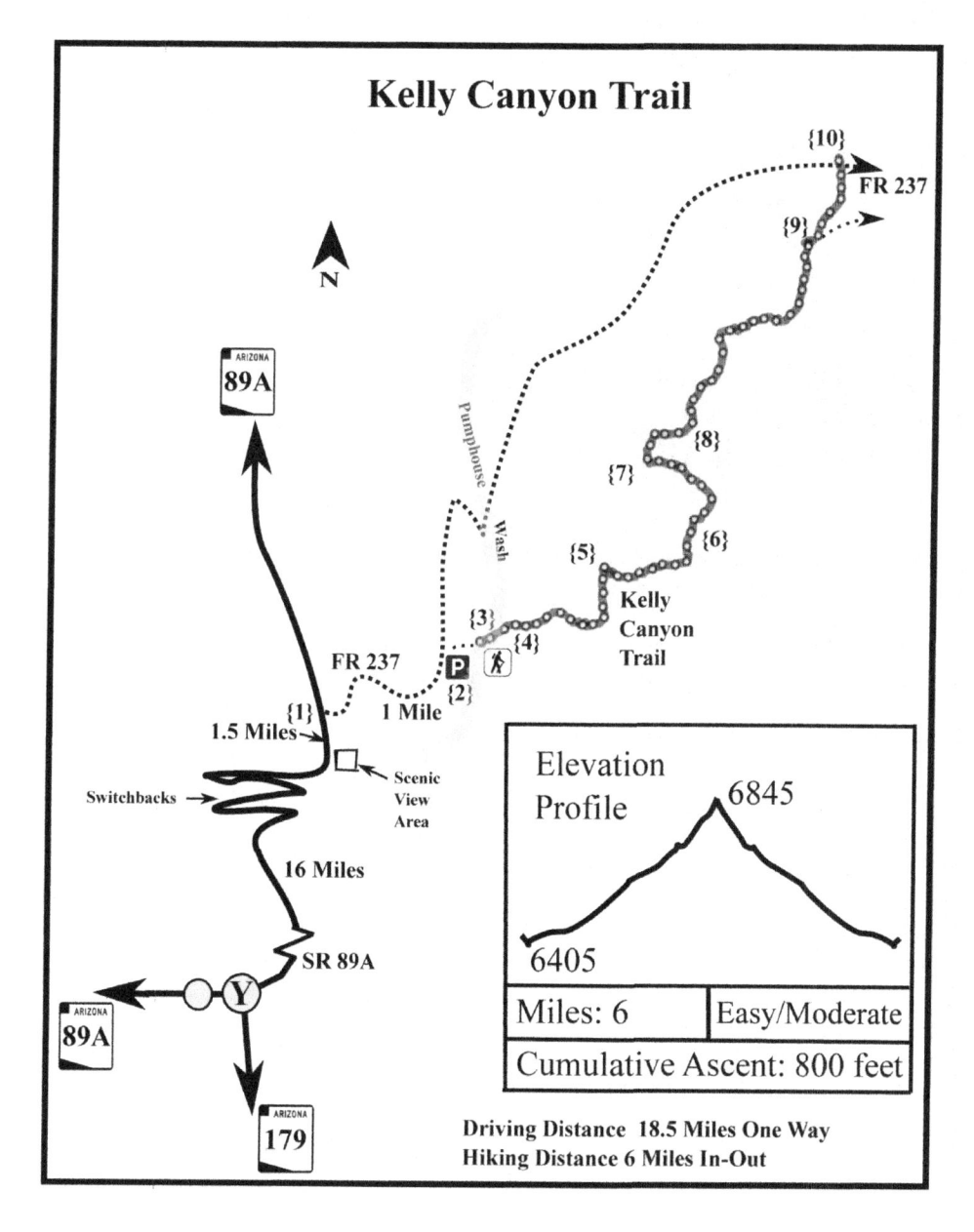

Color Photos: Scan the QR code below for additional color photos of this trail

Kelly Canyon Trail

Elevation Profile
6845
6405

Miles: 6	Easy/Moderate
Cumulative Ascent: 800 feet	

Driving Distance 18.5 Miles One Way
Hiking Distance 6 Miles In-Out

Little Horse Trail ★

Summary: A favorite in-out hike to Chicken Point, a large slick rock knoll with majestic views

Challenge Level: Moderate

Hiking Distance: About 2 miles each way or 4 miles round trip

Hiking Time: About 2 hours round trip

Trail Popularity: 🚶🚶🚶🚶

Trailhead Directions: From the "Y" roundabout (see page 7), drive south on SR 179 about 3.5 miles. Just past the Back O' Beyond roundabout, you'll see a Scenic View sign and a hiking sign on the right side of SR 179 and a left turn lane on the left. Turn left here then proceed across the northbound lane of SR 179 to the parking area {1}. (34°49.433'N; 111°46.555'W) The parking area also serves the Bell Rock Pathway/Templeton Loop and HT/Easy Breezy Loop. There are toilets at the parking area. Parking is limited at these popular trails. Rather than attempting to park at the trailhead, a better choice Thursday through Sunday is to take the shuttle **(see Trailhead Shuttle Service page 5)** if the parking area is full.

Description: You'll begin by hiking south on the Bell Rock Pathway for 0.3 mile until it intersects the beginning of the Little Horse Trail {2}. Turn left here onto the Little Horse Trail. When you come to a deep dry wash, go to the left in the wash then follow the trail east then north toward the Twin Buttes, an impressive red rock formation.

After about 1 mile, you'll intersect the Llama Trail on the right {3}. You will intersect the Chapel Trail at the 1.5 mile mark {4}. If you have the time, follow the Chapel Trail for 0.6 mile until it intersects Chapel Road and go up to visit the Chapel of the Holy Cross {5}.

Returning to the Little Horse Trail, continue on for another 0.5 mile where you'll arrive at an expansive area of slick rock known as Chicken Point. The climb up to Chicken Point isn't hard and is well worth the effort {6}.

Chicken Point is named for thrill-seeking jeep drivers who once dared to drive close to the edge of the point (jeep access is no longer permitted on Chicken Point). If you look to the south, you'll see a chicken-shaped rock high up on the red rock cliff. Chicken

Point is a nice place for a snack break as the views are outstanding. You'll likely encounter some Pink Jeeps as the Broken Arrow tour brings many visitors to this beautiful area.

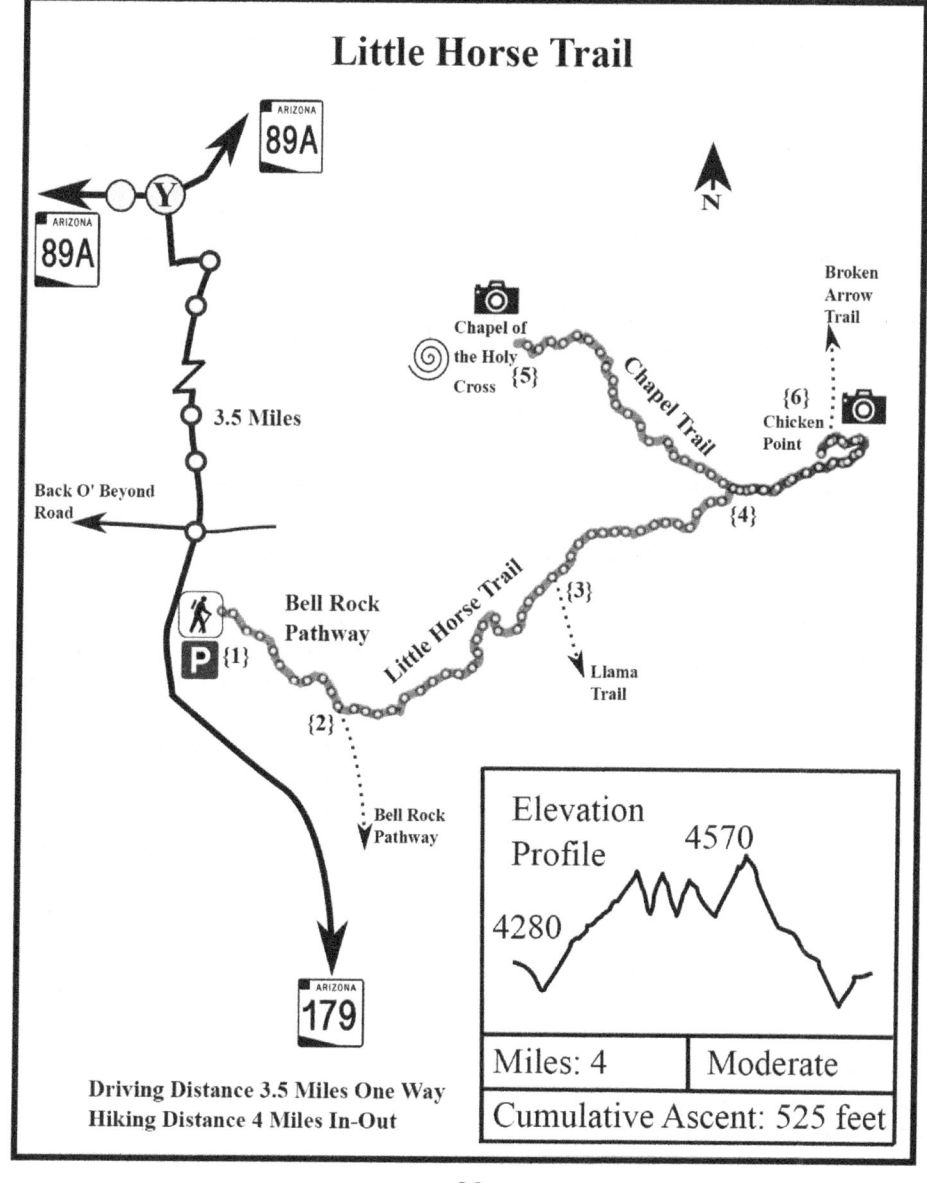

Color Photos: Scan the QR code below for additional color photos of this trail

Little Horse Trail

Driving Distance 3.5 Miles One Way
Hiking Distance 4 Miles In-Out

Elevation Profile: 4280 – 4570

Miles: 4 | Moderate
Cumulative Ascent: 525 feet

Llama/Baby Bell Loop

Summary: A short loop hike with panoramic views of many of Sedona's famous rock formations

Challenge Level: Easy

Hiking Distance: About 1.3 miles loop

Hiking Time: About 1 hour round trip

Trail Popularity: 🚶🚶🚶

Trailhead Directions: From the "Y" roundabout (see page 7), drive south on SR 179 for about 5 miles to the parking area. After you drive about 3.2 miles, just past the Back O' Beyond roundabout, SR 179 becomes a divided highway. Continue driving south. About 1.8 miles beyond the Back O' Beyond roundabout, southbound SR 179 adds a passing lane on the left. From the passing lane, turn left at the sign for the Court House Vista parking area {1}. (34°48.350'N; 111°46.009'W) Before you turn, you'll see Bell Rock ahead of you on the left side of SR 179. This parking area also serves the Bell Rock Climb, Bell Rock Loop, and Courthouse Butte Loop Trails. There are toilets at the parking area. The trail starts on the southeast side of the parking area.

Description: This is a scenic, short loop I like to hike in a clockwise direction, although you can also hike it in the counterclockwise direction. The trails you'll be hiking are a favorite of mountain bikers which you may encounter. From the Court House Vista parking area, look for the Phone Trail on your left about 25 feet past the interpretive signboard. Turn left onto the Phone Trail and you'll see Baby Bell rock on the left. Follow the Phone Trail 0.3 mile then continue north on the Bell Rock Pathway Trail {2} for another 0.1 mile then turn right onto the Baby Bell Trail {3}.

Soon after beginning the Baby Bell Trail, you'll see Rabbit Ears straight ahead. You'll come to a signpost at 0.5 mile where you'll make a right turn to continue on the Baby Bell Trail {4}. Look to the west here for a great view of Cathedral Rock. At 0.7 mile, you'll intersect the Llama Trail and have great red rock views all around {5}. Make a right turn here then continue on the Llama Trail. At 0.8 mile, you'll intersect the Courthouse Butte Loop Trail {6}. Make a right turn then follow Courthouse Butte Loop for 0.1 mile. Continue on the Bell Rock Pathway {7}. At 1.2 miles, you'll intersect the Bell Rock Trail {8}. Turn right here then follow the Bell Rock Trail back to the parking area {1} to complete the loop. There isn't much shade on this trail so it would be a good choice in cooler weather.

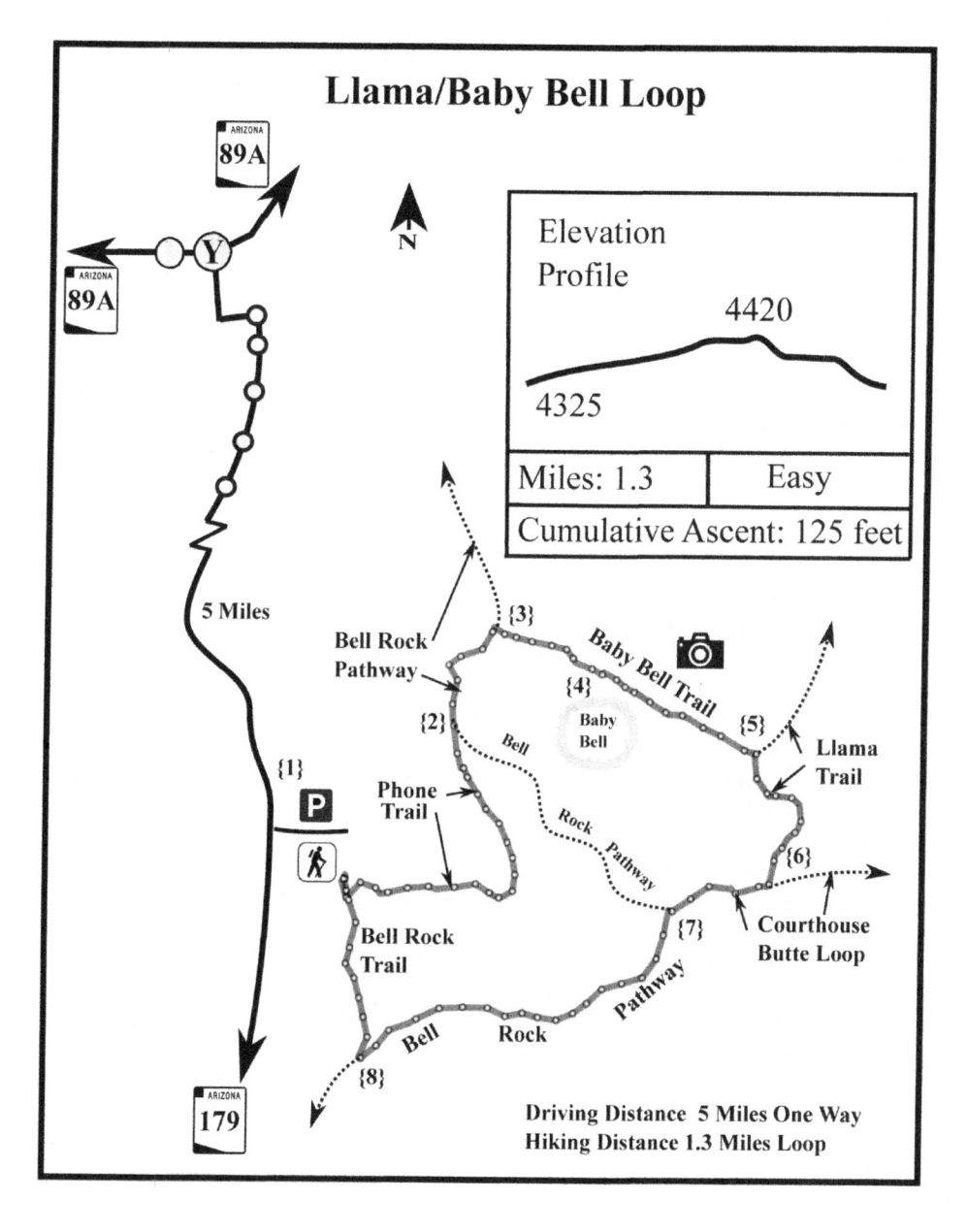

Color Photos: Scan the QR code below for additional color photos of this trail

Llama/Baby Bell Loop

Elevation Profile

4420
4325

| Miles: 1.3 | Easy |

Cumulative Ascent: 125 feet

ARIZONA 89A
ARIZONA 89A
ARIZONA 179

5 Miles

{1} P
{2} Bell Rock Pathway
{3}
{4} Baby Bell
Baby Bell Trail
{5} Llama Trail
Phone Trail
Bell Rock Pathway
{6} Courthouse Butte Loop
{7}
Bell Rock Trail
Bell Rock Pathway
{8}

Driving Distance 5 Miles One Way
Hiking Distance 1.3 Miles Loop

101

Llama/Bail Loop or Llama/Little Horse Loop

Summary: A loop hike with panoramic views of many of Sedona's famous rock formations

Challenge Level:
Easy to Moderate

Hiking Distance: About 4.4 miles for the Llama/ Bail/Bell Rock Pathway loop; about 6 miles for the Llama/ Little Horse/Bell Rock Pathway/Phone Trail loop

Hiking Time: About 2 ¼ hours for the Llama/Bail Loop; about 3 hours round trip for the Llama/Little Horse/Bell Rock Pathway/Phone Trail Loop;

Trail Popularity:

Trailhead Directions: From the "Y" roundabout (see page 7), drive south on SR 179 for about 5 miles to the parking area. After you drive about 3.2 miles, just past the Back O' Beyond roundabout, SR 179 becomes a divided highway. Continue driving south. About 1.8 miles beyond the Back O' Beyond roundabout, southbound SR 179 adds a passing lane on the left. From the passing lane, turn left at the sign for the Court House Vista parking area {1}. This parking area also serves the Bell Rock Climb, Bell Rock Loop, and Courthouse Butte Loop Trails. (34°48.350'N; 111°46.009'W) Before you turn, you'll see Bell Rock ahead of you on the left side of SR 179. This parking area also serves the Bell Rock Climb, Bell Rock Loop, and Courthouse Butte Loop Trails. There are toilets at the parking area. The trail starts on the southeast side of the parking area. There is another Llama trailhead off of the Little Horse Trail {8}. Parking is limited at Little Horse Trail parking area. Rather than attempting to park here, a better choice is to take the shuttle **(see Trailhead Shuttle Service page 5)** if the parking area is full.

Description: The Llama Trail goes from Bell Rock to the Little Horse Trail. It is a favorite of mountain bikers. From the parking area, proceed past the interpretive signboard then follow the Bell Rock Trail 0.1 mile to the intersection with the Bell Rock Pathway {2}. Turn left (northeast) at the sign that says, To Courthouse Butte Loop then follow the Bell Rock Pathway 0.3 mile. Continue straight ahead onto the Courthouse Butte Loop Trail {3}. Follow Courthouse Butte Loop for about 300 feet then turn left onto the Llama Trail {4}.

In 1 mile, you'll come to a scenic area with 8 depressions in the slick rock that are usually filled with water {5}. Continue another 0.9 mile to the intersection with the Bail Trail {6}. You can turn left here then follow the Bail Trail 0.4 mile to the intersection with the Bell Rock Pathway {7}, or proceed another 1.1 miles on the Llama Trail to the Little Horse Trail {8} then turn left to reach the Bell Rock Pathway {9}. Hike south on the Bell Rock Pathway then turn onto the Phone Trail {10} for a shortcut back to the parking area. The Llama Trail approaches Lee Mountain and provides outstanding views of Bell Rock, Courthouse Butte, Twin Buttes and Cathedral Rock. There isn't much shade on this trail so it would be a good choice in cooler weather.

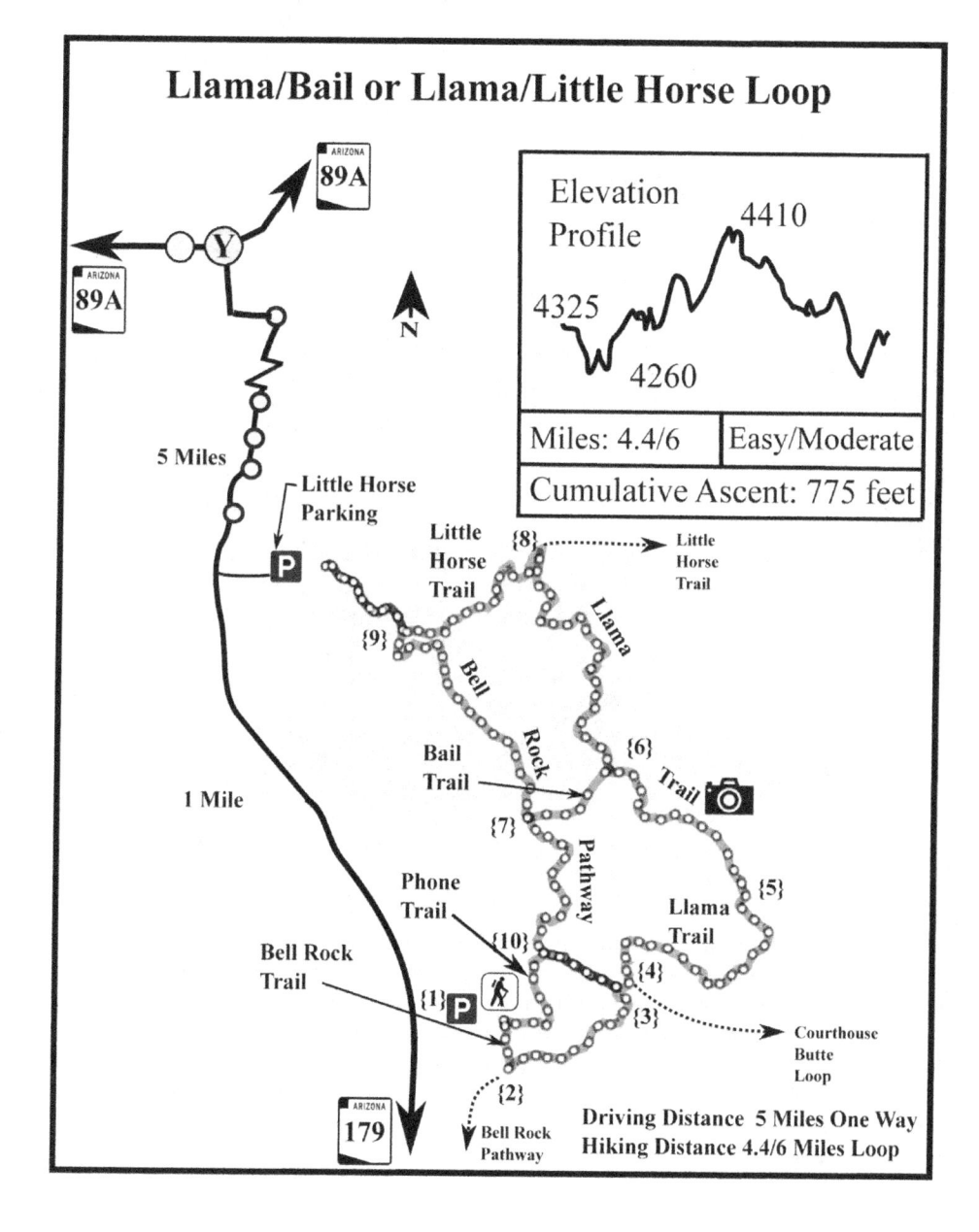

Color Photos: Scan the QR code below for additional color photos of this trail

Llama/Bail or Llama/Little Horse Loop

Elevation Profile
4410
4325
4260

Miles: 4.4/6	Easy/Moderate
Cumulative Ascent: 775 feet	

89A
89A
5 Miles
Little Horse Parking
Little Horse Trail
{8} → Little Horse Trail
{9}
Llama
Bell Rock Pathway
Bail Trail
{6}
Trail
{7}
1 Mile
Phone Trail
{5}
Llama Trail
Bell Rock Trail
{10}
{1}
{4}
{3} → Courthouse Butte Loop
179
{2} ↓ Bell Rock Pathway

Driving Distance 5 Miles One Way
Hiking Distance 4.4/6 Miles Loop

103

Long Canyon Trail

Summary: An in-out hike through a forested canyon with some good red rock views

Challenge Level: Moderate

Hiking Distance: About 3.5 miles each way or 7 miles round trip

Hiking Time: About 3 ½ hours round trip

Trail Popularity: 🚶🚶

Trailhead Directions: From the "Y" roundabout (see page 7), drive west toward Cottonwood on SR 89A about 3 miles. Turn right onto Dry Creek Road. Stay on Dry Creek Road to a stop sign (about 3 miles) then turn right onto Long Canyon Road. Proceed 0.6 mile to the parking area on the left {1}. (34°54.408'N; 111°49.452'W) The trailhead is at the parking area.

Description: This is a nice moderate partially shaded trail through a canyon with red rock views, although some are obstructed. The first 0.75 mile is an old jeep trail. This part of the trail is not shaded and can be very hot in the summer. But once you are in the forest, the trees provide shade. You'll make a left turn after 0.4 mile {2} and come to a Long Canyon sign at 0.6 mile. You intersect the Deadman's Pass Trail after about 1 mile {3}. Soon you'll see the Seven Canyons golf course and development on the right. As you continue, the trail becomes more shaded and you'll cross several washes. I suggest you continue to hike Long Canyon for another 2 miles then begin the return trip {4}.

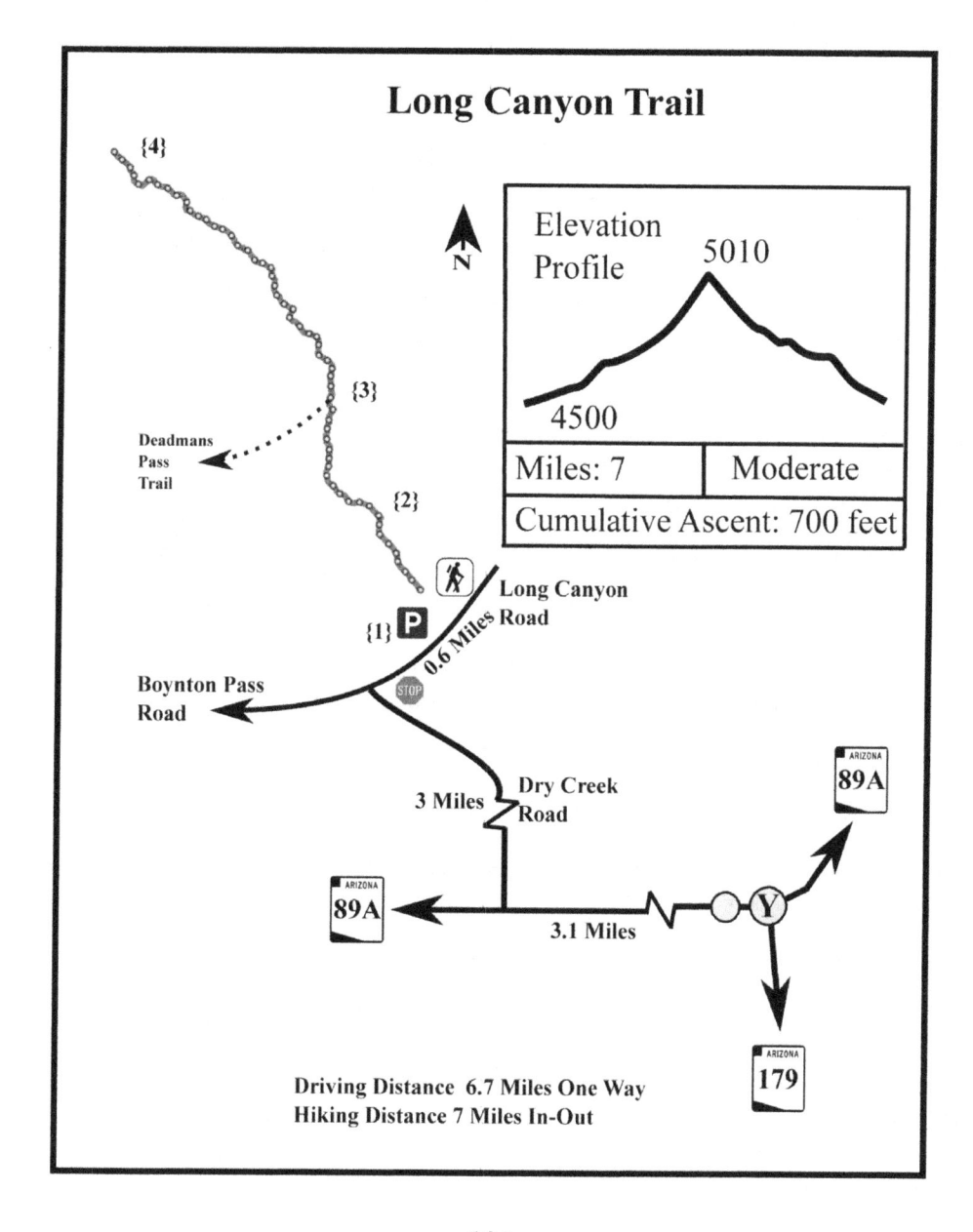

Color Photos: Scan the QR code below for additional color photos of this trail

Long Canyon Trail

{4}

{3}

Deadmans Pass Trail

{2}

{1} 🅿 0.6 Miles

Long Canyon Road

Boynton Pass Road

Elevation Profile
5010
4500

Miles: 7	Moderate
Cumulative Ascent: 700 feet	

3 Miles

Dry Creek Road

ARIZONA 89A

ARIZONA 89A

3.1 Miles

ARIZONA 179

Driving Distance 6.7 Miles One Way
Hiking Distance 7 Miles In-Out

Marg's Draw Trail

Summary: An in-out hike with great red rock views

Challenge Level: Easy to Moderate

Hiking Distance: About 1.3 miles each way from the Sombart Lane trailhead to Schnebly Hill Road or 2.6 miles round trip; about 2.1 miles each way from the Morgan Road trailhead to Schnebly Hill Road or 4.2 miles round trip

Hiking Time: About 1 ½ hours from Sombart Lane to Schnebly Hill Road round trip; about 2 1/2 hours from Morgan Road to Schnebly Hill Road round trip

Trail Popularity:

Trailhead Directions: There are actually three trailheads for this trail: At the south end, at the north end and in the middle of the trail. The south trailhead is at the end of Morgan Road. From the "Y" roundabout (see page 7), drive south on SR 179 1.5 miles to Morgan Road roundabout. Take the third exit then proceed on Morgan Road for 0.6 mile to the trailhead parking on your left (the last part is a dirt road) {1}. (34°50.738'N; 111°45.424'W) This parking area also serves the Broken Arrow Trail.

The middle trailhead is at the end of Sombart Lane, which is located 0.7 mile south of the "Y" off of SR 179 {3}. (34°51.427'N; 111°45.677'W)

The north trailhead is located on Schnebly Hill Road. From the "Y" roundabout, drive south on SR 179 about 0.3 mile to the Schnebly Hill roundabout then take the second exit. Proceed on the paved Schnebly Hill Road for 1 mile then turn left into the parking area {6}. (34°52.000'N; 111°44.925'W) This parking area also serves the Huckaby and Mund's Wagon Trails. There are toilets at this parking area. Hike west on the Huckaby Trail for about 0.2 mile then turn left onto the Marg's Draw Trail {5}.

Description: The trail essentially goes north and south, parallel with SR 179. You'll encounter a number of social trails along the way. For example, about 0.8 mile north of the Broken Arrow trailhead, be sure you take the main trail to the northeast rather than the social trail to the west after you cross a wash {2}. Hiking from the middle trailhead is steep for the first 0.1 mile then is relatively flat {4}. The trail is close to town so there are residences at either end. But in the middle you are in wilderness and won't see any homes. You'll have nice views of Snoopy and Lucy rock formations.

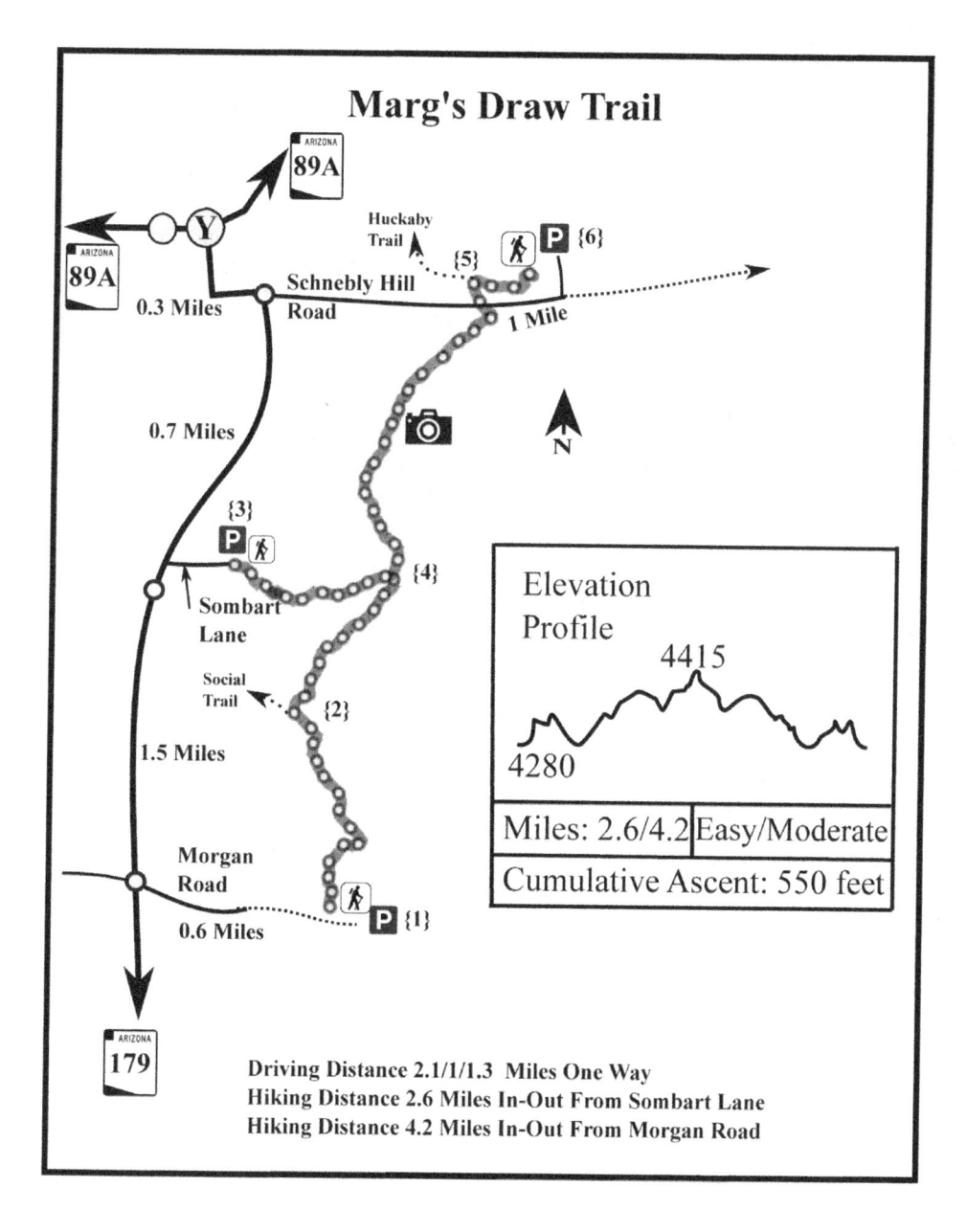

Color Photos: Scan the QR code below for additional color photos of this trail

Marg's Draw Trail

ARIZONA 89A

ARIZONA 89A
0.3 Miles

Huckaby Trail

Schnebly Hill Road

{5}

P {6}

1 Mile

0.7 Miles

N

{3}
P

Sombart Lane

{4}

Social Trail

{2}

1.5 Miles

Elevation Profile

4415

4280

Miles: 2.6/4.2 | Easy/Moderate

Cumulative Ascent: 550 feet

Morgan Road

0.6 Miles

P {1}

ARIZONA 179

Driving Distance 2.1/1/1.3 Miles One Way
Hiking Distance 2.6 Miles In-Out From Sombart Lane
Hiking Distance 4.2 Miles In-Out From Morgan Road

Mescal/Long Canyon Loop ★

Summary: A favorite in-out hike that skirts the base of Mescal Mountain with both panoramic and up close red rock views with the option for a loop hike

Challenge Level: Easy to Moderate

Hiking Distance: About 2.4 miles each way to the Deadman's Pass Trail intersection or 4.8 miles round trip; about 5 miles for Mescal Trail to Deadman's Pass Trail to Long Canyon Trail loop

Hiking Time: About 2 ½ hours for the in-out hike to Deadman's Pass Trail round trip; about 3 hours for the Mescal/Long Canyon loop round trip

Trail Popularity: 🚶🚶🚶

Trailhead Directions: From the "Y" roundabout (see page 7), drive west toward Cottonwood on SR 89A about 3 miles. Turn right onto Dry Creek Road. Stay on Dry Creek Road to a stop sign (about 3 miles) then turn right onto Long Canyon Road. Proceed 0.3 mile to the Mescal Day Use Trailhead parking area on the left on the left {1} (34°54.100'N; 111°49.667'W) or on the right {2}. There are toilets and picnic tables here. These parking areas also serve the Devil's Bridge and Chuck Wagon Trails. The trail begins near the signboard in parking area {1} or across the road from parking area {2}.

Description: This is a favorite trail that provides both close-up and distant red rock views. After the first 0.1 mile, the trail begins to gently rise as you approach the base of Mescal Mountain. At 0.25 mile, you'll intersect the connector trail to Long Canyon Trail on your right {3}. Continue straight ahead. At 0.4 mile, you are on the top of a high bluff with good red rock views all around. You'll pass a cairn and trail marker for the Yucca Trail {4} then at the 1 mile mark, look up high to the right where you'll observe a large cave in the side of Mescal Mountain {5}. Soon the trail becomes very narrow in places with steep drop offs – watch your footing. You'll find signs indicating difficult and extreme portions of the trail for the mountain bikers. I recommend you hike the difficult path. After 1.75 miles, you'll come to a cairn and trail marker for the Canyon of Fools Trail [6]. Just beyond you can see Kachina Woman and the Warrior in Boynton Canyon, Cockscomb, Doe Mountain, Bear Mountain and Courthouse Butte in the distance.

As you proceed, the views get better and better. At 2.2 miles [7], the trail begins to descend some 85 feet in 0.25 mile and intersects the Deadman's Pass Trail [8]. Turn around here or, if you wish to hike a loop, turn right onto the Deadman's Pass Trail then hike for 0.9 mile to the Long Canyon Trail. Turn right onto the Long Canyon Trail {9} then follow it back toward Long Canyon Road. You'll see a connector trail just before the parking area on Long Canyon Road {10}. Turn right to follow the connector trail back to the Mescal Trail. Turn left when you reach the intersection with the Mescal Trail {3} to return to the parking areas {1} {2}.

Note: Don't attempt this trail if it is snowy or the trail is icy. There are some places where the trail is narrow with drop offs on the side.

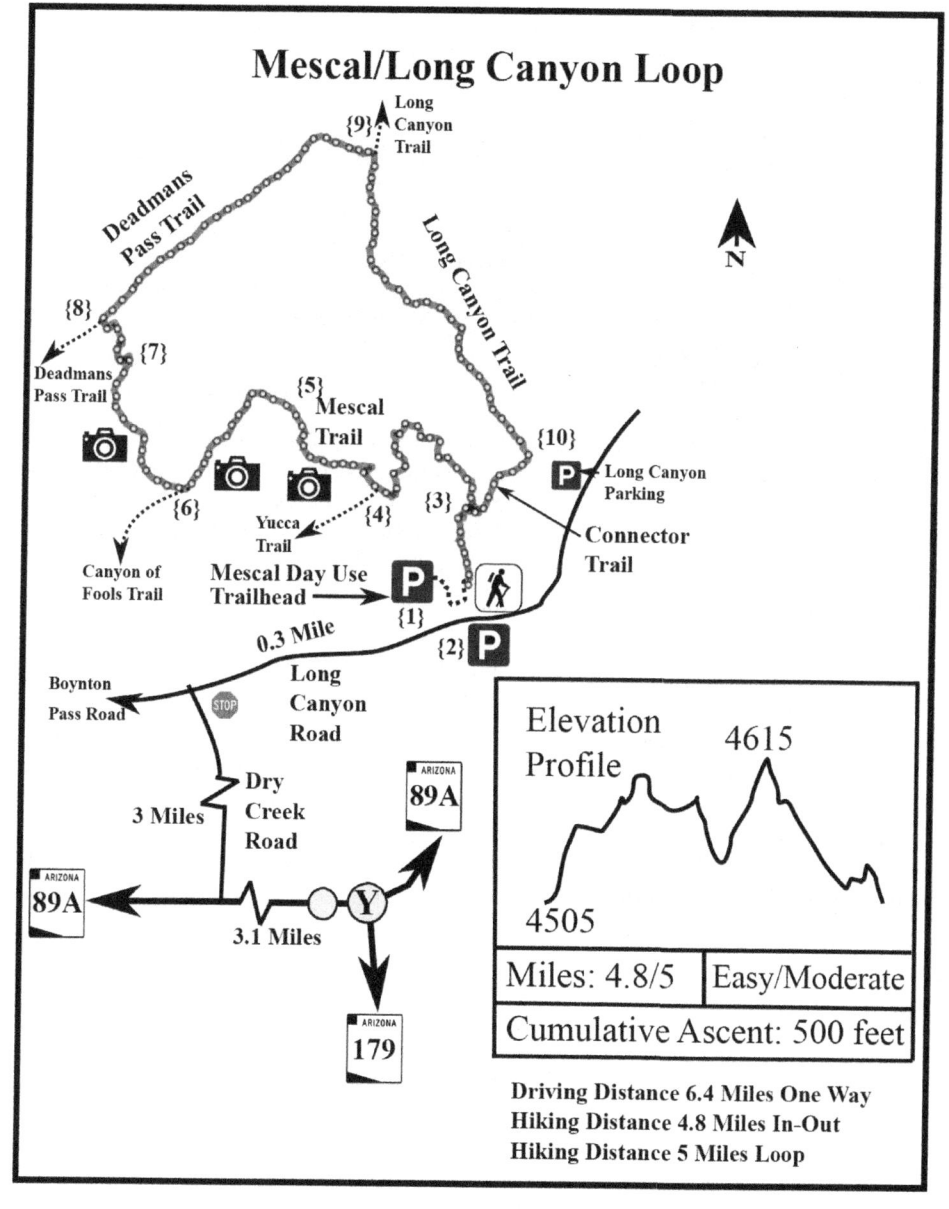

Color Photos: Scan the QR code below for additional color photos of this trail

Mescal/Long Canyon Loop

- {9} Long Canyon Trail
- Deadmans Pass Trail
- Long Canyon Trail
- {8}
- {7}
- Deadmans Pass Trail
- {5} Mescal Trail
- {10}
- Long Canyon Parking
- {6}
- Yucca Trail
- {4}
- {3}
- Connector Trail
- Canyon of Fools Trail
- Mescal Day Use Trailhead
- {1}
- {2}
- 0.3 Mile
- Boynton Pass Road
- Long Canyon Road
- Dry Creek Road
- 3 Miles
- 89A
- 89A
- 3.1 Miles
- Y
- 179

Elevation Profile 4615
4505

Miles: 4.8/5	Easy/Moderate
Cumulative Ascent: 500 feet	

Driving Distance 6.4 Miles One Way
Hiking Distance 4.8 Miles In-Out
Hiking Distance 5 Miles Loop

Munds Wagon Trail

Summary: A moderate in-out hike following an old wagon road and stream bed parallel to Schnebly Hill Road

Challenge Level: Moderate

Hiking Distance: About 2.8 miles each way or 5.6 miles round trip

Hiking Time: About 3 hours round trip

Trail Popularity: 🚶🚶

Trailhead Directions:
From the "Y" roundabout (see page 7), drive south on SR 179 about 0.3 mile to the Schnebly Hill roundabout then take the second exit. Proceed on Schnebly Hill Road for 1 mile then turn left into the parking area {1}. (34°52.000'N; 111° 44.925'W) This parking area also serves the Huckaby and Marg's Draw Trails. The trail begins on the east side of the parking area. There are toilets at the parking area.

Description: This partially shaded trail follows an old wagon road along Schnebly Hill Road. Shortly after you start out, you'll cross Schnebly Hill Road, hike a short distance then cross back over. The trail begins a gentle descent for 0.2 miles. If you have a snack with you, there are picnic tables about 1.3 miles from the parking area {2}.

At 1.75 miles, you'll intersect the Hangover Trail on your left {3}. At 2.1 miles, there is a social trail on your right that leads up to Schnebly Hill Road. Don't make the turn here, but continue straight ahead and slightly to the left to stay on the main trail {4}. After about 2.5 miles {5}, you'll be looking up at the Cow Pies (see Cow Pies Trail). Continue on another 0.3 mile where you'll cross Schnebly Hill Road {6} then make a left {7} to go to the Cow Pies Trail parking area.

The trail is much prettier when there is water flowing from snow runoff, which usually happens in the spring.

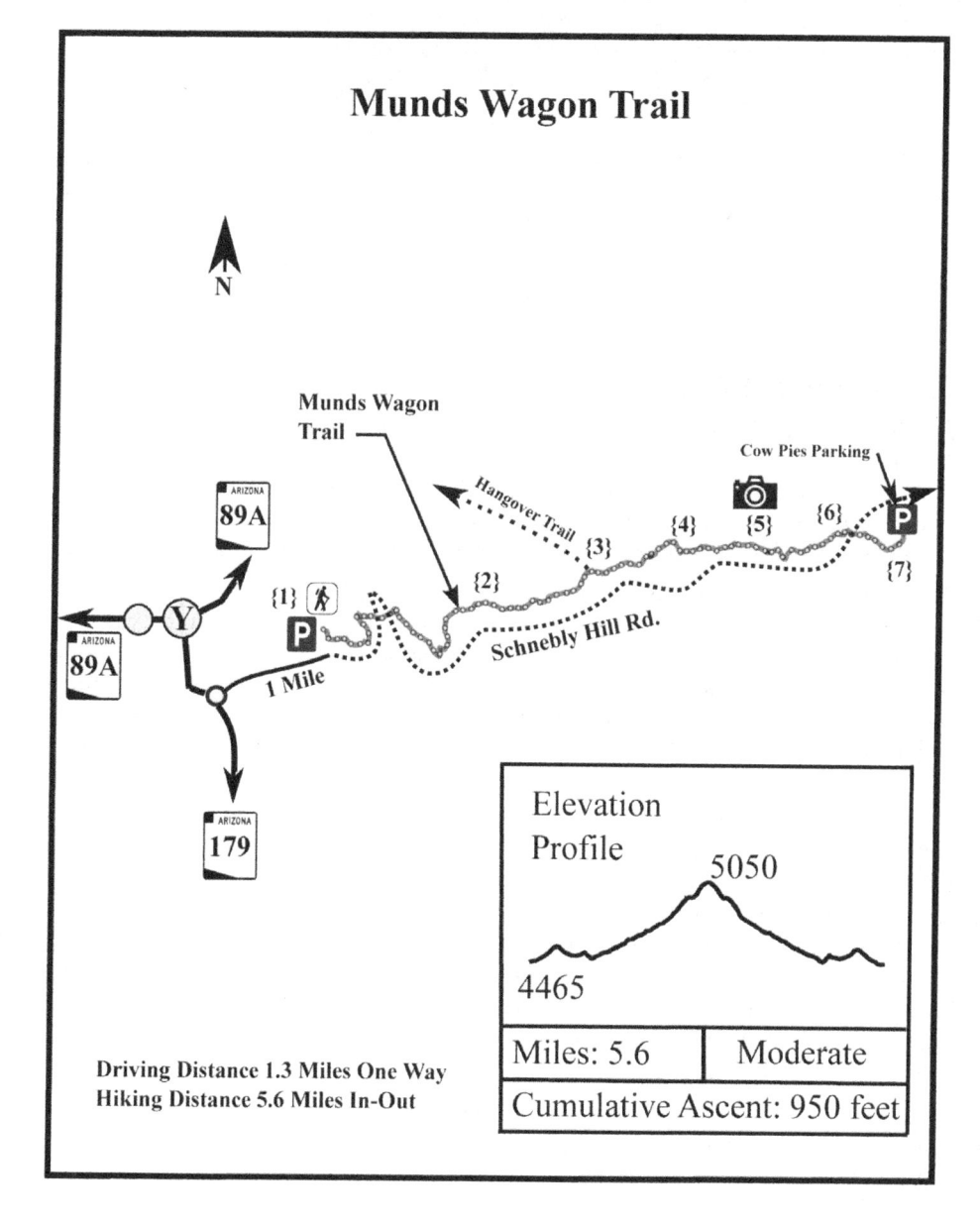

Color Photos: Scan the QR code below for additional color photos of this trail

Munds Wagon Trail

Munds Wagon Trail

Hangover Trail

Cow Pies Parking

Schnebly Hill Rd.

1 Mile

Elevation Profile
5050
4465

Miles: 5.6	Moderate
Cumulative Ascent: 950 feet	

Driving Distance 1.3 Miles One Way
Hiking Distance 5.6 Miles In-Out

Old Post/Carroll Canyon Loop

Summary: A loop hike using a series of connected trails west of Sedona featuring some nice views but with little shade

Challenge Level: Moderate

Hiking Distance: About 5 miles round trip for the Old Post/Carroll Canyon loop hike

Hiking Time: About 2½ hours round trip

Trail Popularity:

Trailhead Directions: From the "Y" roundabout (see page 7), drive west toward Cottonwood on SR 89A about 4.25 miles. Turn left onto Upper Red Rock Loop Road. You'll pass Sedona High School on your right. Continue for 1.8 miles then turn left onto Chavez Ranch Road. Drive 0.2 miles to the parking area on the left {1}. (34°49.990'N; 111°48.618'W) There is room for about 8 vehicles. The trail begins at the parking area.

Description: You'll begin by following an old road, used for mail delivery long ago. After hiking 0.3 mile, you'll intersect the Ramshead Trail on the right {2} and the Herkenham Trail to the left at 0.7 mile mark {3}. Periodically look behind you for some nice views of Cathedral Rock and Courthouse Butte. You'll come to the southern intersection of the Carroll Canyon Trail at the 1 mile mark {4}. Stay on the Old Post Trail rather than turn onto the Carroll Canyon Trail (you'll be back to this point on your return hike).

After hiking an additional 0.4 mile, you'll intersect the Skywalker Trail on the left {5}. The trail begins a gradual descent here and you'll have a nice view of Thunder Mountain ahead. After hiking 2.2 miles from the parking area, you'll intersect the north end of the Carroll Canyon Trail {6}. Turn right onto the Carroll Canyon Trail here.

The Ridge Trail joins the Carroll Canyon Trail after another 0.6 mile {7}; they are a combined trail for 0.2 mile {8}. When they split, stay on the Carroll Canyon Trail. After hiking 4 miles from the parking area, you'll be back at the southern intersection of the Carroll Canyon and Old Post Trails {4}. Turn left onto the Old Post Trail here then hike 1 mile to the parking area {1}.

I've seen many wildflowers on these trails in late April and early May.

Note: There is very little shade on this hike so it would be a good choice in cooler weather.

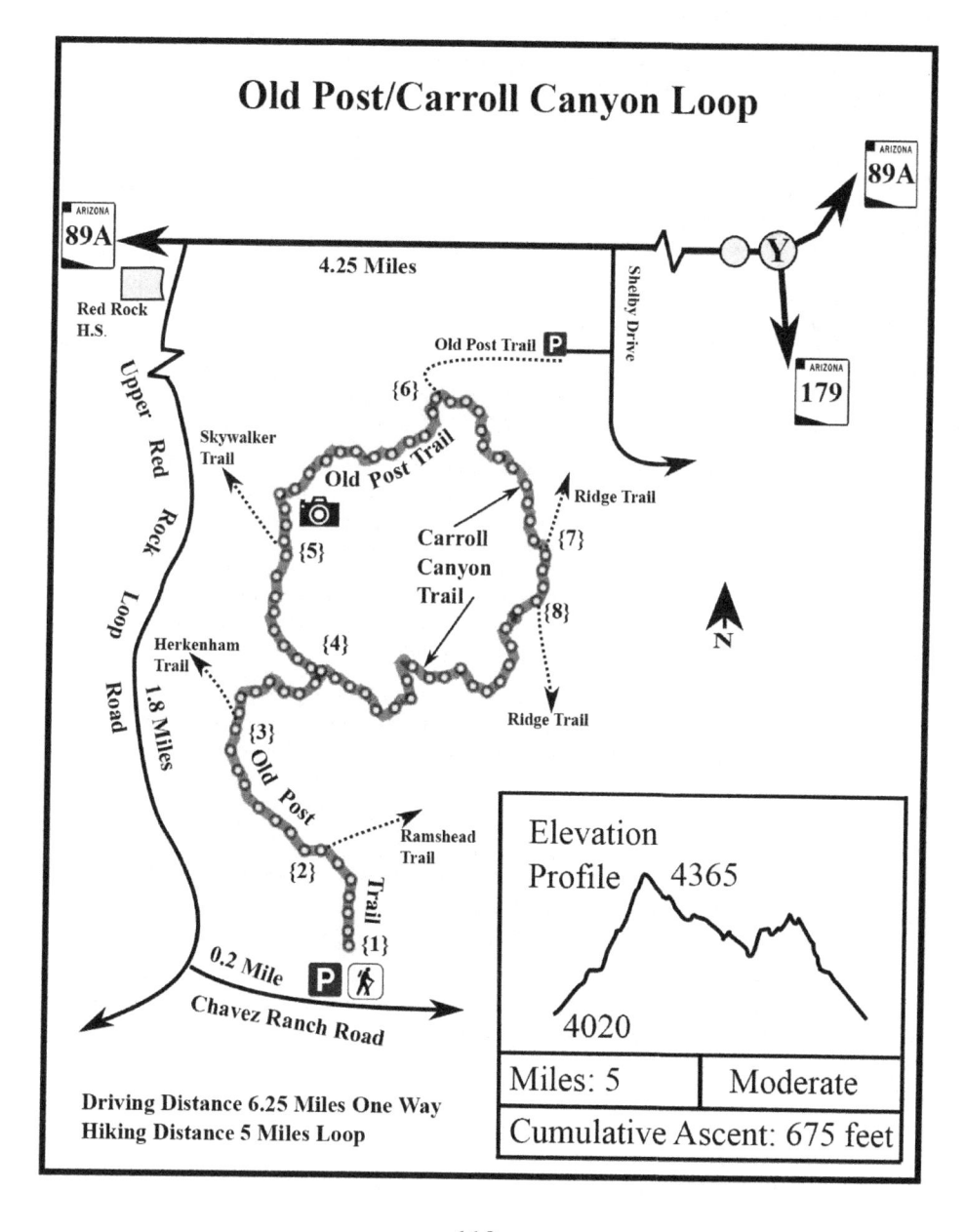

Color Photos: Scan the QR code below for additional color photos of this trail

Old Post/Carroll Canyon Loop

ARIZONA 89A

4.25 Miles

Shelby Drive

ARIZONA 89A

Red Rock H.S.

Old Post Trail 🅿

{6}

ARIZONA 179

Upper Red Rock Loop Road 1.8 Miles

Skywalker Trail

Old Post Trail

📷 {5}

Carroll Canyon Trail

Ridge Trail

{7}

{8}

N

Herkenham Trail

{4}

Ridge Trail

{3}

Old Post

Ramshead Trail

{2}

Trail

{1}

0.2 Mile 🅿 🚶

Chavez Ranch Road

Elevation Profile 4365

4020

Miles: 5	Moderate
Cumulative Ascent: 675 feet	

Driving Distance 6.25 Miles One Way
Hiking Distance 5 Miles Loop

113

Pyramid/Scorpion Loop

Summary: A loop hike circling Sedona's Pyramid with great views of Cathedral Rock

Challenge Level: Easy to Moderate

Hiking Distance: About 2.3 miles loop

Hiking Time: About 1 ½ hours round trip

Trail Popularity:

Trailhead Directions: From the "Y" roundabout (see page 7), drive west on SR 89A about 4.25 miles then turn left onto the Upper Red Rock Loop Road. Sedona High School is on your right. Follow the Upper Red Rock Loop Road for 1.8 miles to the intersection of Chavez Ranch Road then park on the right side of the road {1}. (34°49.982'N; 111°48.801'W) This parking area also serves the Scorpion Trail. There is room for about 12 vehicles here. You'll see the trailhead to the west from the parking area.

Description: The Pyramid Trail (combined with the Scorpion Trail) circles around the base of the Pyramid rock formation. You'll need good hiking boots with excellent traction because there are places where the trail is steep with loose gravel.

To hike the loop, you'll hike part of both the Scorpion and the Pyramid Trails. From the parking area, hike west for 300 feet to the signpost at the intersection of the Scorpion and the Pyramid Trail {2}. You'll come back here on the return trip. I suggest you hike the loop in the counterclockwise direction for the best views. So turn right then follow the Scorpion Trail. This trail gently rises for the next mile. You'll pass by a fence after 0.5 mile {3} and have a nice view behind you after 0.8 mile {4}. After 1 mile, you'll intersect the Pyramid Trail on your left at the signpost with large cairn {5}. Make a very sharp left turn here to follow the Pyramid Trail.

The Pyramid Trail is relatively flat for about the next 0.4 mile. You'll come to another nice view of Cathedral Rock {6} then begin a rather steep descent. There are excellent views all along this section of the trail. But the trail here is very narrow, with loose dirt and rocks as well as uneven in places with large drop offs so watch your footing. There's a nice place to stop for a snack just before you make a sharp right turn at about the 1.6 mile mark {7}. You'll have continuing views of Cathedral Rock on your way back to the intersection of the Pyramid and the Scorpion Trail {2}. When you arrive back, continue straight ahead to return to the parking area {1}.

Note: There is little shade on this trail so it is a good choice for cooler weather.

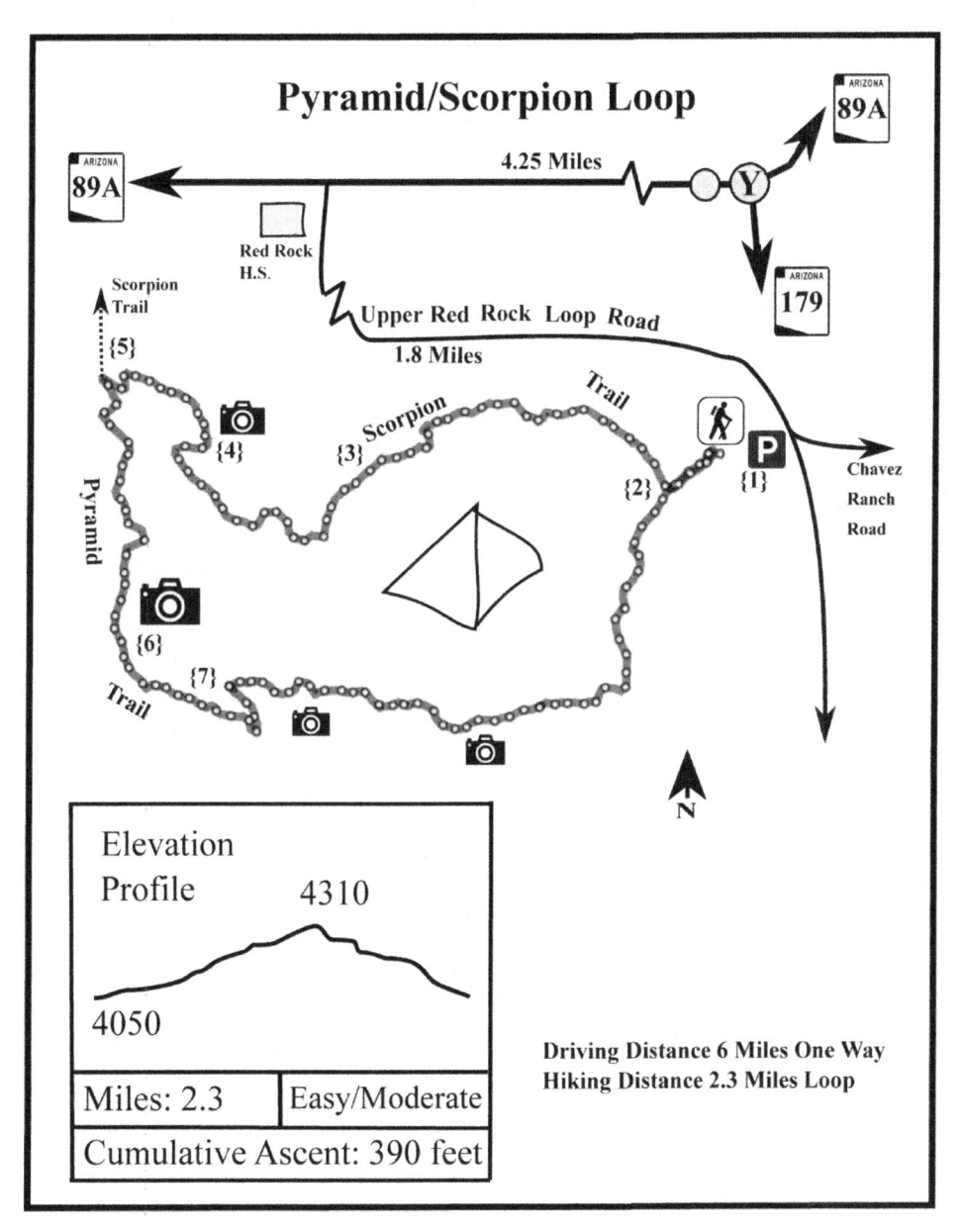

Color Photos: Scan the QR code below for additional color photos of this trail

Pyramid/Scorpion Loop

Elevation Profile
4310
4050

Miles: 2.3 | Easy/Moderate
Cumulative Ascent: 390 feet

Driving Distance 6 Miles One Way
Hiking Distance 2.3 Miles Loop

115

Rabbit Ears Trail

Summary: An in-out hike to the base of a very distinct rock formation

Challenge Level: Moderate

Hiking Distance: About 2.5 miles each way from the Bell Rock Vista parking area or 5 miles round trip; about 1.5 miles each way from the Jacks Canyon parking area or 3 miles round trip

Hiking Time: About 2 ½ hours from the Bell Rock Vista parking area round trip; about 1 ½ hours from the Jacks Canyon Road parking area round trip

Trail Popularity:

Trailhead Directions: There are two trailheads for this trail: Bell Rock Vista and Jacks Canyon Road. From the "Y" roundabout (see page 7), proceed south on SR 179 about 6.25 miles. You'll pass the Court House Vista parking area on your left, just north of Bell Rock. Continue on SR 179 another 3/4 mile or so, you'll see another parking area on your left, south of Bell Rock. Turn left here into the Bell Rock Vista parking area {1}. (34°47.501'N; 111°45.669'W)

To reach the Jacks Canyon Road trailhead, continue south on SR 179, past the Bell Rock Vista parking area about 1 mile to the Jacks Canyon/Verde Valley School Road roundabout. Take the third exit then continue on Jacks Canyon Road. Watch for a sharp right turn after about 1 mile and continue on Jacks Canyon Road for a total of 2 miles. The parking area is up the access road on the right located across the road from Canyon Ridge Trail Road {2}. (34°47.081'N; 111°43.941'W)

Description: From the Bell Rock Vista parking area, hike past the interpretive signboard for 0.1 mile then turn right to go to the Big Park Loop Trail {3}. You'll intersect the Big Park Loop Trail in about 175 feet {4}. Turn right onto the Big Park Loop Trail. You'll intersect the Middle Trail after about 0.5 mile {5} and the intersection of the Little Rock Trail as you hike east then north. After 1.2 miles, you'll see a sign for the Rabbit Ears Trail {6}. Turn right. As you hike east, the trail gently rises and in 0.4 mile you'll have a good view of the Rabbit Ears formation {7}. You'll come to an unmarked trail on the left after another 0.7 mile at a directional trail sign {8}. This trail takes you to the base of Rabbit Ears and an outstanding view, but it is unmaintained, steep and narrow so watch your step.

From the Jacks Canyon Road parking area {2}, you'll see the sign for Rabbit Ears on the north side of the parking area. Follow the gently descending trail for about 400 feet and proceed through each gate on both sides of Jacks Canyon Road. In 0.7 mile, you'll intersect the Little Rock Trail {10}. You'll have good views of Lee Mountain throughout the hike. After 1.4 miles, you'll begin to have good views of Rabbit Ears {9}. In a short distance, you'll come to the steep downward trail that leads to the base of Rabbit Ears {8}.

The best views of Rabbit Ears are when you hike from the Bell Rock Vista parking area. There isn't much shade on either of the ways to get to Rabbit Ears so they can be hot hikes in the summer.

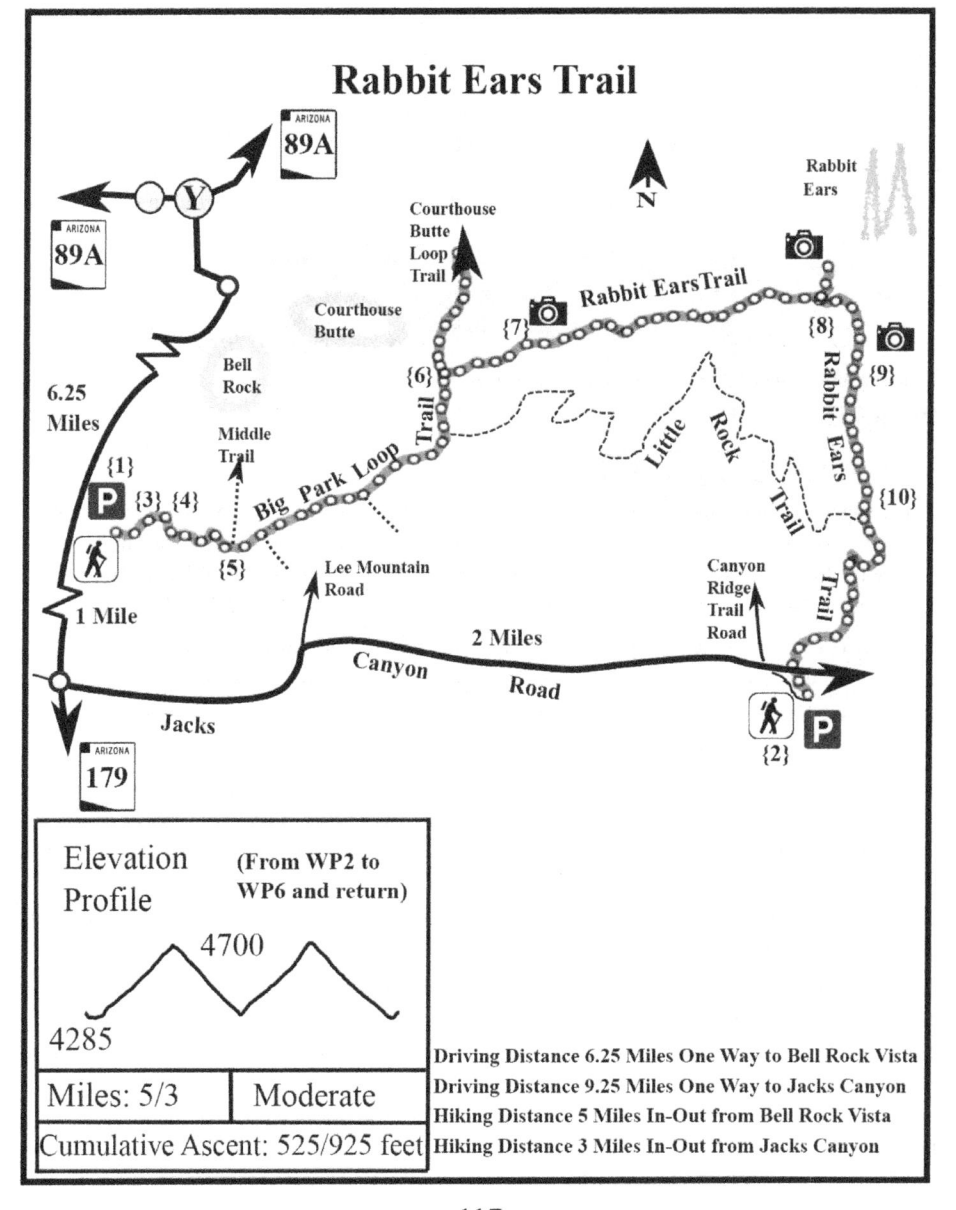

Color Photos: Scan the QR code below for additional color photos of this trail

Rabbit Ears Trail

Elevation Profile (From WP2 to WP6 and return)

4700
4285

Miles: 5/3	Moderate
Cumulative Ascent: 525/925 feet	

Driving Distance 6.25 Miles One Way to Bell Rock Vista
Driving Distance 9.25 Miles One Way to Jacks Canyon
Hiking Distance 5 Miles In-Out from Bell Rock Vista
Hiking Distance 3 Miles In-Out from Jacks Canyon

Red Rock State Park Trails

Summary: Red Rock State Park is a 286 acre nature preserve and environmental education center with excellent scenery. It features 10 trails, 7 of which are described below. Hikes led by naturalists are available daily – call the Park at (928) 282-6907

Challenge Level: Easy to Moderate

Hiking Distance: Varies (see descriptions)
Hiking Time: Varies
Trail Popularity: 🚶🚶🚶

Trailhead Directions: From the "Y" roundabout (see page 7), drive west on SR 89A about 5.5 miles then turn left onto the Lower Red Rock Loop Road. Continue on the Lower Red Rock Loop for 3 miles and turn right at the sign for the Red Rock State Park. You'll come to the entry station. An entry fee is required. (34°49.082'N; 11149.920'W)

Description: Red Rock State Park has 5 miles of maintained trails ranging from easy trails to moderate trails. Descriptions of the most popular trails follows.

Bunkhouse Trail: This easy 0.4 mile loop from the Visitor Center is a good way to get to Kingfisher Bridge, which crosses Oak Creek

Smoke Trail: This easy 0.4 mile trail features a walk along Oak Creek

Yavapai Ridge Trail: This moderate short trail is somewhat hilly. You can access it by crossing Kingfisher Bridge, continuing a short distance on the Apache Fire Trail and then turning left.

Kisva Trail: After crossing Kingfisher Bridge, turn right at the first trail and follow this easy trail along an old ranch road.

Apache Fire Trail: After crossing the Kingfisher Bridge, watch for the Apache Fire loop. This moderate trail includes a possible side trip to the House of Apache Fires.

Javelina Trail: This moderate trail includes scenic overlooks with views of Cathedral Rock.

Eagle's Nest Trail: This moderate trail includes a 200 foot climb. But the views from the vista are very nice and worth the climb.

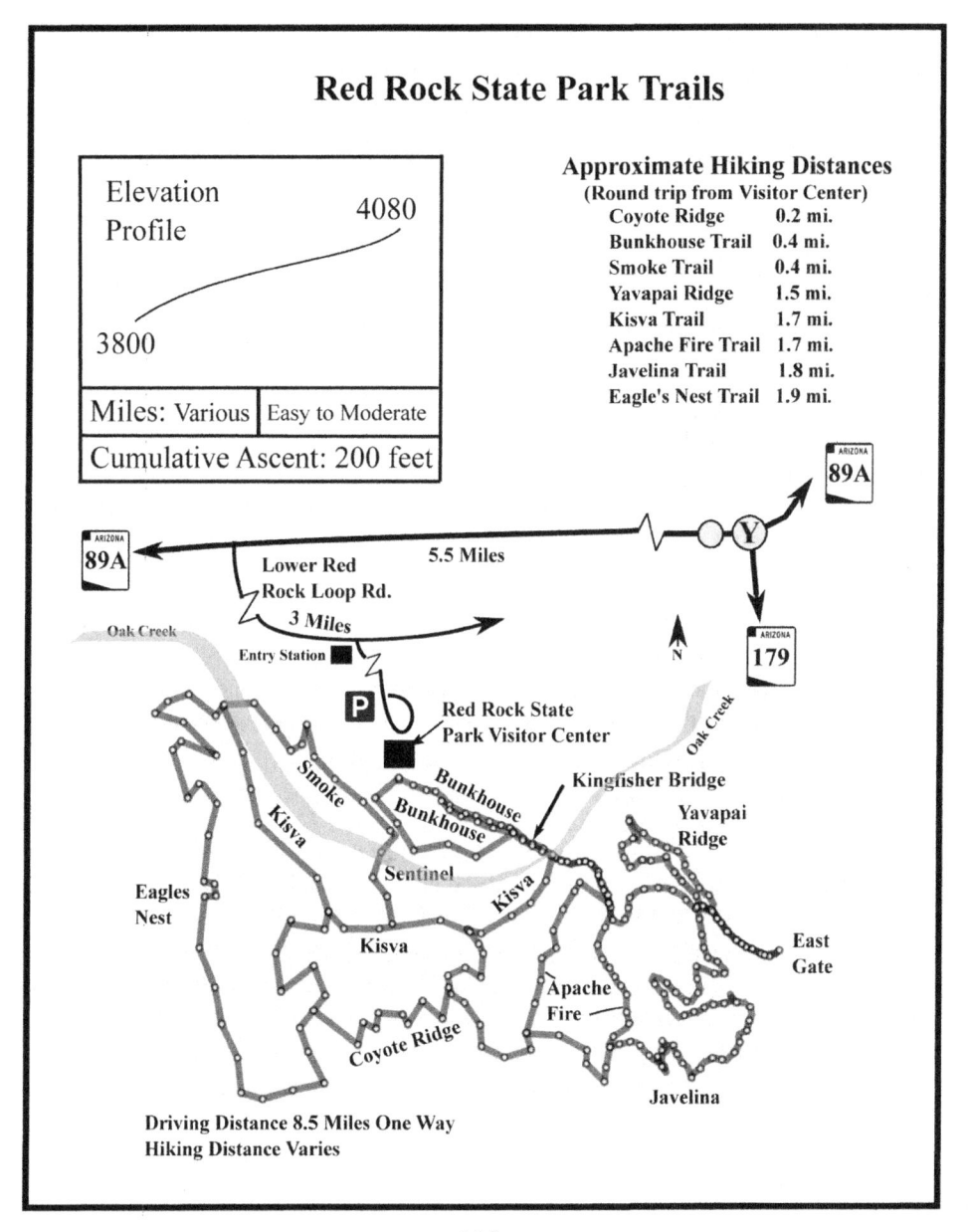

Color Photos: Scan the QR code below for additional color photos of these trails

Red Rock State Park Trails

Elevation Profile
4080
3800

Miles: Various — Easy to Moderate
Cumulative Ascent: 200 feet

Approximate Hiking Distances
(Round trip from Visitor Center)
Coyote Ridge	0.2 mi.
Bunkhouse Trail	0.4 mi.
Smoke Trail	0.4 mi.
Yavapai Ridge	1.5 mi.
Kisva Trail	1.7 mi.
Apache Fire Trail	1.7 mi.
Javelina Trail	1.8 mi.
Eagle's Nest Trail	1.9 mi.

89A
Lower Red Rock Loop Rd.
5.5 Miles
3 Miles
Oak Creek
Entry Station
89A
179
Red Rock State Park Visitor Center
Smoke
Kisva
Bunkhouse
Bunkhouse
Kingfisher Bridge
Yavapai Ridge
Oak Creek
Sentinel
Eagles Nest
Kisva
Kisva
East Gate
Coyote Ridge
Apache Fire
Javelina

Driving Distance 8.5 Miles One Way
Hiking Distance Varies

Scheurman Mountain Vista Trail ★

Summary:
A favorite in-out hike up the side of a mountain with great panoramic views of Cathedral Rock and other notable landmarks

Challenge Level: Moderate

Hiking Distance: About 0.5 mile to the top then another 0.25 miles to the southern overlook, and another 0.25 mile to the northern overlook or 2 miles round trip

Hiking Time: About 1 ½ hours round trip

Trail Popularity: 🚶🚶

Trailhead Directions: From the "Y" roundabout (see page 7), drive west toward Cottonwood on SR 89A about 4.25 miles. Turn left onto the Upper Red Rock Loop Road. There is a sign for the Sedona Shuttle Park & Ride at the first driveway on the right. Continue on and turn right at the fourth driveway (it's behind the high school) then drive past 10 parking places on the left and look for the sign to the trailhead parking area on the left {1}. (34°50.762'N; 111°49.716'W) If the parking area is blocked off, return to the Upper Red Rock Loop Road and park along the road {6} or go back to the Sedona Shuttle Park & Ride parking lot {7}. Then walk on the sidewalk and road 0.25 mile to the trailhead. These parking areas also serve the Scorpion and Skywalker Trails.

Description: Scheurman Mountain Vista Trail provides great views of Cathedral Rock and other red rock views to the south. You begin by hiking behind the Red Rock High School where you'll intersect the Scorpion Trail on the left {2} then see a large array of solar panels as big as the school's football field. After 0.2 mile, the trail goes around a gate, placed there when cattle once grazed the area. The trail up is steep in places, so watch your footing. If you hike in April, you may encounter wildflowers blooming.

When you get to the top {3}, you'll see a Scheurman Mountain Trail sign pointing straight ahead (west). I don't recommend hiking this trail because the views are limited. Rather, take the trail to the left (south) marked Scheurman Mountain Vista for a good view of Cathedral Rock {4}.

The best views of Cathedral Rock from the southern view point are in the afternoon. You can also take the faint (and unmarked) trail to the right to the top to look northwest toward the Verde Valley and Mingus Mountain {5}. Note that the trail up and on top of Scheurman Mountain is very rocky in places.

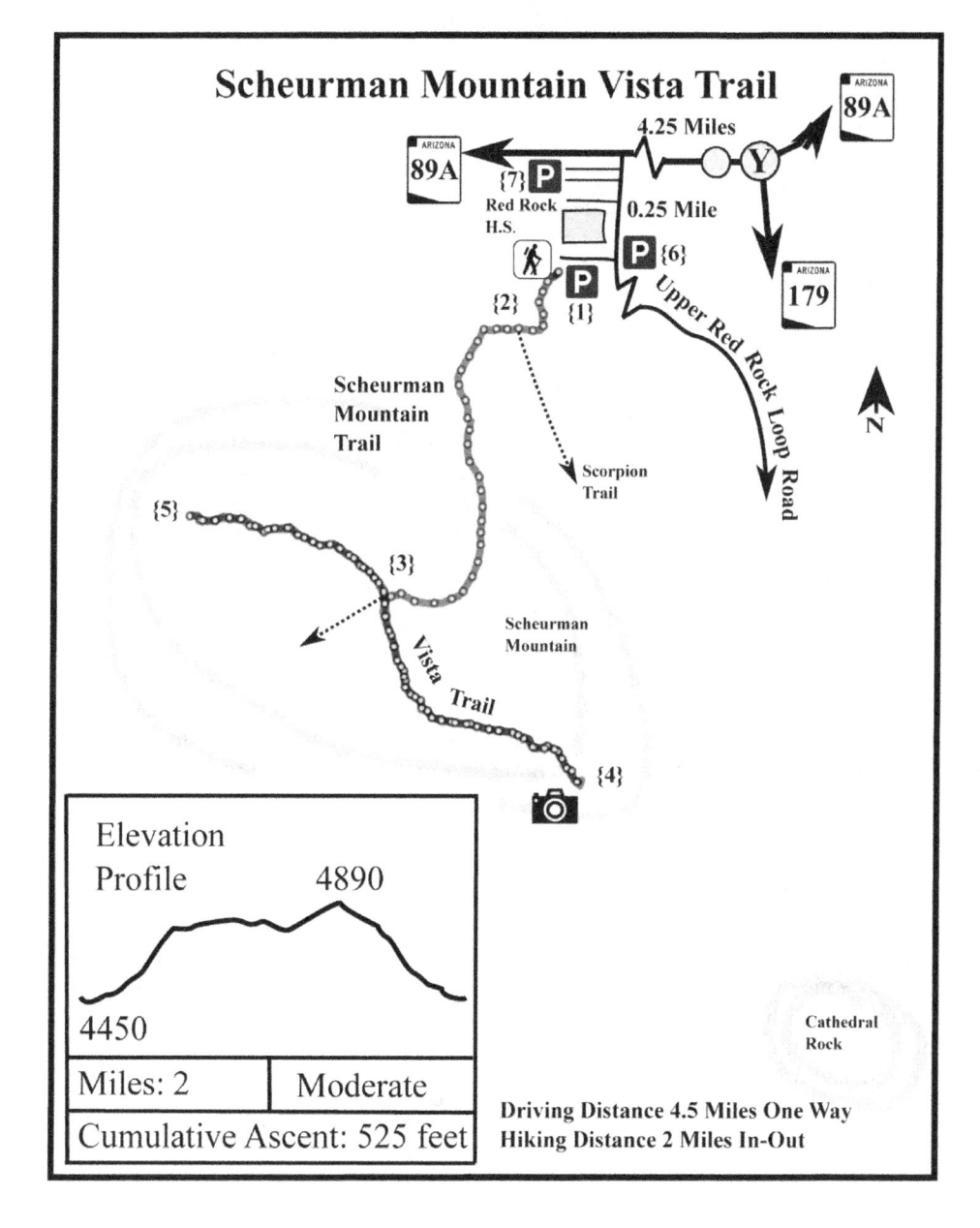

Color Photos: Scan the QR code below for additional color photos of this trail

Scheurman Mountain Vista Trail

4.25 Miles
89A
{7} P
Red Rock H.S.
0.25 Mile
P {6}
89A
{2}
P {1}
Upper Red Rock Loop Road
179
Scheurman Mountain Trail
Scorpion Trail
N
{5}
{3}
Scheurman Mountain
Vista Trail
{4}

Elevation Profile   4890

4450

Miles: 2	Moderate
Cumulative Ascent: 525 feet	

Cathedral Rock

Driving Distance 4.5 Miles One Way
Hiking Distance 2 Miles In-Out

121

Scorpion Trail

Summary: An in-out hike around the northeast side of Sedona's Pyramid with great views of Cathedral Rock

Challenge Level: Moderate

Hiking Distance: About 2.1 miles each way or 4.2 miles round trip from the parking area behind the High School {1} to the parking area on the Upper Red Rock Loop Road {2} and return

Hiking Time: About 2 1/2 hours from the parking behind the High School to the parking on Red Rock Loop Road and return round trip

Trail Popularity:

Trailhead Directions: There are two trailheads you can use for this trail. From the "Y" roundabout (see page 7), drive west toward Cottonwood on SR 89A about 4.25 miles. Turn left onto the Upper Red Rock Loop Road. There is a sign for the Sedona Shuttle Park & Ride at the first driveway on the right. Continue on and turn right at the fourth driveway (it's behind the high school) then drive past 10 parking places on the left and look for the sign to the trailhead parking area on the left {1}. (34°50.762'N; 111°49.716'W) If the parking area is blocked off, return to the Upper Red Rock Loop Road and park along the road {9} or go back to the Sedona Shuttle Park & Ride parking lot {10}. Then walk on the sidewalk and road 0.25 mile to the trailhead. These parking areas also serve the Scheurman Mountain Vista and Skywalker Trails. To get to the second parking area, follow the Upper Red Rock Loop Road for 1.8 miles to the intersection of Chavez Ranch Road then park on the right side of the road {2}. (34°49.982'N; 111°48.801'W) This parking area also serves the Pyramid Loop. You'll see the trail heading west from the parking area.

Description: From the parking area behind the high school {1}, hike the Scheurman Mountain Trail for about 500 feet. Turn left (south) at the sign for the Scorpion Trail {3} located about 50 paces beyond the telephone pole. Follow this narrow, rocky former mountain bike trail. You'll have excellent views of the Pyramid and Cathedral Rock as you hike south. At 1.1 miles, you'll intersect the Pyramid Trail on the right {4} then come to a nice view of Cathedral Rock at 1.2 miles {5}. As you continue skirting the Pyramid, you'll have some nice views {6}, pass through a fence {7} then come to the intersection with the other end of the Pyramid Trail {8}. The Pyramid Trail skirts the southern and western side of the Pyramid.

If you begin the hike from the second parking area on Red Rock Loop Road {2}, go west from the parking area for 350 feet to the signpost at the intersection of the Scorpion and the Pyramid Trail {8}. Make a right turn here to follow the Scorpion Trail north.

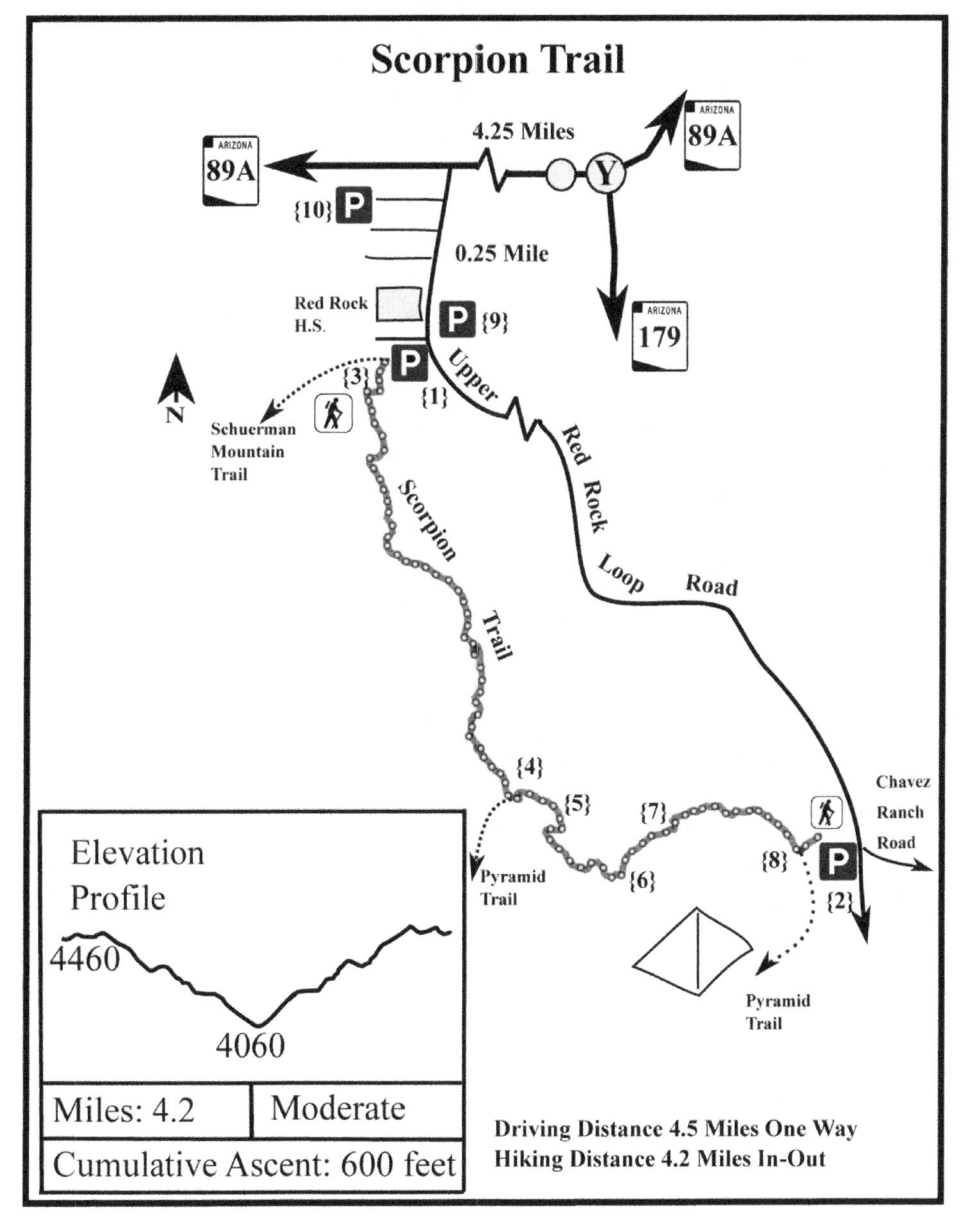

Color Photos: Scan the QR code below for additional color photos of this trail

Scorpion Trail

4.25 Miles

ARIZONA 89A

ARIZONA 89A

{10} P

0.25 Mile

ARIZONA 179

Red Rock H.S.

P {9}

P {1}

Upper

{3}

Schuerman Mountain Trail

N

Scorpion Trail

Red Rock Loop Road

{4}

{5}

{7}

Chavez Ranch Road

Pyramid Trail

{6}

{8}

P {2}

Pyramid Trail

Elevation Profile

4460

4060

Miles: 4.2 | Moderate
Cumulative Ascent: 600 feet

Driving Distance 4.5 Miles One Way
Hiking Distance 4.2 Miles In-Out

123

Secret Canyon Trail

Summary: A solitary in-out hike up a beautiful red rock canyon with the option for a loop hike

Challenge Level: Moderate to Hard

Hiking Distance: About 2.4 miles each way or 4.8 miles round trip

Hiking Time: About 2 ½ hours as an in-out hike round trip

Trail Popularity:

Trailhead Directions: From the "Y" roundabout (see page 7), drive west toward Cottonwood on SR 89A about 3 miles. Turn right onto Dry Creek Road. Stay on Dry Creek Road for 2 miles then turn right onto Forest Road (FR) 152. Proceed on FR 152 for 3.4 miles to the parking area on your left {1}. (34°55.797'N; 111°48.391'W) This parking area also serves the HS Canyon Trail.

Note: FR 152 is an extremely rough road beyond the 0.2 mile paved section; a high clearance vehicle and 4WD are strongly recommended.

Description: I like this trail for its solitude. It is hard to get to (see description of FR 152 above), in the Wilderness and mountain bikers are not permitted on the trail. The trail goes up a very picturesque canyon. You'll intersect the HS Canyon Trail about 0.7 mile into the hike {2}. You'll cross a large wash at the 1.2 mile mark {3} and intersect the David Miller Trail about 1.75 miles into the hike {4}.

If you wish to hike a loop, see Secret Canyon/Bear Sign Loop for directions on the 6.6 mile loop hike.

If you would rather hike in-out, continue on the Secret Canyon Trail. At about 2.4 miles, you'll be in a pine forest. Look to your left for a deep wash then follow the wash to the right for a short distance. If you are lucky, you may see a seasonal waterfall {5}. I usually stop after hiking 2.4 miles {5}, but the trail continues on another 2 miles, becoming steeper and rockier.

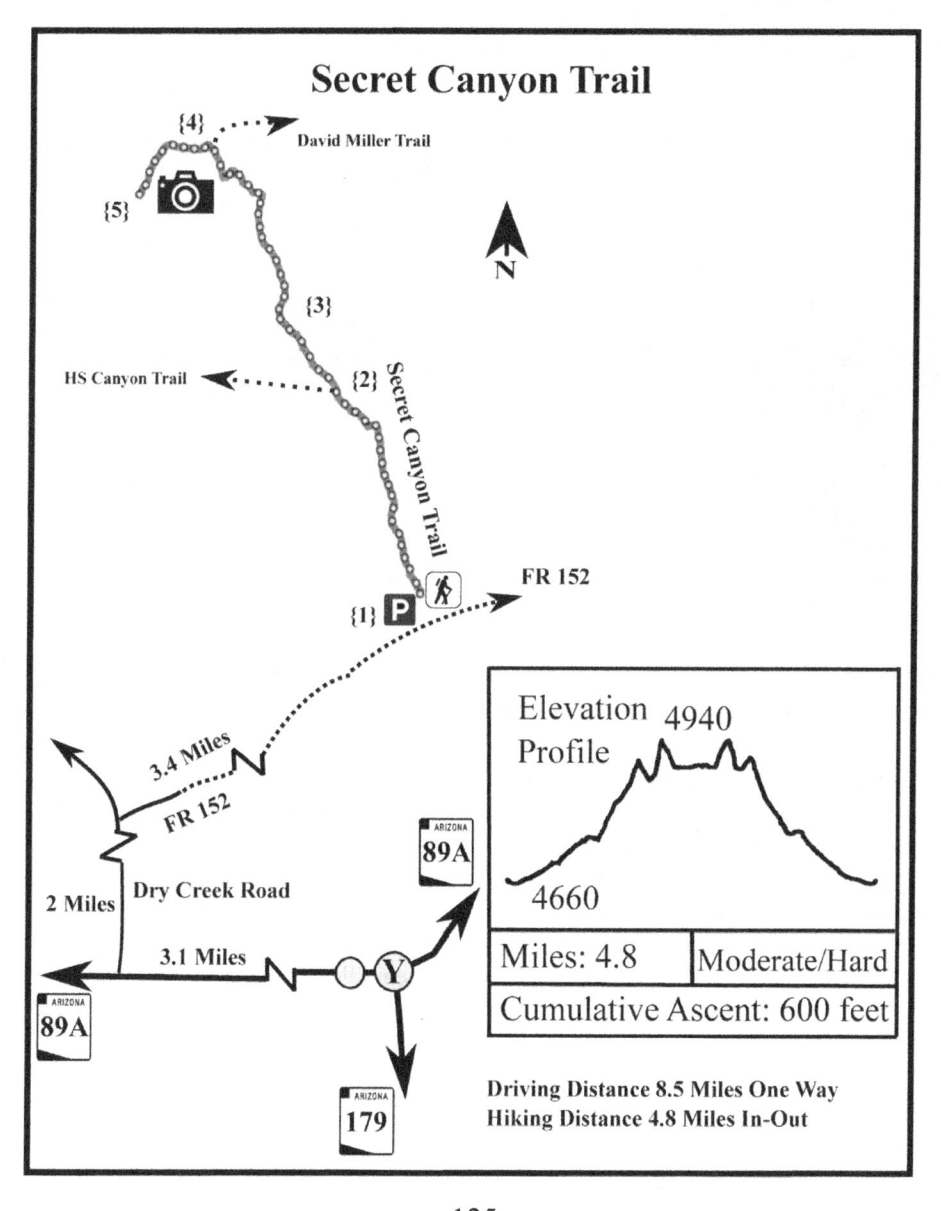

Color Photos: Scan the QR code below for additional color photos of this trail

Secret Canyon Trail

{4} David Miller Trail
{5}
N
{3}
HS Canyon Trail
{2}
Secret Canyon Trail
{1} P 🚶 FR 152

3.4 Miles
FR 152

2 Miles Dry Creek Road
3.1 Miles
Y
ARIZONA 89A
ARIZONA 89A
ARIZONA 179

Elevation Profile 4940
4660

Miles: 4.8	Moderate/Hard
Cumulative Ascent: 600 feet	

Driving Distance 8.5 Miles One Way
Hiking Distance 4.8 Miles In-Out

125

Secret Canyon/Bear Sign Loop

Summary: A solitary loop hike through several beautiful red rock canyons

Challenge Level: Hard

Hiking Distance: 6.6 mile loop hike

Hiking Time: About 4 hours round trip

Trail Popularity:

Trailhead Directions: From the "Y" roundabout (see page 7), drive west toward Cottonwood on SR 89A about 3 miles. Turn right onto Dry Creek Road. Stay on Dry Creek Road for 2 miles then turn right onto Forest Road (FR) 152. Proceed on FR 152 for 3.4 miles to the Secret Canyon parking area on your left {1}. (34°55.797'N; 111°48.391'W) This parking area also serves the HS Canyon Trail.

Note: FR 152 is an extremely rough road beyond the 0.2 mile paved section; a high clearance vehicle and 4WD are strongly recommended.

Description: I like this trail for its solitude although it is hard to get to (see description of FR 152 above). Mountain bikers are not permitted on the trail. The trail goes up a very picturesque canyon. You'll intersect the HS Canyon Trail about 0.7 mile into the hike {2}. You'll cross a large wash at the 1.2 mile mark {3}.

The David Miller Trail (named after a forest ranger who went missing in the area) appears after 1.75 miles {4}. Make a right turn here onto the David Miller Trail then begin a rather steep uphill climb then steep downhill for the next 0.6 mile. When you come to the Bear Sign Trail, make a right turn to begin the journey back {5}. Bear Sign crosses several washes and has the feeling of deep wilderness. After hiking Bear Sign for 2.2 miles, you'll intersect the Dry Creek Trail on your left {6}. Continue on Bear Sign for another 0.6 mile back to FR 152 {7}. Make a right onto FR 152 then walk down the road for about 1 mile to return to the Secret Canyon parking area {1}.

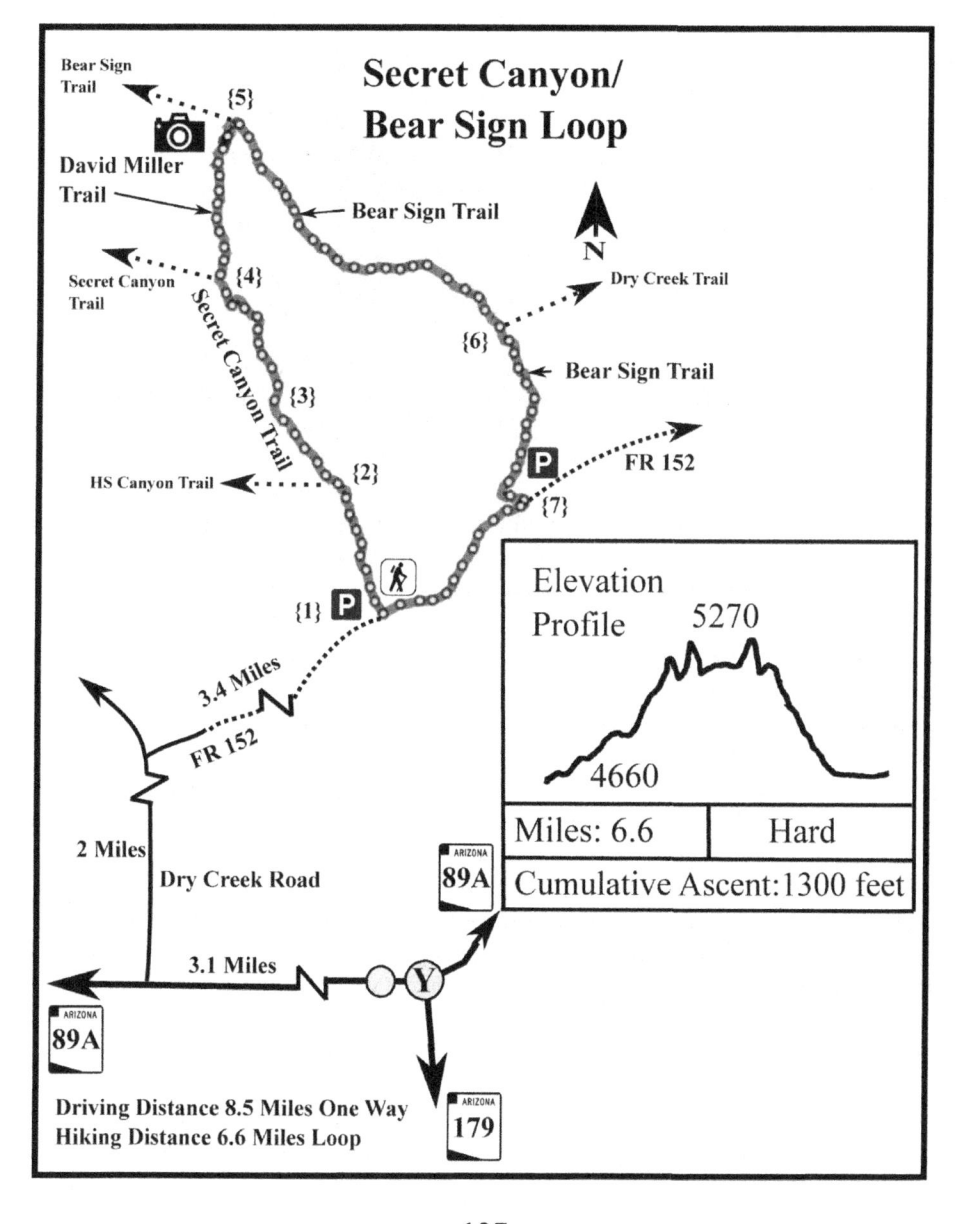

Color Photos: Scan the QR code below for additional color photos of this trail

Secret Canyon/ Bear Sign Loop

- Bear Sign Trail
- {5}
- David Miller Trail
- Bear Sign Trail
- Secret Canyon Trail
- {4}
- Secret Canyon Trail
- N
- Dry Creek Trail
- {3}
- {6}
- Bear Sign Trail
- HS Canyon Trail
- {2}
- P
- FR 152
- {7}
- {1} P

3.4 Miles
FR 152

2 Miles
Dry Creek Road

ARIZONA 89A

3.1 Miles

Y

ARIZONA 89A

Driving Distance 8.5 Miles One Way
Hiking Distance 6.6 Miles Loop

ARIZONA 179

Elevation Profile
5270
4660

Miles: 6.6	Hard
Cumulative Ascent: 1300 feet	

127

Skywalker/Herkenham Loop

Summary: A loop hike on the western edge of Sedona featuring views of Cathedral Rock, Courthouse Butte and West Sedona

Challenge Level: Moderate

Hiking Distance: About 3.8 mile loop hike

Hiking Time: About 2 ½ hours round trip

Trail Popularity:

Trailhead Directions: From the "Y" roundabout (see page 7), drive west toward Cottonwood on SR 89A about 4.25 miles. Turn left onto the Upper Red Rock Loop Road. There is a sign for the Sedona Shuttle Park & Ride at the first driveway on the right. Continue on and turn right at the fourth driveway (it's behind the high school) then drive past 10 parking places on the left and look for the sign to the trailhead parking area on the left {1}. (34°50.762'N; 111°49.716'W) If the parking area is blocked off, return to the Upper Red Rock Loop Road and park along the road {10} or go back to the Sedona Shuttle Park & Ride parking lot {11}. Then walk on the sidewalk and cross the road to the trailhead {2}. These parking areas also serve the Scheurman Mountain Vista and Scorpion Trails. The trail begins on the east side of Upper Red Rock Loop Road {2}.

Description: You'll be hiking three trails to complete the loop which are Skywalker, Old Post and Herkenham trails. Skywalker and Herkenham are narrow with ups and downs while Old Post is a gentle downhill hike. An afternoon hike will give you excellent views to the south.

Begin by hiking Skywalker. In 0.2 mile, you'll intersect the Over Easy Trail, which is a little loop trail. You'll intersect it again after 0.5 mile. At 0.7 mile, you'll come to a bench with nice views to the south {3}. Just beyond the bench the trail becomes very narrow with a large drop off for 0.2 mile so watch your footing.

You'll see houses all along the Skywalker Trail but they really don't distract from the pleasant views. At 1.1 miles, you'll come to the highest point on the trail {4} and have a nice view of West Sedona to the north. At 1.3 miles, you'll be under a power line {5}, then in 2 miles you'll intersect the Old Post Trail {6}. Make a right turn here onto the Old Post Trail but look north here for a nice view of Thunder Mountain.

After 0.5 mile, you'll intersect the Carroll Canyon Trail on the left {7}. Continue on the Old Post Trail. You'll intersect the Herkenham Trail at 2.9 miles {8}. Turn right here onto the Herkenham Trail then begin a series of ups and downs as you head northwest.

At 3.3 miles, the trail turns left at the bottom of a wash {9}. Continue on Herkenham back to the trailhead {2} and the parking area {1}.
Color Photos: Scan the QR code below for additional color photos of this trail

Skywalker/Herkenham Loop

Elevation Profile
4580
4450
4140

Miles: 3.8 | Moderate
Cumulative Ascent: 650 feet

Driving Distance 4.5 Miles One Way
Hiking Distance 3.8 Miles Loop

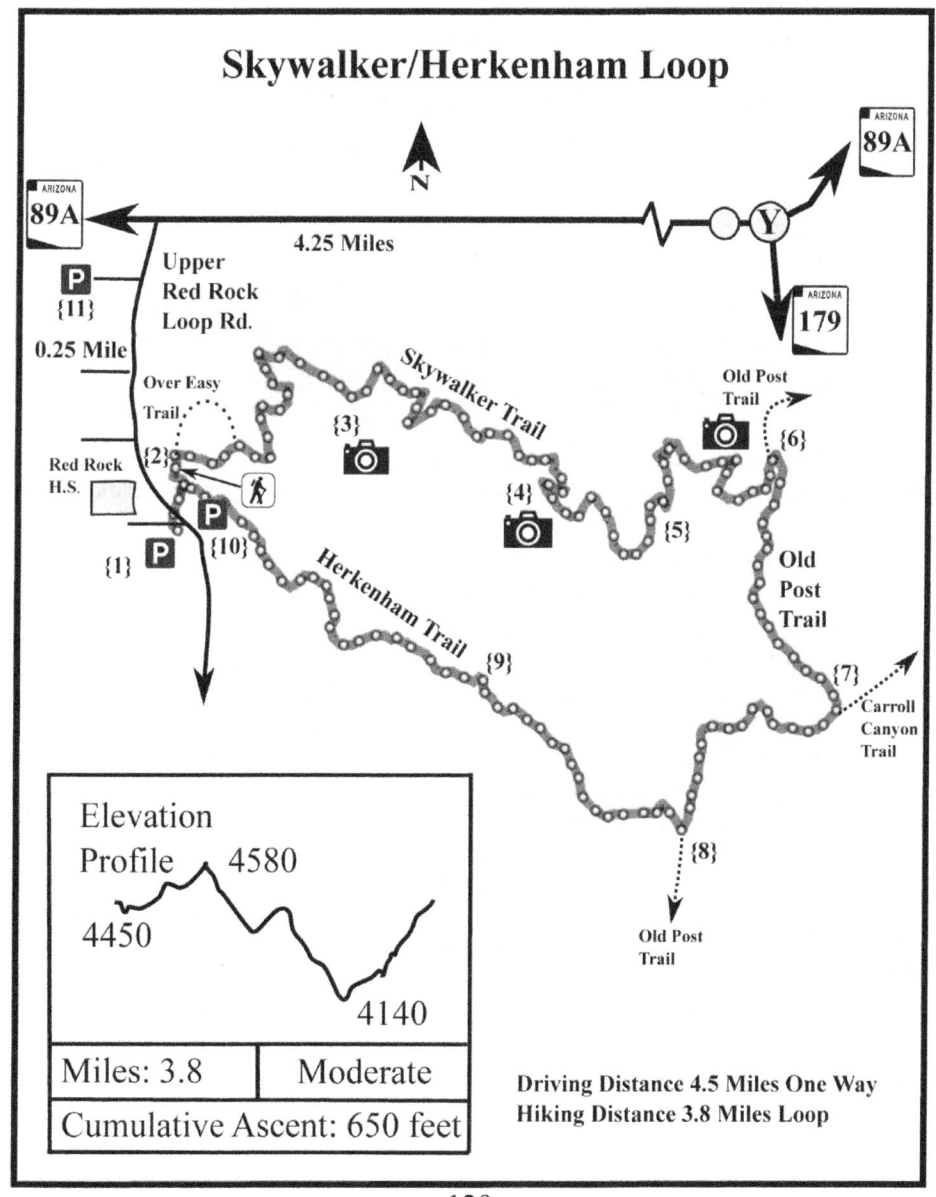

Slim Shady/Hermit Loop

Summary:
A partially shaded loop hike using several popular mountain biking trails with nice red rock views

Challenge Level:
Easy

Hiking Distance:
About 2.7 miles loop

Hiking Time:
About 2 hours round trip

Trail Popularity:

Trailhead Directions: From the "Y" roundabout (see page 7), drive south on SR 179 about 4.8 miles to mile marker 308.5 then turn right into the Yavapai Vista parking area {1}. (34°48.442'N; 111°46.174'W).

Note: The parking area is accessible only from southbound SR 179. The trail begins on the southwest side of the parking area near the interpretive signboard.

Description: There are a number of short, interconnected trails here but I prefer to hike the short loop hike described below in the clockwise direction. An afternoon hike will produce the best photos. Just past the interpretive signboard, turn left onto an unmarked connector trail. (If you were to continue straight ahead, you will come to the intersection of the Kaibab and Yavapai Vista Trails {2}.) Follow the short connector trail for about 200 feet until you intersect the Coconino Trail {3}. Turn right then follow the Coconino Trail for 0.3 mile then make a right turn onto the Slim Shady Trail {4}. You'll come to the intersection of the HiLine Trail on the left after 0.1 mile and the Kaibab Trail on the right after 0.2 mile {5}. Continue on the Slim Shady Trail. You'll soon be in a wash which provides shade in the summer for the next 0.2 mile. Look to the right for good views of Lee Mountain, the Two Nuns and Rabbit Ears. At 1.1 miles from the parking area, you'll come to an open area that makes a nice snack spot {6}.

After 1.7 miles from the parking area, you'll come to the intersection of the Templeton and HT Trails {7}. Make a right then follow the Templeton Trail. After another 0.3 mile, you'll intersect the Easy Breezy Trail on the left {8}. Continue on the Templeton Trail for another 0.2 mile to the intersection with the Hermit Trail {9}. Turn right then follow the Hermit Trail for 0.4 mile back to the parking area.

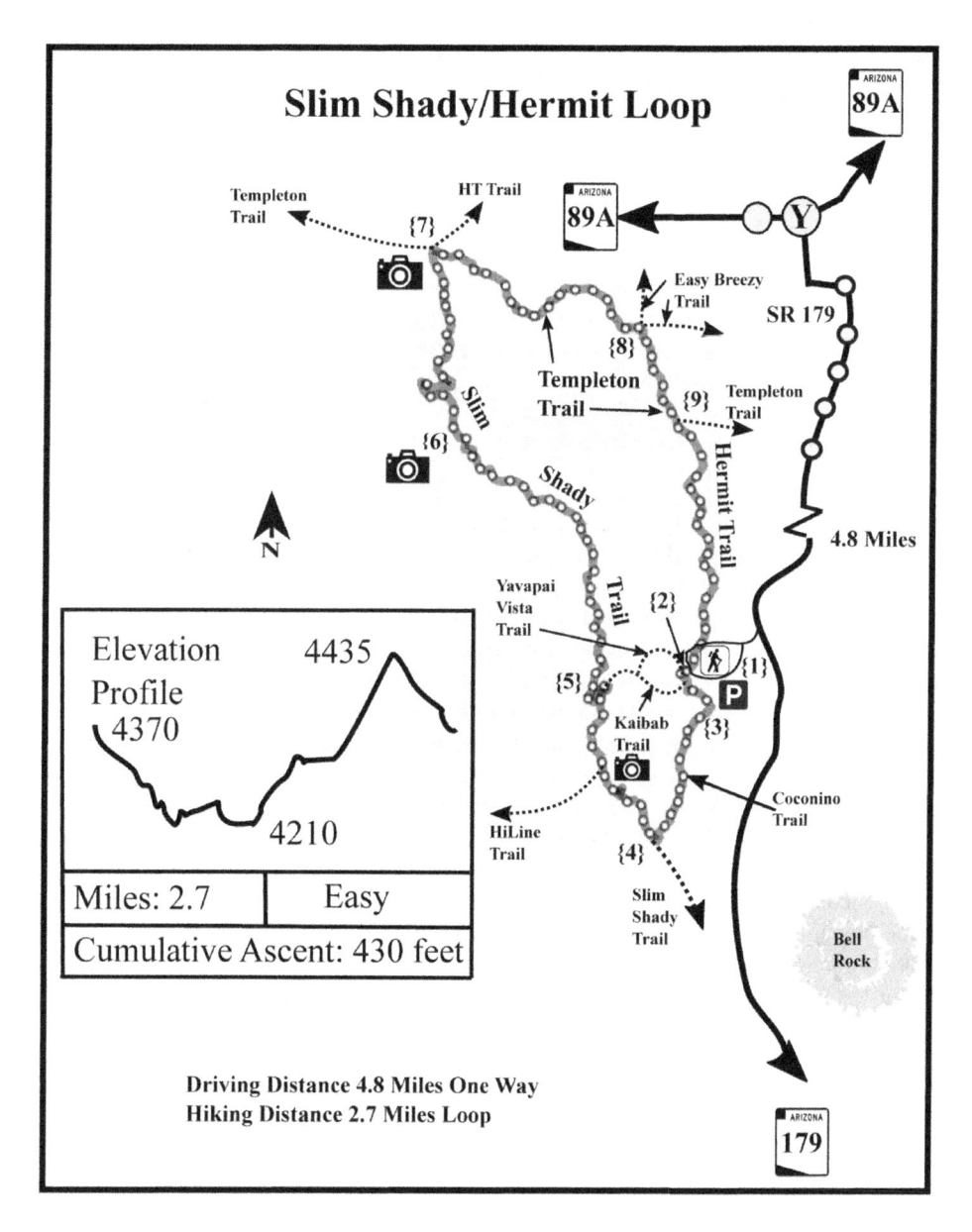

Color Photos: Scan the QR code below for additional color photos of this trail

Slim Shady/Hermit Loop

- Templeton Trail
- HT Trail
- {7}
- ARIZONA 89A
- Easy Breezy Trail
- {8}
- Templeton Trail
- {9} Templeton Trail
- SR 179
- Slim Shady Trail
- {6}
- Hermit Trail
- 4.8 Miles
- Yavapai Vista Trail
- {2}
- {5}
- {1}
- P
- Kaibab Trail
- {3}
- Coconino Trail
- HiLine Trail
- {4}
- Slim Shady Trail
- Bell Rock
- ARIZONA 89A
- ARIZONA 179
- Y

Elevation Profile
4370
4435
4210

Miles: 2.7	Easy
Cumulative Ascent: 430 feet	

Driving Distance 4.8 Miles One Way
Hiking Distance 2.7 Miles Loop

131

Soldier Pass Trail ★

Summary: A favorite in-out hike with stops at the Devil's Kitchen and the Seven Sacred Pools along with a side trip to some impressive red rock arches

Challenge Level: Moderate

Hiking Distance:
About 2.1 miles one way to the Brins Mesa Trail or 4.2 miles round trip from the trailhead parking lot; add 2.5 miles from the Posse Grounds Park & Ride parking lot

Hiking Time:
About 3 hours round trip or 4 hours from Posse Grounds Park & Ride parking lot

Trail Popularity:
🚶🚶🚶🚶

Trailhead Directions: From the "Y" roundabout (see page 7), drive west toward Cottonwood on SR 89A for 1.25 miles then turn right onto Soldiers Pass Road. Proceed on Soldiers Pass Road for 1.5 miles. Note Carruth Road on the left after 0.5 mile. Continue another 1 mile and turn right onto Rim Shadows. Go about 0.25 mile then turn left into the parking area {1}. (34°53.057'N; 111°47.028'W)

Parking is very limited at this popular trail. If you are hiking Thursday thru Sunday, you must take the shuttle because the parking area is closed. **(see Trailhead Shuttle Service page 5)** or park at the Posse Grounds Park & Ride lot {9} located on Carruth Road and follow the mixed-use trail along Soldiers Pass Road to reach the Soldier Pass trailhead.

Description: Shortly after beginning the Soldier Pass Trail, you'll descend into the deep Soldier Wash then climb up to the Devil's Kitchen (about 0.2 mile) {2}. This is the largest sinkhole in the Sedona area. After another 0.4 mile, you'll come to the Seven Sacred Pools, which are small depressions in the red rock that hold water even in dry periods {3}. These two areas are very popular with hikers and visitors on jeep rides. You won't encounter jeeps or as many other hikers on the rest of the trail. There is partial shade beginning at about the 1 mile mark and the trees tend to block some of the red rock views.

About 1.3 miles from the trailhead, look to the right for a faint trail up to the Soldier Pass Arches {4}. It's a steep climb of about 275 feet with drop offs so be extremely careful if you attempt to go to the arches {5}. Return to the main trail. As you continue, the trail becomes rockier and steeper as it approaches Brins Mesa. Once on top of Brins Mesa, you'll come to a fork at the 2 mile mark {6}. Take the right fork to an overlook {8} or take the left fork to the intersection with the Brins Mesa Trail after another 0.1 mile {7}. Turn around here, or you can hike a loop by turning right onto the Brins Mesa Trail (see Brins Mesa/Soldier Pass Loop).

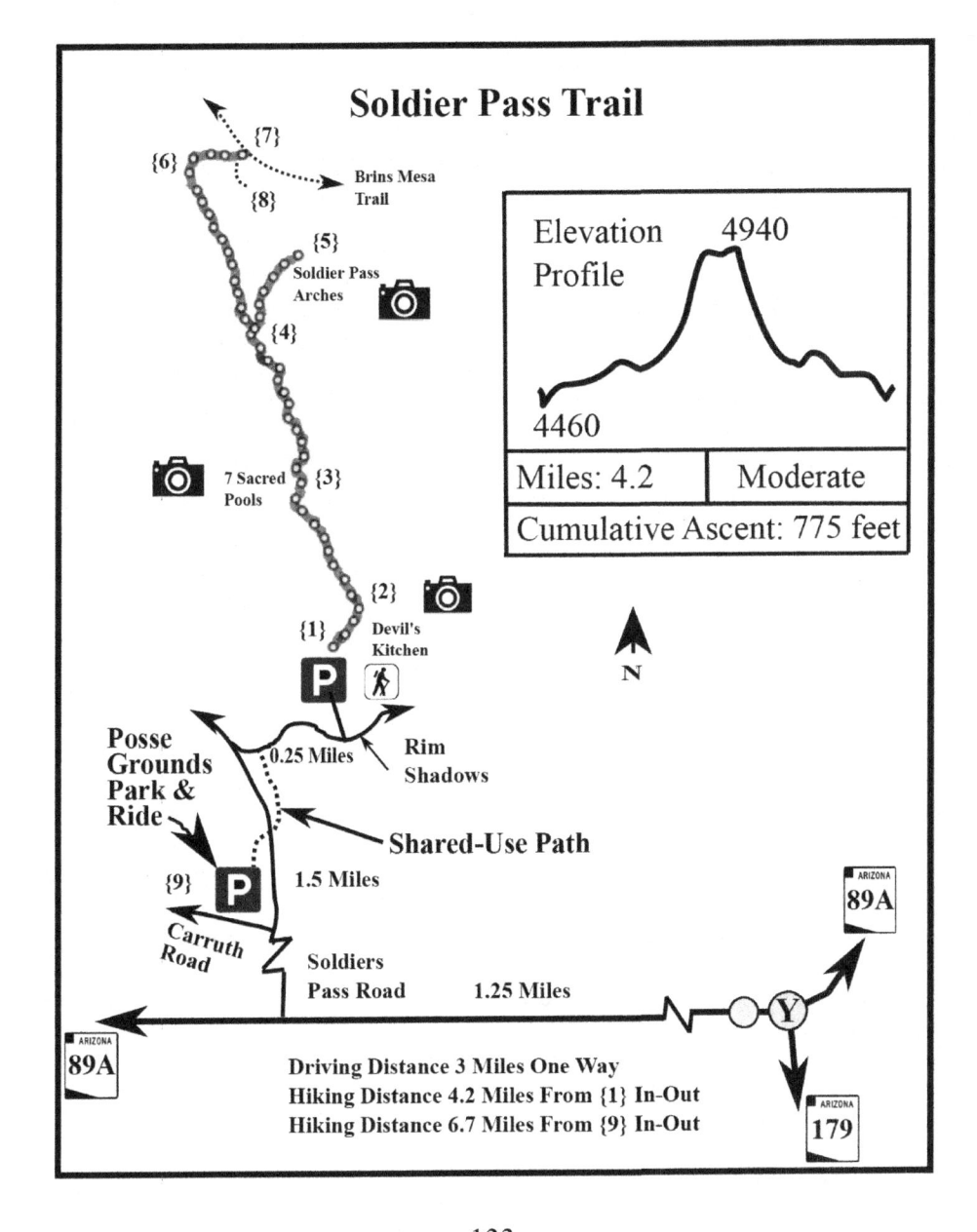

Color Photos: Scan the QR code below for additional color photos of this trail

Soldier Pass Trail

{7}
{6}
{8} → Brins Mesa Trail
{5} Soldier Pass Arches
{4}
{3} 7 Sacred Pools
{2} Devil's Kitchen
{1}

Elevation Profile 4940
4460

Miles: 4.2	Moderate
Cumulative Ascent: 775 feet	

N

Posse Grounds Park & Ride
0.25 Miles
Rim Shadows
Shared-Use Path
{9}
1.5 Miles
Carruth Road
Soldiers Pass Road
1.25 Miles

89A
89A
179

Driving Distance 3 Miles One Way
Hiking Distance 4.2 Miles From {1} In-Out
Hiking Distance 6.7 Miles From {9} In-Out

Soldier Wash Trails
Adobe Jack/Javelina Loop

Summary: A loop hike that offers a short detour to a beautiful overlook with wonderful views

Challenge Level: Moderate

Hiking Distance: About a 4.6 mile loop (including the side trip to the top of Ant Hill)

Hiking Time: About 2 ½ hours round trip

Trail Popularity: 🚶🚶

Trailhead Directions: From the "Y" roundabout (see page 7), drive west toward Cottonwood 0.8 mile then turn right into the small parking area along SR 89A. {1} (34°51.908'N; 111°46.593'W) There are only 5 parking spaces here but you can squeeze in 2 more vehicles.

Description: There are seven connecting trails within the Soldier Wash Trail System,. This is a loop by hiking up the western side of the system on the Adobe Jack Trail, stopping at a beautiful overlook then continuing back on the east side via the Javelina Trail. The views improve the further north you hike.

From the parking area, follow the signs for the Adobe Jack Trail. After 350 feet, you descend into a large wash, then intersect the Crusty Trail {2}. You'll be returning via the Crusty Trail. For now, continue on Adobe Jack. Throughout this hike all of the trails rise and fall. You'll intersect the Coyote Trail {3} after 0.8 mile then the Power Line Plunge Trail after 1 mile {4}. Make a right turn onto Power Line Plunge.

As you hike Power Line Plunge, you'll intersect the Shorty Trail {5} and after 1.4 miles, you'll intersect the Grand Central Trail {6}. Here I suggest you make a left then follow the Grand Central Trail for 0.6 mile to the top of Ant Hill {9} for fantastic views. You'll pass the Shorty Trail {7} and the Ant Hill Loop {8} on the way. The Grand Central Trail rises gently between {6} and {8} but is very steep between {8} and {9} so watch your footing.

Once you've enjoyed the views from the top of Ant Hill, return to the Power Line Plunge Trail then make a left turn to continue on. At 2.75 miles, continue across an open area {10}. At 2.8 miles, you'll intersect the Javelina Trail {11}. Make a right turn here to begin the hike back. You"ll intersect the Manzanita Trail {12} at 3.2 miles and the Grand Central Trail again at 4 miles {13}. Continue west on the Grand Central Trail. You'll be following a large wash parallel to SR 89A. You'll intersect the end of the Crusty Trail at 4.2 miles {14}. Continue west on the Crusty Trail for another 0.5 mile to the intersection of the Crusty Trail and Adobe Jack {2}. Make a left turn here and follow Adobe Jack a short distance back to the parking area {1} for a 4.6 mile loop hike.

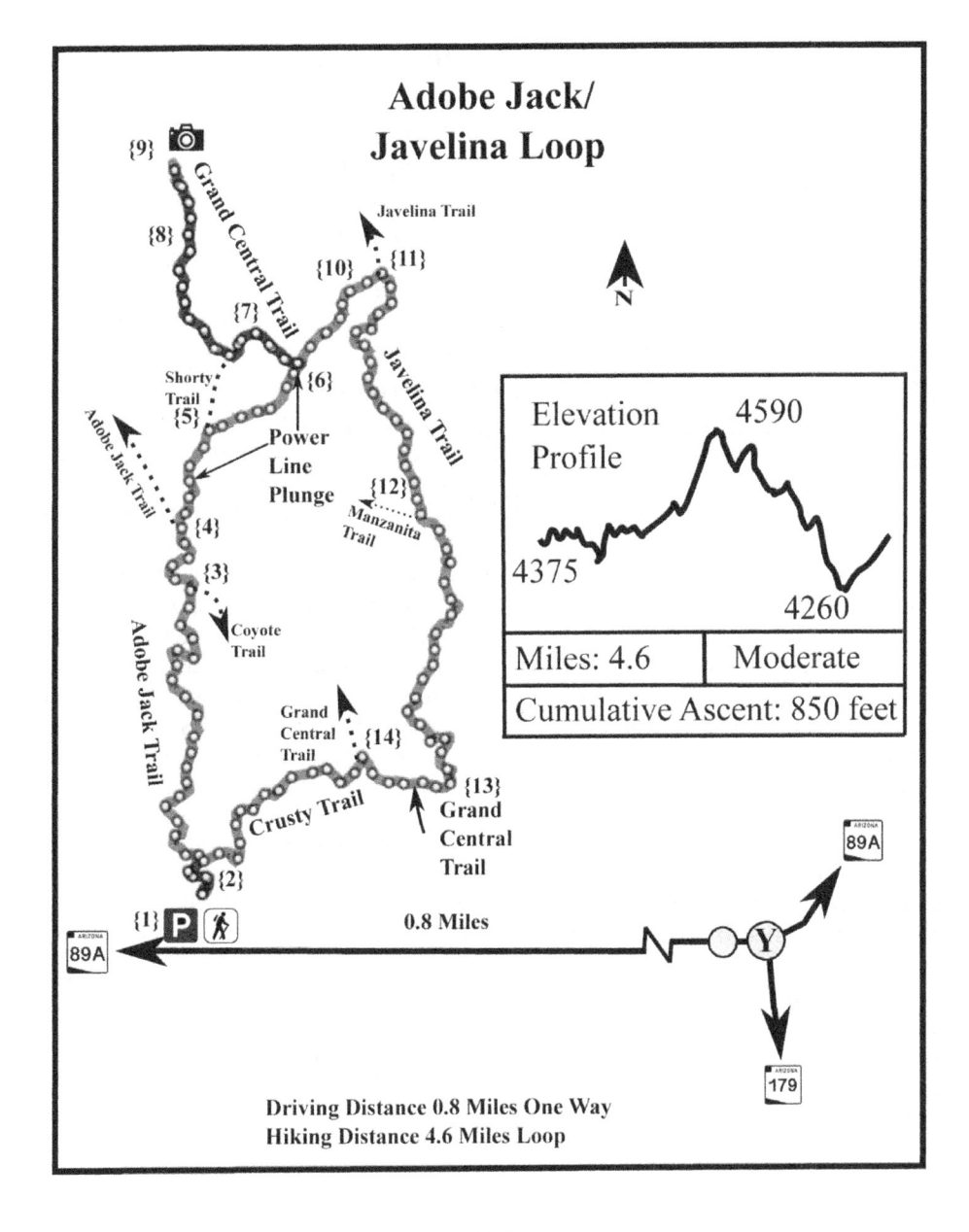

Color Photos: Scan the QR code below for additional color photos of this trail

Adobe Jack/ Javelina Loop

{9}
{8} Grand Central Trail
Javelina Trail
{10} {11}
{7}
Shorty Trail
{5} {6}
Adobe Jack Trail
Power Line Plunge
Javelina Trail
{4}
{12}
Manzanita Trail
{3}
Coyote Trail
Adobe Jack Trail
Grand Central Trail {14}
{13} Grand Central Trail
Crusty Trail
{2}
{1} P
0.8 Miles

N

Elevation Profile	4590
4375	4260
Miles: 4.6	Moderate
Cumulative Ascent: 850 feet	

89A
Y
179

Driving Distance 0.8 Miles One Way
Hiking Distance 4.6 Miles Loop

135

Soldier Wash Trails
Grand Central/Javelina Loop

Summary: A loop hike that passes a beautiful overlook with wonderful views

Challenge Level: Moderate

Hiking Distance: About a 5 mile loop

Hiking Time: About 2 ½ hours round trip

Trail Popularity:

Trailhead Directions: From the "Y" roundabout (see page 7), drive towards Cottonwood 0.8 mile then turn right into the small parking area along SR 89A. {1} (34°51.908'N; 111°46.593'W) There are only 5 parking spaces here but you can squeeze in 2 more vehicles

Description: There are seven connecting trails within the Soldier Wash Trail System. This is a loop by hiking up the center of the system on the Grand Central Trail, stopping at a beautiful overlook then continuing back on the east side via the Javelina Trail. The views improve the further north you hike.

From the parking area, follow the signs for the Adobe Jack Trail. After 350 feet, you descend into a large wash then hike up to make a sharp right turn onto the Crusty Trail. As you proceed, you cross back and forth and hike in the wash for a large part of the way. After 0.6 mile, you'll intersect the Grand Central Trail (GCT) {2}. Make a left turn then begin hiking north for 1.4 miles. The GCT is very shaded for the first 0.5 mile. As you hike along, you'll intersect the Coyote, Power Line Plunge and Shorty Trails. When you intersect the Ant Hill Loop Trail, turn left; walk 7 paces then turn right to continue on the GCT. The trail now becomes steep and there is loose rock so watch your footing. After 0.1 mile, look to the left for a high red rock knoll known as Ant Hill which is a great place to stop for photos and a snack {3}. You'll have 360 degree views and can see Bell Rock, Courthouse Butte, Sugarloaf, Chimney Rock, Snoopy, Lucy and other Sedona landmarks. If you like, this is a good place to turn around and return to the parking area for a 4 mile round trip hike.

To hike the loop, continue north on the GCT for 0.3 mile then make a right turn onto the Ant Hill Loop Trail {4}. Follow the Ant Hill Loop Trail for 0.2 mile then make a right turn (east) onto the Jordan Trail {5}. Follow the Jordan Trail for 0.5 mile then turn right (south) onto the Javelina Trail {6}. Follow the Javelina Trail for 1.2 miles then turn right (west) onto the GCT {7}. Follow the GCT for 0.1 mile then continue on the Crusty Trail {2} for 0.6 mile back to the parking area {1}.

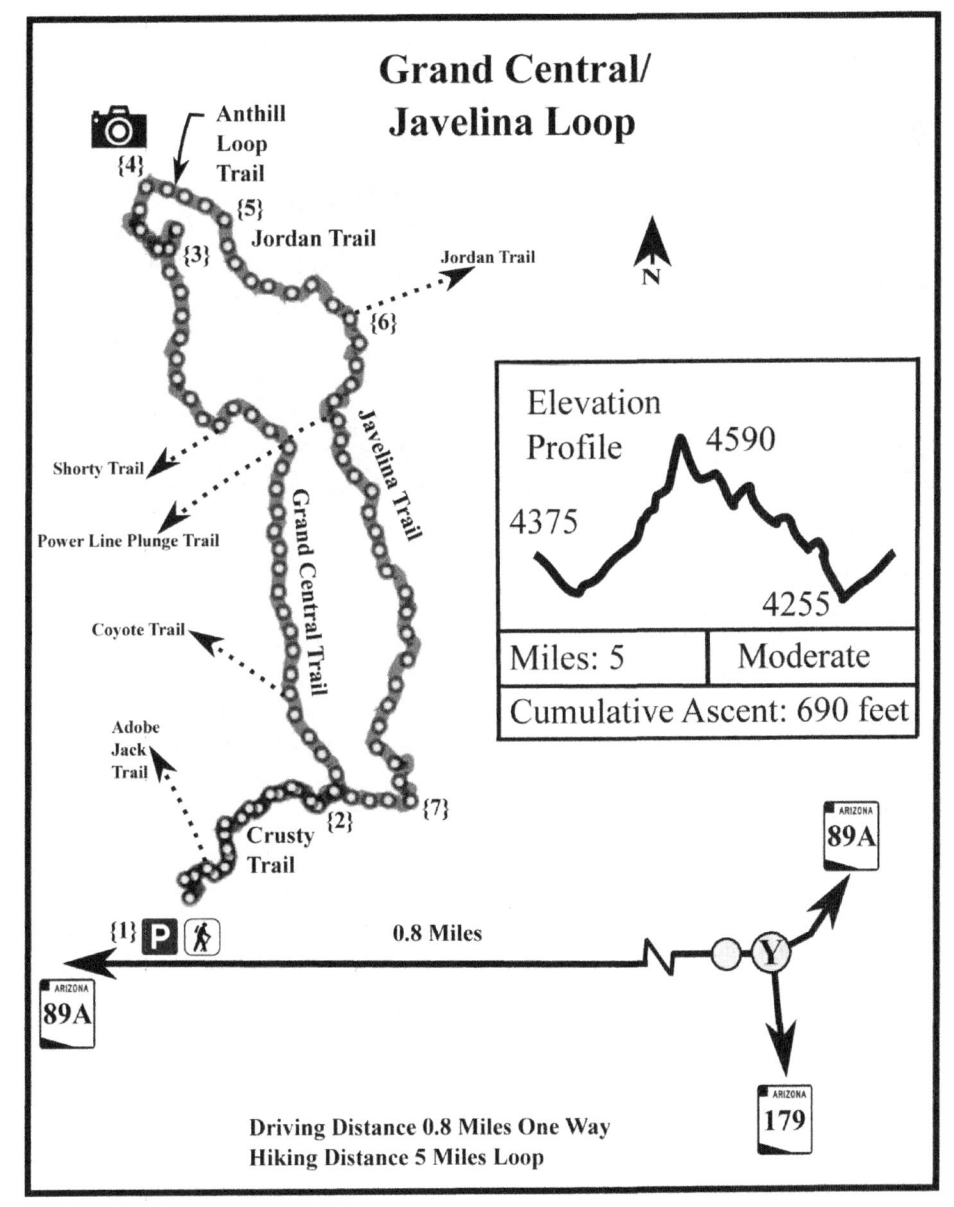

Color Photos: Scan the QR code below for additional color photos of this trail

Grand Central/Javelina Loop

{4} Anthill Loop Trail
{5} Jordan Trail
{3}
Jordan Trail
{6}
Shorty Trail
Power Line Plunge Trail
Javelina Trail
Grand Central Trail
Coyote Trail
Adobe Jack Trail
{2} {7}
Crusty Trail
{1} 0.8 Miles

N

Elevation Profile
4590
4375
4255

Miles: 5	Moderate
Cumulative Ascent: 690 feet	

ARIZONA 89A
ARIZONA 89A
ARIZONA 179

Driving Distance 0.8 Miles One Way
Hiking Distance 5 Miles Loop

137

Sterling Pass to Vultee Arch Trail

Summary: An in-out hike up the west side of Oak Creek Canyon and an alternative way to reach Vultee Arch

Challenge Level: Hard

Hiking Distance: About 2.6 miles each way from Sterling Pass trailhead to Vultee Arch or 5.2 miles round trip

Hiking Time: About 3 ½ hours to Vultee Arch and return round trip

Trail Popularity:

Trailhead Directions: From the "Y" roundabout (see page 7), drive north on SR 89A about 6.25 miles. You'll need to find a wide spot in the road to park on the west side of SR 89A near mile mark 380.5, about 300 feet north of the Manzanita campground located on the east side of SR 89A. {1} (34°56.201'N; 111°44.826'W) Be careful when you make the U-turn as traffic can move pretty fast on SR 89A. The trail starts on the west side of SR 89A.

Description: You can reach Vultee Arch {4} from the Sterling Pass Trail. Sterling Pass is very steep with areas you have to climb up, has loose rock in places and can be overgrown but is easy to follow. Watch for poison ivy along the trail.

You'll hike up about 1150 feet to reach the saddle {2}. The saddle is about 1.4 miles from the SR 89A parking area. As you continue from the saddle, you'll enter a pine forest and the trail begins a steady descent. While there aren't many red rock views on this trail, the scenery is very nice.

About 2.4 miles in, you've reached the end of the Sterling Pass Trail and you'll see a sign for Vultee Arch on the right {3}. Turn right here then hike 0.2 mile down the Vultee Arch Trail to see Vultee Arch, an impressive sight {4} (see Vultee Arch Trail).

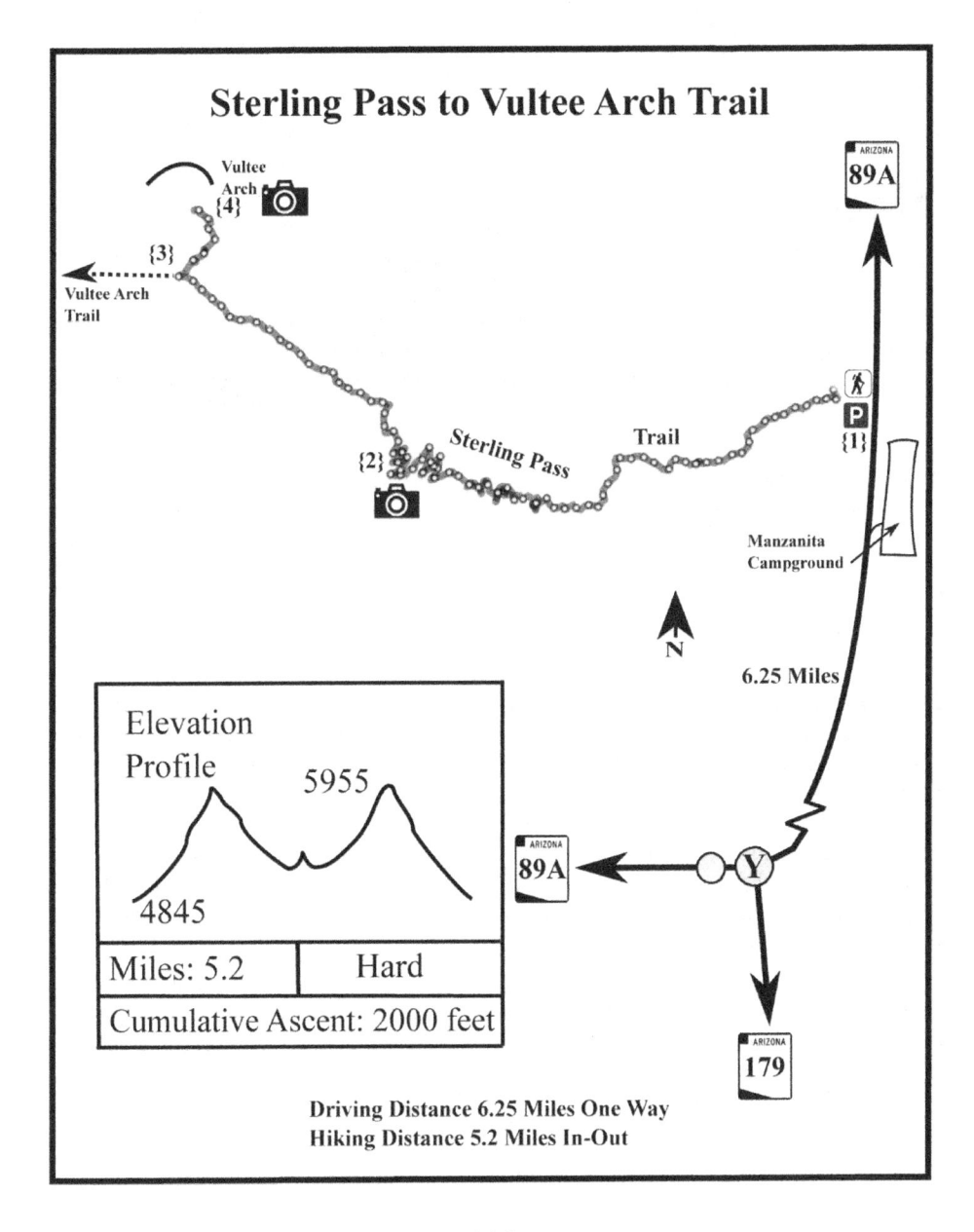

Color Photos: Scan the QR code below for additional color photos of this trail

Sterling Pass to Vultee Arch Trail

Vultee Arch {4}

{3}

Vultee Arch Trail

{2} Sterling Pass Trail

{1}

89A

Manzanita Campground

N

6.25 Miles

89A

Y

179

Elevation Profile
5955
4845

Miles: 5.2	Hard
Cumulative Ascent: 2000 feet	

Driving Distance 6.25 Miles One Way
Hiking Distance 5.2 Miles In-Out

139

Sugarloaf Trail

Summary: A short hike to the top of a large rock mound with nice views of Thunder Mountain, Coffeepot and Sedona

Challenge Level: Moderate

Hiking Distance: About 2 miles round trip

Hiking Time: About 1 hour round trip

Trail Popularity:

Trailhead Directions: From the "Y" roundabout (see page 7), drive west toward Cottonwood on SR 89A for just under 2 miles then turn right onto Coffeepot Drive. Drive about 0.5 mile then turn left at the stop sign onto Sanborn. Continue to the second street then turn right onto Little Elf. Little Elf ends at Buena Vista so turn right onto Buena Vista then turn left into the parking area {1}. (34°52.458'N; 111°47.793'W) This parking area also serves the Coffeepot, Teacup and Thunder Mountain Trails. It has only 14 spots so can fill quickly.

Description: About 50 feet past the interpretive signboard near the parking area, look for a sign on the right {2}. Follow the Teacup/Sugarloaf Summit Trail for 0.3 mile. There are many social trails in this area so be sure to follow the cairns. Turn right at the next sign {3} then continue on the Teacup Trail. You'll soon come to a sign for the western end of the Sugarloaf Summit Loop Trail {4}. Continue straight ahead on the Teacup Trail for another 0.15 mile and you'll intersect an unmarked trail on your left that will lead you to the base of Coffeepot Rock {5} (see Coffeepot Trail). About 0.1 mile further on, turn right onto the Sugarloaf Summit Trail {6} at a trail marker where you'll have a nice view of Coffeepot Rock.

Hike south then turn west under a power line. After 0.4 mile, you'll see a post on the right, opposite of where the trail to Sugarloaf Summit begins on your left {7}. After climbing to the summit (a scramble of some 0.2 mile that gains 200 feet in elevation) {8}, return to the Sugarloaf Loop Trail. Turn left (west) then continue on for another 0.1 mile. Turn left onto the Teacup Trail {4} then hike back to the parking area.

While you'll see rooftops on this in-town trail, the views of Thunder Mountain and Coffeepot Rock are beautiful. There is little shade, however, so the hike can be hot in the summer months.

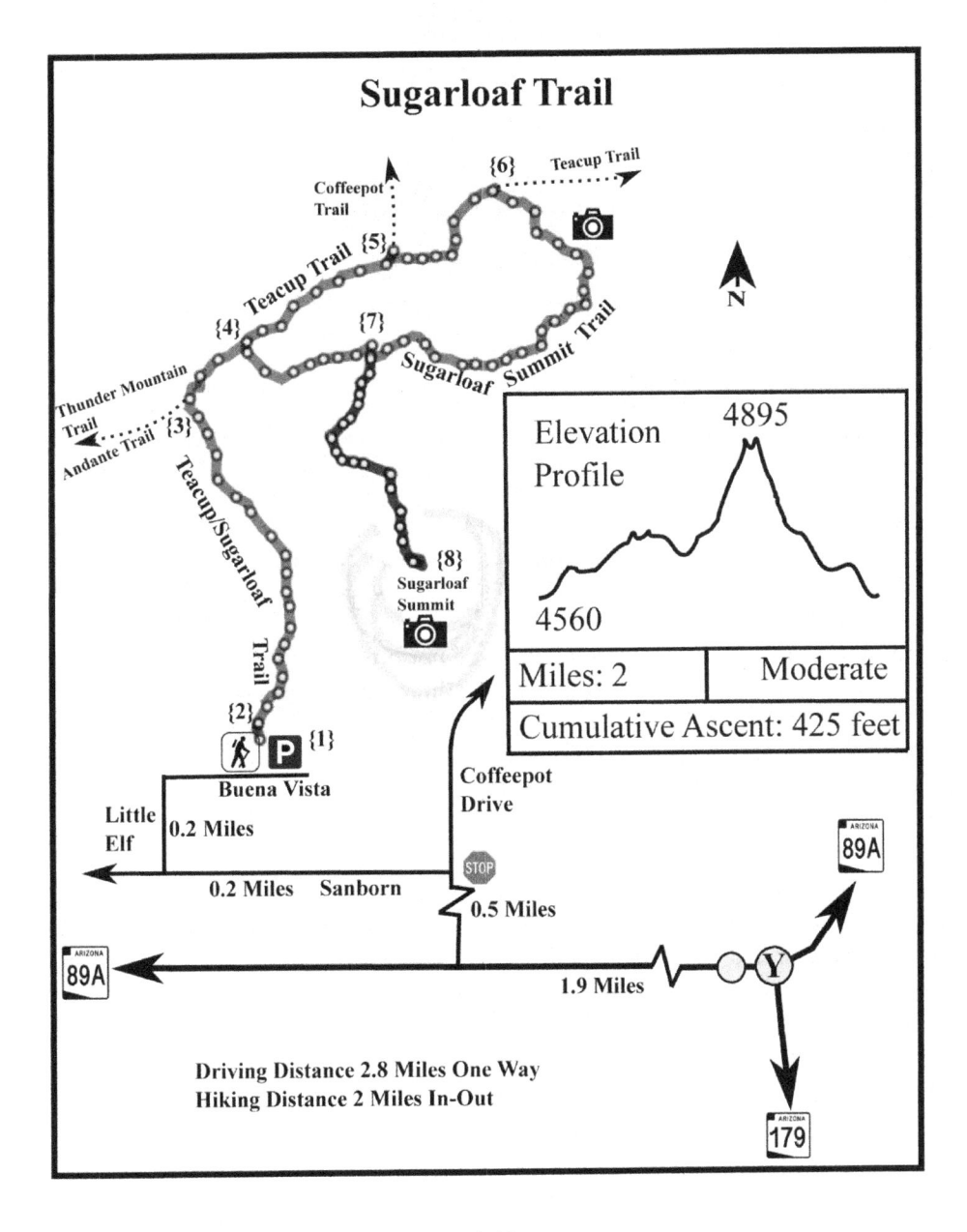

Color Photos: Scan the QR code below for additional color photos of this trail

Sugarloaf Trail

- Teacup Trail
- Coffeepot Trail
- {6}
- {5}
- {4}
- Teacup Trail
- {7}
- Sugarloaf Summit Trail
- Thunder Mountain Trail
- Andante Trail {3}
- Teacup/Sugarloaf Trail
- {8} Sugarloaf Summit
- {2}
- {1}
- Buena Vista
- Little Elf
- 0.2 Miles
- 0.2 Miles Sanborn
- Coffeepot Drive
- 0.5 Miles
- 1.9 Miles
- ARIZONA 89A
- ARIZONA 89A
- Y
- ARIZONA 179

Elevation Profile 4895 — 4560

| Miles: 2 | Moderate |

Cumulative Ascent: 425 feet

Driving Distance 2.8 Miles One Way
Hiking Distance 2 Miles In-Out

141

Teacup Trail

Summary: A sunny in-town trail with the option to visit the Devil's Kitchen and Seven Sacred Pools

Challenge Level: Moderate

Hiking Distance: About 2.1 miles each way to view Devil's Kitchen or 4.2 miles round trip. Add 0.4 mile each way to visit the Seven Sacred Pools or 5 miles round trip.

Hiking Time: About 3 hours round trip

Trail Popularity:

Trailhead Directions: From the "Y" roundabout (see page 7), drive west toward Cottonwood on SR 89A for just under 2 miles then turn right onto Coffeepot Drive. Drive about 0.5 mile then turn left at the stop sign onto Sanborn. Continue to the second street then turn right onto Little Elf. Little Elf ends at Buena Vista so turn right onto Buena Vista then turn left into the parking area {1}. (34°52.458'N; 111°47.793'W) This parking area also serves the Coffeepot, Thunder Mountain and Sugarloaf Trails. It has only 14 spots so can fill quickly.

Description: From the parking lot, proceed north for 0.3 mile to the intersection with the Thunder Mountain Trail {2}. Continue on the Teacup Trail and you'll soon come to the west end of the Sugarloaf Summit Trail {3} and then the east end of the Sugarloaf Summit Trail after 0.7 mile {4}. The Teacup Trail begins a descent and there are some drop offs after about 1 mile {5}. After 1.25 miles, you'll come to a nice area for a break {6}. Beyond this point the rooftops you've seen all along will disappear.

After 1.85 miles, look to the left for a distant view of Devil's Kitchen, the largest sink hole in the Sedona Area. At 2 miles, you'll intersect a road. This is the end of the Teacup Trail {7}. If you'd like to visit Devil's Kitchen, turn left and follow the road for about 160 feet, then turn right continuing on the road for another 0.1 mile {8}. At the Soldier Pass/To Sinkhole sign, turn right and follow the road for 375 feet to Devil's Kitchen {9}.

If you'd like to visit the Seven Sacred Pools, return to the Soldier Pass Trail sign {8} and follow the Soldier Pass Trail north for 0.4 mile. (See Soldier Pass Trail)

This trail has little shade so it will be a hot hike in the summer.

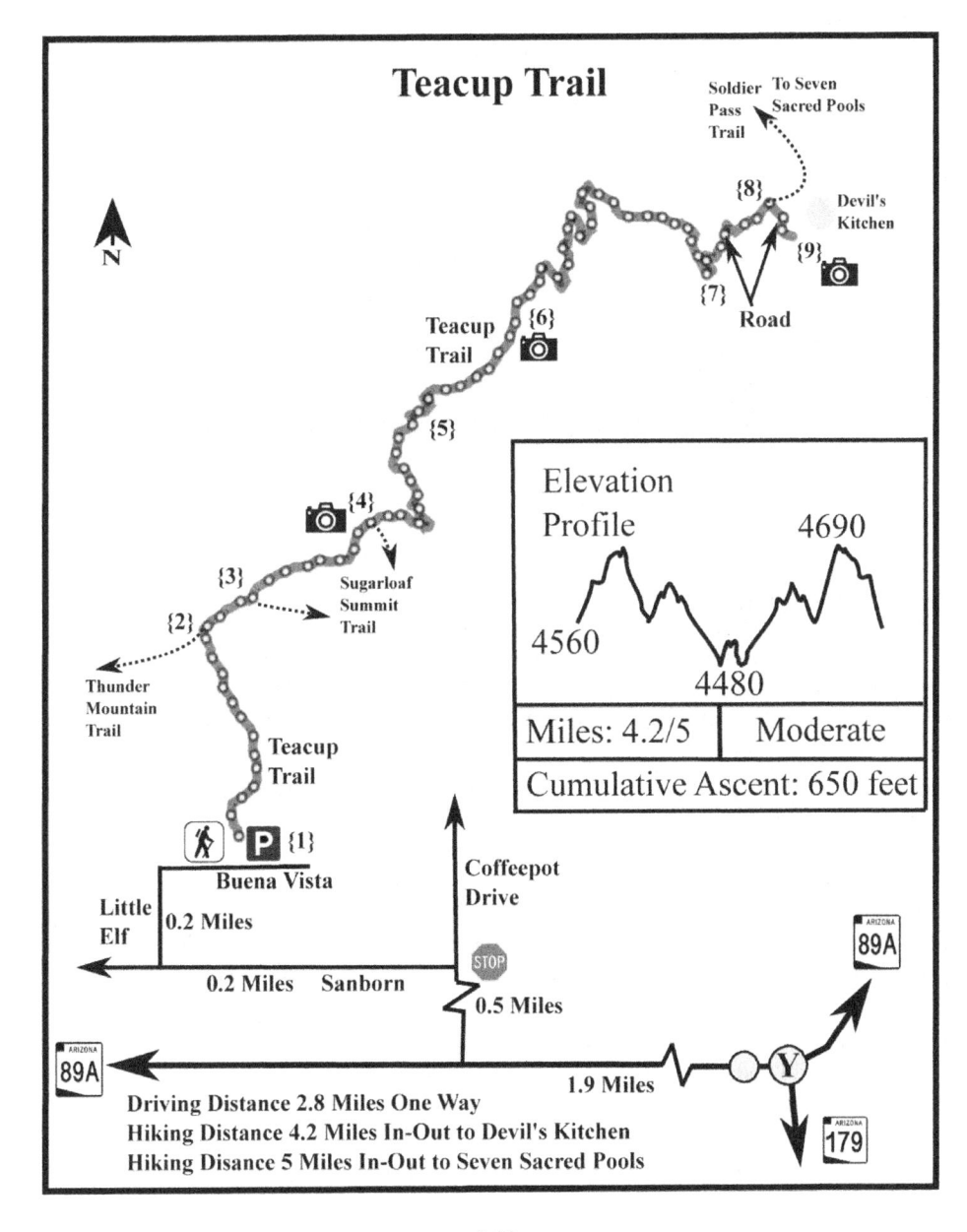

Color Photos: Scan the QR code below for additional color photos of this trail

Teacup Trail

To Seven Sacred Pools
Soldier Pass Trail
{8}
Devil's Kitchen
{9}
{7}
Road

N

Teacup Trail {6}

{5}

{4}

{3}
{2}
Sugarloaf Summit Trail

Thunder Mountain Trail

Teacup Trail

{1}
Buena Vista
0.2 Miles
Little Elf
0.2 Miles   Sanborn

Coffeepot Drive

STOP
0.5 Miles

ARIZONA 89A

1.9 Miles

ARIZONA 89A
ARIZONA 179

Elevation Profile
4560
4480
4690

| Miles: 4.2/5 | Moderate |

Cumulative Ascent: 650 feet

Driving Distance 2.8 Miles One Way
Hiking Distance 4.2 Miles In-Out to Devil's Kitchen
Hiking Disance 5 Miles In-Out to Seven Sacred Pools

Telephone Trail

Summary: A short but steep hike up the east side of Oak Creek Canyon leading to amazing window rock formations

Challenge Level: Hard

Hiking Distance: About 1.3 miles each way or 2.6 miles round trip

Hiking Time: About 2 hours round trip

Trail Popularity:

Trailhead Directions: From the "Y" roundabout (see page 7), drive north on SR 89A about 10.9 miles to mile post 385.1. The parking area is 0.4 mile north of the turn to the West Fork Trail parking area. Park on the east side of SR 89A on the paved shoulder beneath a 25 foot high cliff. {1} (34°59.457'N; 111°44.150'W) Walk north along SR 89A for 475 feet to the trail sign on your right {2}. There you'll see a dark rust color sign for the Telephone Trail.

Description: The trail begins by following SR 89A under a telephone line (hence the name of the trail). After 0.3 mile, you'll begin a series of steep ascents up to several nice ridges {3}. Because this trail is seldom used, you'll likely find loose rock, sand and pine needles which can make the trail slippery. Along the way there are some very nice rock formations and scenic views of Oak Creek Canyon. At 0.6 mile and a rather steep descent, you'll come to a series of unique window or keyhole rocks {4}. This would be a good place to have a snack, take some photos then turn back if you don't want to continue on the very steep trail ahead.

If you continue on, the trail becomes very steep with loose sand, rock and pine needles {5}{6}. The trail ends when you reach the top of the east wall of Oak Creek Canyon {7} but you can bushwhack about 1.6 miles to the north and intersect the Harding Springs Trail. For this endeavor, I recommend you use a GPS unit.

Note: The trail is very steep in places with loose sand and rock; do not attempt if the trail is wet or snow is present.

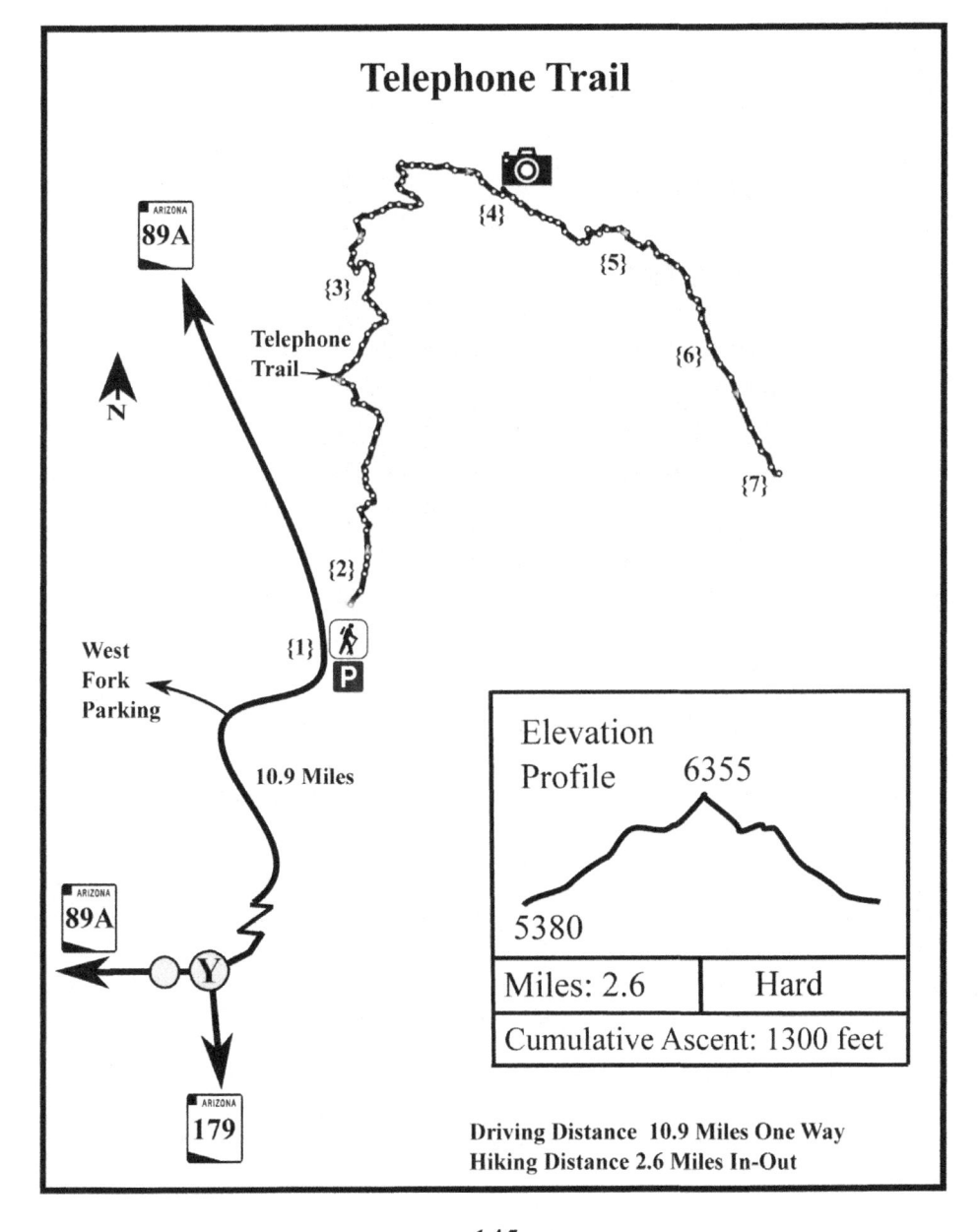

Color Photos: Scan the QR code below for additional color photos of this trail

Telephone Trail

{4}
{5}
{3}
Telephone Trail →
{6}
{7}
{2}
{1}
West Fork Parking
10.9 Miles
ARIZONA 89A
ARIZONA 89A
Y
ARIZONA 179
N

Elevation Profile 6355

5380

Miles: 2.6	Hard
Cumulative Ascent: 1300 feet	

Driving Distance 10.9 Miles One Way
Hiking Distance 2.6 Miles In-Out

145

Templeton Trail

Summary: An in-out hike with views of Sedona's major rock formations

Challenge Level: Moderate

Hiking Distance: About 4.1 miles each way from the Court House Vista parking area to the intersection of the Baldwin Loop Trail; about 8.2 miles round trip

Hiking Time: About 5 hours as an in-out hike from the Court House Vista parking area to the intersection of Baldwin Loop Trail and return

Trail Popularity: 🚶🚶🚶

Trailhead Directions: From the "Y" roundabout (see page 7), drive south on SR 179 for about 5 miles to the parking area. After you drive about 3.2 miles, just past the Back O' Beyond roundabout, SR 179 becomes a divided highway. Continue driving south. About 1.8 miles beyond the Back O' Beyond roundabout, southbound SR 179 adds a passing lane on the left. From the passing lane, turn left at the sign for the Court House Vista parking area {1}. (34°48.350'N; 111°46.009'W) Before you turn, you'll see Bell Rock ahead of you on the left side of SR 179. There are toilets at the parking area. This parking area also serves the Bell Rock, Llama and Courthouse Butte Loop Trails. The trail starts just beyond the interpretive signboard.

Description: The Templeton Trail extends northwest from the Bell Rock Pathway, just north of Bell Rock and Courthouse Butte to the Baldwin Loop trail near Oak Creek and Red Rock Crossing. It provides excellent views of Bell Rock, Courthouse Butte, Lee Mountain, Cathedral Rock and many other rock formations. You can access the east end of the Templeton Trail {6} from the Baldwin Loop parking area {7}.

If you hike from the Court House Vista parking area, which most people do, look for the Phone Trail on your left about 25 feet past the interpretive signboard {2}. Follow the Phone Trail 0.3 mile then continue north (left) on the Bell Rock Pathway Trail. In 0.1 mile turn left onto the Templeton Trail {3} then follow it beneath both the northbound and southbound lanes of SR 179. You'll have excellent views of Cathedral Rock ahead and, in 1 mile, you'll intersect the HT Trail on your right {4}. As you approach Cathedral Rock, the landscape becomes high desert.

You'll intersect the Cathedral Rock Trail in another 1.3 miles on your right {5} and the short but steep trail to the saddle of Cathedral Rock in another 200 feet on your left. As you continue on the Templeton Trail, you'll descend a series of switchbacks. In 0.8 mile, you'll be adjacent to Oak Creek, across from Buddha Beach and Red Rock Crossing. The Templeton Trail continues on for another 0.2 mile where it ends at the Baldwin Loop trail {6}. Turn around here for a hike of 8.2 miles. The Baldwin Loop Trail parking area is another 0.5 mile further {7}.

146

Color Photos: Scan the QR code below for additional color photos of this trail

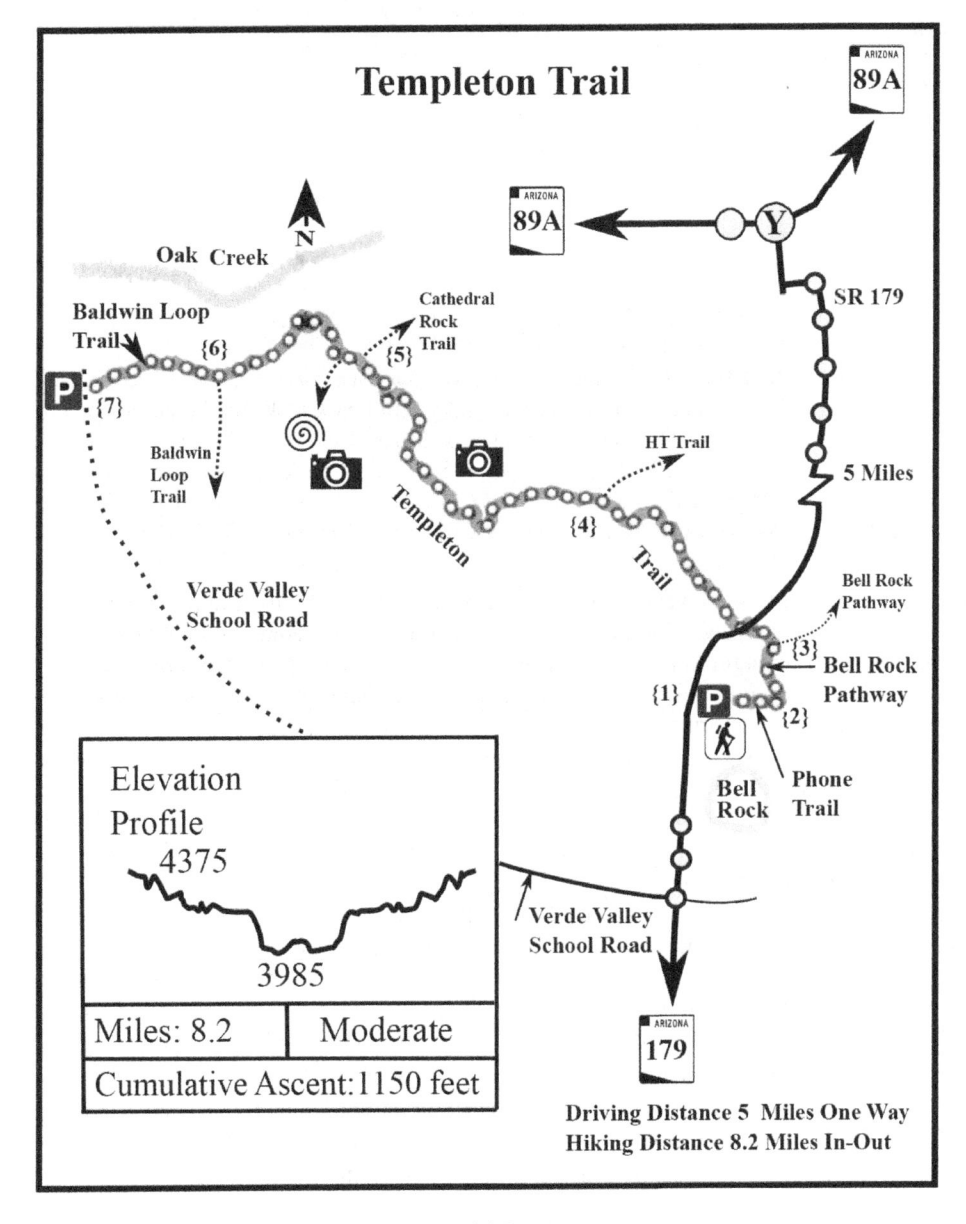

Templeton Trail

Oak Creek
Baldwin Loop Trail
{6}
{7}
Baldwin Loop Trail
Cathedral Rock Trail
{5}
Templeton Trail
{4}
HT Trail
Verde Valley School Road
Bell Rock Pathway
{3}
Bell Rock Pathway
{1}
{2}
Bell Rock
Phone Trail
Verde Valley School Road

ARIZONA 89A
ARIZONA 89A
SR 179
5 Miles
ARIZONA 179

Elevation Profile
4375
3985

Miles: 8.2	Moderate
Cumulative Ascent: 1150 feet	

Driving Distance 5 Miles One Way
Hiking Distance 8.2 Miles In-Out

147

Thunder Mountain/Andante Loop ★

Summary:
A favorite sunny in-town hike with excellent views

Challenge Level: Moderate

Hiking Distance: About 3 miles loop

Hiking Time: About 2 hours round trip

Trail Popularity:

Trailhead Directions: From the "Y" roundabout (see page 7), drive west toward Cottonwood on SR 89A about 3 miles. Turn right onto Dry Creek Road then proceed for 0.5 mile. Turn right onto Thunder Mountain Road then drive 0.7 mile. The parking area is on your left {1}. (34°52.325'N; 111°48.735'W) This parking area also serves the Chimney Rock Upper and Lower Loop. The entrance gate opens each day at 8:00 am and closes at dusk. You can also park at the Coffeepot, Sugarloaf, Teacup Trail parking area

Description: From the parking area, go west past the signboard for about 100 feet then turn right onto the Lower Chimney Trail. In 0.1 miles, you'll come to the intersection of the Thunder Mountain Trail {2}. Turn right onto the Thunder Mountain Trail and you'll soon intersect a social trail after 0.4 mile {3}. After another 0.1 mile, you'll intersect the Andante Trail {4}. Turn right here and follow the Andante Trail. You'll be following overhead power lines and see many rooftops to the south. But the views are excellent to the north. After 0.6 mile, you'll come to the Andante Road parking area {5} and be next to a large green water tank. Continue across the access road and at 0.8 mile you'll come to a nice scenic area {6}. At 1.25 miles, you'll intersect the Thunder Mountain Trail which is the end of the Andante Trail. {7}.

If you follow the Thunder Mountain Trail to the right (east), you'll intersect the Teacup Trail in 0.25 mile. Rather than that, continue straight ahead and follow the Thunder Mountain Trail west. The views along this portion of Thunder Mountain Trail are excellent and there are no rooftops in view. There are some narrow portions of the trail here so watch your footing. At 2 miles, you'll come to a huge rock along the trail {8}.

You'll come to the intersection of the Thunder Mountain and Chimney Pass Trails after 2.5 miles {9}. Make a left here and continue south on the Thunder Mountain Trail back to the parking area to complete the 3 mile loop.

Note: This trail has little shade so it will be a hot hike in the summer.

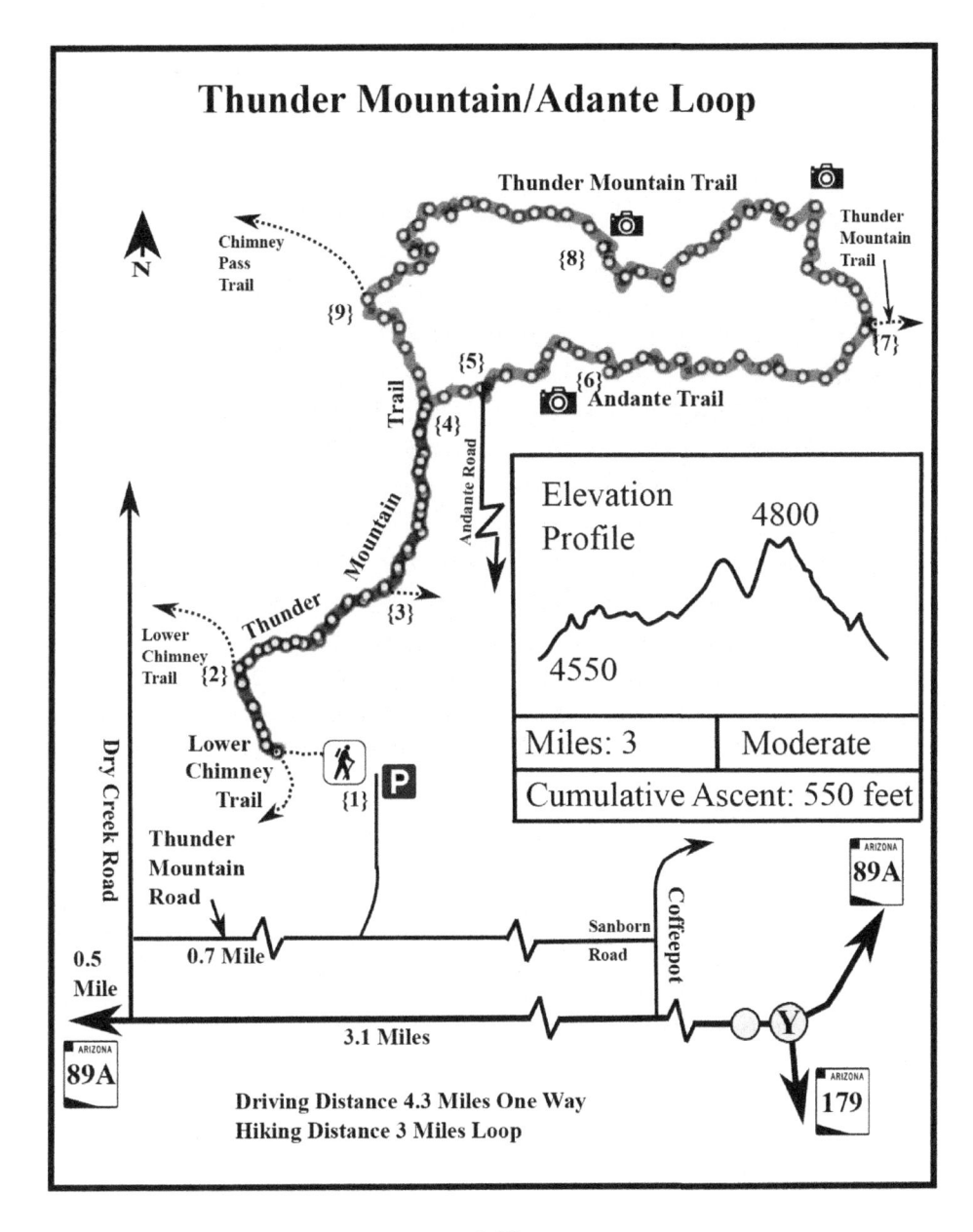

Color Photos: Scan the QR code below for additional color photos of this trail

Thunder Mountain/Adante Loop

Thunder Mountain Trail

Chimney Pass Trail {9}

{8}

Thunder Mountain Trail

{5}

{6} Andante Trail

{4}

Andante Road

Thunder Mountain Trail

{3}

Lower Chimney Trail {2}

Lower Chimney Trail {1}

Thunder Mountain Road

Elevation Profile 4800

4550

Miles: 3	Moderate
Cumulative Ascent: 550 feet	

Dry Creek Road

0.5 Mile

0.7 Mile

Sanborn Road

Coffeepot

ARIZONA 89A

3.1 Miles

Y

ARIZONA 89A

ARIZONA 179

Driving Distance 4.3 Miles One Way
Hiking Distance 3 Miles Loop

149

Transept Trail

Summary: An in-out hike to observe a unique rock formation then onward for some great red rock views

Challenge Level:
Moderate

Hiking Distance:
About 3.1 miles each way or 6.2 miles round trip

Hiking Time:
About 4 hours round trip

Trail Popularity:

Trailhead Directions:
From the "Y" roundabout (see page 7), drive south on SR 179 about 7 miles to the Jacks Canyon and Verde Valley School Road roundabout. Take the first exit onto Verde Valley School Road. Drive 2 miles to the parking area on the left, just beyond the Camping/Camp Fires Prohibited sign {1}. (34°47.428'N; 111°47.572'W) The trail begins across the road.

Description: The Transept Trail, connects Verde Valley School Road and the HiLine Trail. After 0.25 mile, look to the right for rock hoodoo which has a very unusual shape {2}. Some people believe it looks like a Mayan maiden (see photo above). You'll come to a nice view to the right at 0.4 mile {3} then begin climbing.

As you climb higher, you are rewarded with some spectacular views of the Village of Oak Creek, the green fairways of the Sedona Golf Resort and Cathedral Rock in the distance.

At 0.8 mile, the trail becomes steep, narrow and off camber and you'll climb up some natural limestone steps. At 1.1 miles, you'll see a wash on the right {4}. This side trip requires a scramble up some 60 feet to reach two nice overlooks {5} {6} of Big Park and the Oak Creek Country Club below. Return to the main trail and continue on another 2 miles to the intersection with the HiLine Trail {7}. There are some excellent views along the way.

There isn't much shade on this trail so it would be a good choice for cooler weather. There are places that are moderately steep with loose rock and sand and places that are very narrow so watch your footing.

Color Photos: Scan the QR code below for additional color photos of this trail

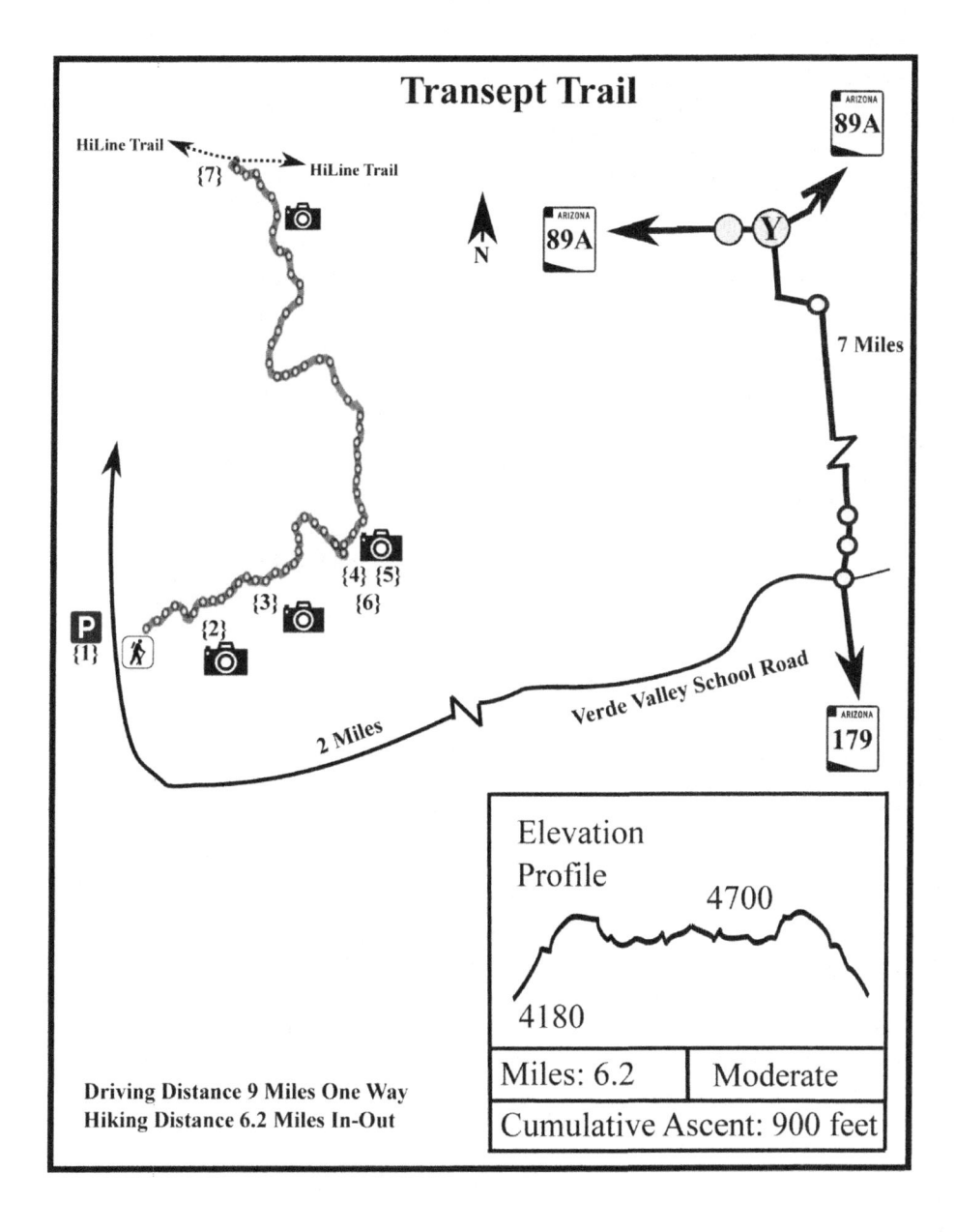

Transept Trail

HiLine Trail
{7}
HiLine Trail

ARIZONA 89A
ARIZONA 89A
Y
7 Miles

{1} P {2} {3} {4} {5} {6}

2 Miles

Verde Valley School Road

ARIZONA 179

Elevation Profile
4700
4180

Miles: 6.2	Moderate
Cumulative Ascent: 900 feet	

Driving Distance 9 Miles One Way
Hiking Distance 6.2 Miles In-Out

Vultee Arch Trail

Summary:
A shady in-out hike to a natural red rock arch

Challenge Level:
Easy to Moderate

Hiking Distance:
About 1.9 miles each way to view the arch, add another 0.3 mile to climb up on the arch or 3.8 miles round trip

Hiking Time: About 2 hours round trip

Trail Popularity:

Trailhead Directions: From the "Y" roundabout (see page 7), drive west toward Cottonwood on SR 89A about 3 miles. Turn right onto Dry Creek Road. Stay on Dry Creek Road for 2 miles then turn right onto Forest Road (FR) 152. Proceed to the end of FR 152 (about 4.3 miles) to the parking area on the left {1}. (34°56.236'N; 111°47.678'W) The parking area also serves the Bear Sign and Dry Creek Trails. The Vultee Arch Trail begins on the east side of the parking area, on the right side of the interpretive signboard.

Note: FR 152 is an extremely rough road beyond the 0.2 mile paved section; a high clearance vehicle and 4WD are strongly recommended.

Description: The trail to the arch viewpoint is a relatively easy hike, but it is a scramble (thus the moderate trail rating) to get onto the arch {6} so be careful if you attempt this. The trail isn't used much because of the difficult drive on FR 152 to the trailhead, as a result this shaded trail can be overgrown. Even though it can be overgrown, it is easy to follow. Watch for poison ivy in some of the wash crossings {2} {3}.

The trail forks at a signpost {4} after about 1.6 miles. Follow the left fork to see the arch. The right fork becomes the Sterling Pass Trail which proceeds to SR 89A in Oak Creek Canyon (see Sterling Pass to Vultee Arch Trail). The arch is visible to the north from the view area {5}. Vultee Arch {6} is named after Gerald and Sylvia Vultee who crashed their plane and died nearby in 1938. There is a plaque dedicated to them near the view area for the arch. There are usually many wildflowers along the trail in late April/early May.

Note: The Forest Service reports that the arch is unstable so proceed onto the arch at your own risk.

Note: See Sterling Pass to Vultee Arch Trail for an alternate way to get to Vultee Arch.

Color Photos: Scan the QR code below for additional color photos of this trail

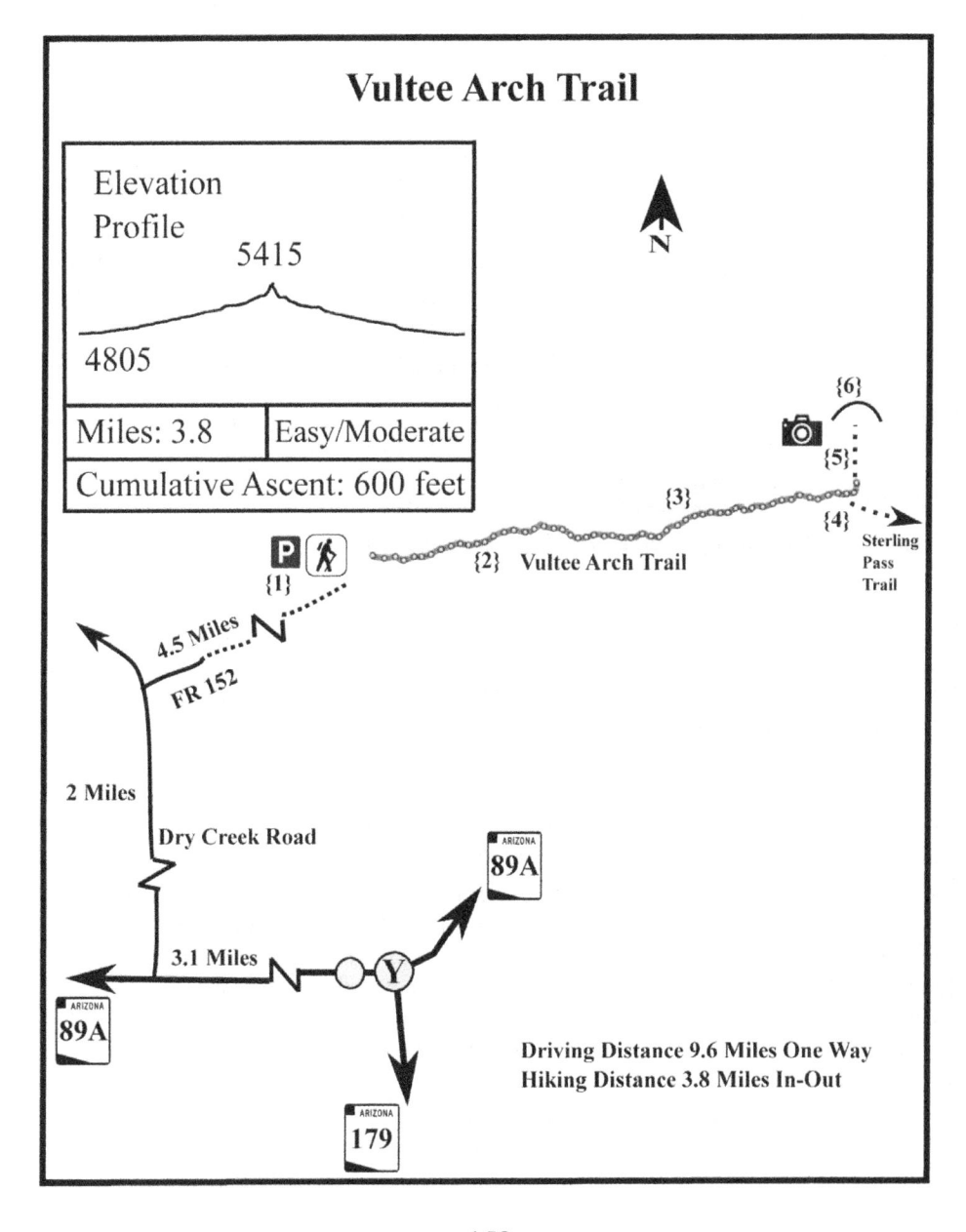

Vultee Arch Trail

Elevation Profile
5415
4805

Miles: 3.8	Easy/Moderate
Cumulative Ascent: 600 feet	

N

{1} P 🚶
{2} Vultee Arch Trail
{3}
{4}
{5}
{6} 📷

Sterling Pass Trail

4.5 Miles
FR 152

2 Miles

Dry Creek Road

ARIZONA 89A

3.1 Miles

Y

ARIZONA 89A

ARIZONA 179

Driving Distance 9.6 Miles One Way
Hiking Distance 3.8 Miles In-Out

153

Western Gateway Trails
Centennial Trail

Summary:
A short barrier free paved path to a nice overlook on the western edge of Sedona

Challenge Level: Easy

Hiking Distance: About 0.38 mile each way to the viewpoint or 0.75 mile round trip

Hiking Time: About 1/2 hour round trip

Trail Popularity: 🚶🚶🚶

Trailhead Directions: From the "Y" roundabout (see page 7), drive west toward Cottonwood on SR 89A for about 4.25 miles then turn right onto Cultural Park Place. Continue straight ahead 0.3 mile to the large unpaved parking lot on the right {1}. (34° 51.150'N; 111° 49.889'W) The parking area also serves the Girdner/Remnant/Roundabout Loop. The paved road is not well maintained but you won't need a high clearance vehicle to access the parking lot. There are two picnic tables near the trailhead.

Description: The Centennial Trail is one of the few barrier free trails in Sedona. As a result wheelchairs and strollers can successfully traverse the trail, although this partially maintained trail has large cracks, dirt and rocks on the asphalt pathway. It is perfect for families with small children as it is flat and short.

Just past the signboard you'll immediately come to the sign for the Centennial Trail. Turn right onto the 4' wide paved path. You'll likely find gravel on the pathway. In 0.1 mile you'll come to a bench on the left where you can sit and enjoy some outstanding views {2}. Continue on and you'll soon intersect the Girdner Trail, then a sign for the Outer Limits Trail {3}. Continue on the paved path and at 0.2 mile you'll cross a gravel road {4}. Continue straight across the road to follow the paved path.

The Centennial Trail begins a gentle rise and at 0.35 mile you'll come to a sign, View Loop. It's 0.1 mile around the loop and the best views are on the north side of the loop. Return to the parking area by retracing your steps on the Centennial Trail.

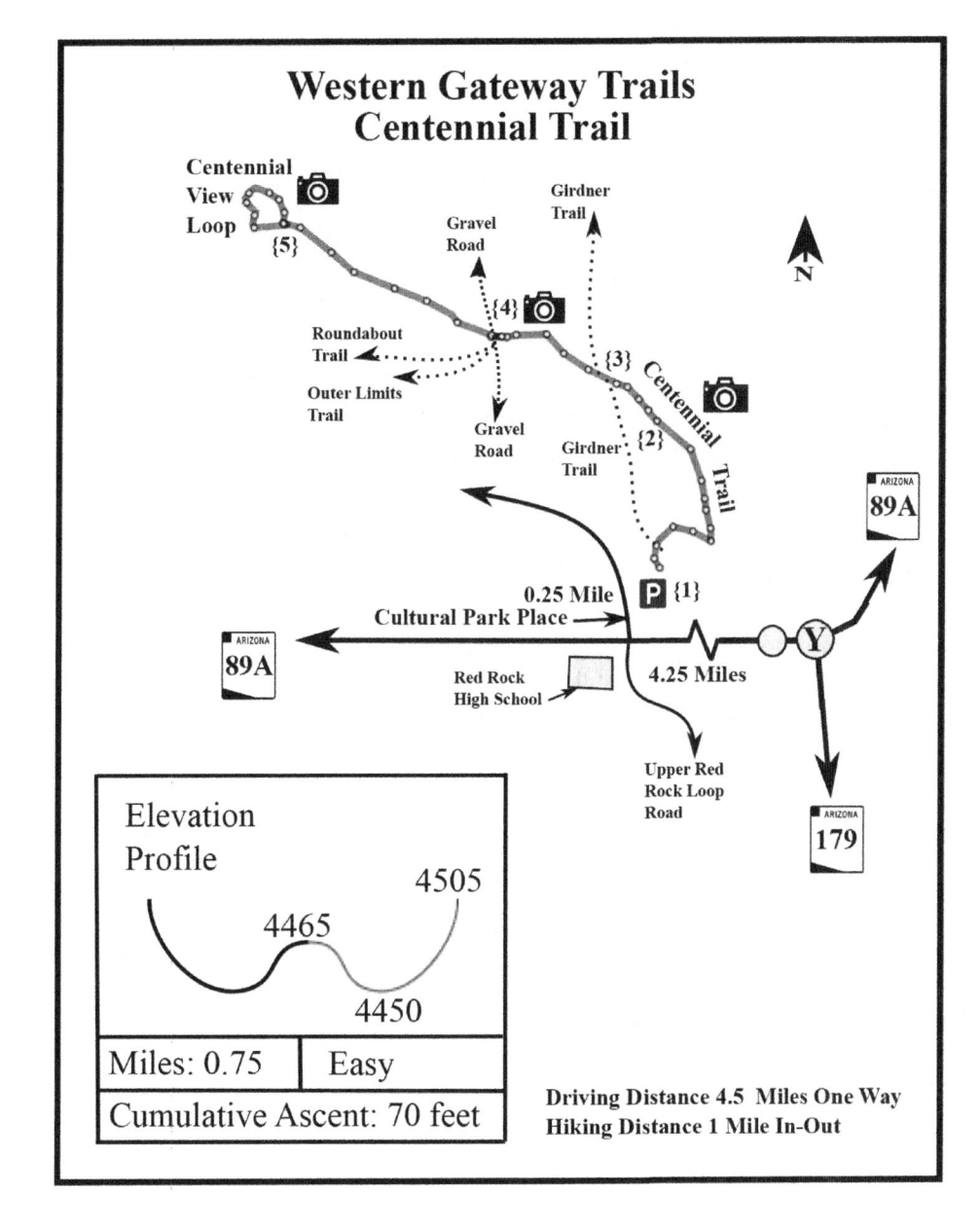

Color Photos: Scan the QR code below for additional color photos of this trail

Western Gateway Trails
Centennial Trail

Centennial View Loop {5}

Girdner Trail

Gravel Road

{4}

Roundabout Trail

Outer Limits Trail

Gravel Road

Girdner Trail {2}

{3}

Centennial Trail

N

ARIZONA 89A

{1}

0.25 Mile
Cultural Park Place

ARIZONA 89A

Red Rock High School

4.25 Miles

Upper Red Rock Loop Road

ARIZONA 179

Elevation Profile

4505
4465
4450

Miles: 0.75 | Easy
Cumulative Ascent: 70 feet

Driving Distance 4.5 Miles One Way
Hiking Distance 1 Mile In-Out

155

Western Gateway Trails
Girdner/Remnant/Roundabout Loop

Summary: A loop with panoramic views using several interconnected trails on the western edge of Sedona

Challenge Level: Moderate

Hiking Distance: About 2.7 miles loop

Hiking Time: About 2 hours round trip

Trail Popularity:

Trailhead Directions: From the "Y" roundabout (see page 7), drive west toward Cottonwood on SR 89A for about 4.25 miles then turn right onto Cultural Park Place. Continue straight ahead 0.3 mile to the large unpaved parking lot on the right {1}. (34° 51.150'N; 111° 49.889'W) The parking area also serves the Centennial Trail. The paved road is not well maintained but you won't need a high clearance vehicle to access the parking lot. There are two picnic tables near the trailhead.

Description: There are a number of interconnected trails in the Western Gateway area. This is a nice loop hike using 3 of the trails which feature some outstanding panoramic views. Hike past the signboard on the Girdner Trail and you'll note the Centennial Trail then in about 500 feet you'll intersect the eastern end of the Roundabout Trail {2}. You'll be returning here. Continue straight ahead and you'll soon intersect the Stirrup Trail {3} and then the Axis Trail {4}. As you continue in a northwest direction, the views to the north gradually improve. After 0.6 mile you'll intersect the western end of the Roundabout Trail {5}. Continue on the Girdner Trail then watch for some great views on the left {6}.

After hiking about 0.9 mile you'll intersect the Remnant Trail {7} and the Girdner Trail goes to the right. Turn onto the Remnant Trail. Soon the trail becomes narrow with drop offs so watch your footing. But turn around every so often for views behind you. You'll intersect the Roundabout Trail after 1.6 miles. Turn onto the Roundabout Trail and follow it for about 0.9 mile where you'll intersect the Outer Limits Trail. Proceed across the gravel road to continue on the Roundabout Trail. The trail is a paved path for about 0.1 mile. You'll pass through a fence and intersect a signpost for the Centennial, Girdner and Outer Limits trails. Continue on for about 25 feet then make a slight right turn onto the unpaved Girdner Trail {2}. Continue on for about 500 feet back to the parking area {1}.

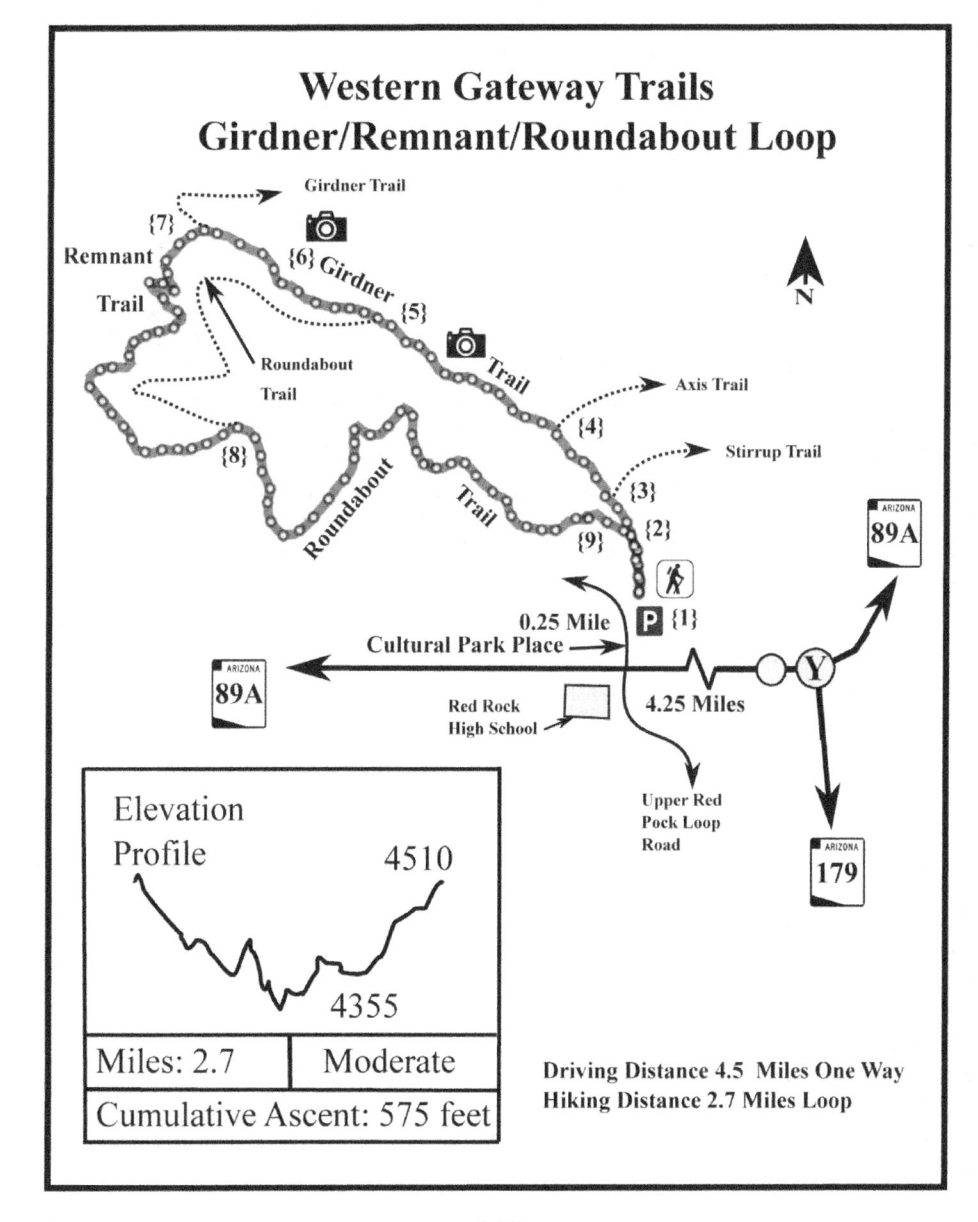

Color Photos: Scan the QR code below for additional color photos of this trail

Western Gateway Trails
Girdner/Remnant/Roundabout Loop

Girdner Trail
{7}
Remnant Trail
{6} Girdner
{5}
Roundabout Trail
{8}
Roundabout Trail
{4} Axis Trail
{3} Stirrup Trail
{9} {2}
{1}
0.25 Mile
Cultural Park Place
ARIZONA 89A
ARIZONA 89A
4.25 Miles
Red Rock High School
Upper Red Rock Loop Road
ARIZONA 179

Elevation Profile 4510
4355

Miles: 2.7	Moderate
Cumulative Ascent: 575 feet	

Driving Distance 4.5 Miles One Way
Hiking Distance 2.7 Miles Loop

157

West Fork Trail ★

Summary:
A favorite, shady in-out hike along the West Fork of Oak Creek

Challenge Level:
Moderate

Hiking Distance:
About 3.6 miles each way or 7.2 miles round trip

Hiking Time:
About 4 hours round trip

Trail Popularity:
🚶🚶🚶🚶

Trailhead Directions: From the "Y" roundabout (see page 7), drive north on SR 89A about 10.5 miles. Turn left into the parking area {1}. (34°59.446'N; 111°44.570'W) If left turns are prohibited into the parking area, continue north on SR 89A for 1.2 miles and turn around at the Cave Springs campground. The trail starts on the far side of the parking area, furthest away from the entrance. There are toilets at the parking area. The gate to the parking area opens at 8:00 am. It is a special fee area (see Red Rock Pass Fee Program, page 11). The parking area fills quickly so arrive early in the morning.

Description: West Fork is considered by many to be the most beautiful trail in the Sedona area. You'll be crossing the water 13 times as you hike the trail. You have to step from stone to stone to cross, so the trail isn't recommended in high water times (you'll get your feet wet!).

After 0.3 mile, you'll come to the remains of Mayhew's Lodge, built in the 1880s. It was remodeled in 1895 then burned down in 1980 {2}. At the 0.4 mile mark, you'll come to the first of the 13 creek crossings {3}.

As you continue along, look to the sides for some amazing red rock bluffs. There is a nice spot to stop and enjoy the creek after 1.1 miles {4}. At 2.8 miles, the trail is next to a large overhang where the water has eroded the rock {5}. Walk about 25 feet west toward the creek and look down. This is a nice place for a break. Continue another 0.4 mile and watch for a short side trail to a cave on your left {6}. At 3.6 miles, you'll come to a sign marking the end of the trail {7}. Sometimes you can continue a little further, depending on the water level but usually you'll have to wade through the water to go further.

West Fork has two wonderful seasons, spring and fall. The most beautiful is fall, when the deciduous trees display glorious colors. The third or fourth week in October seems to be when the colors are usually at their peak.

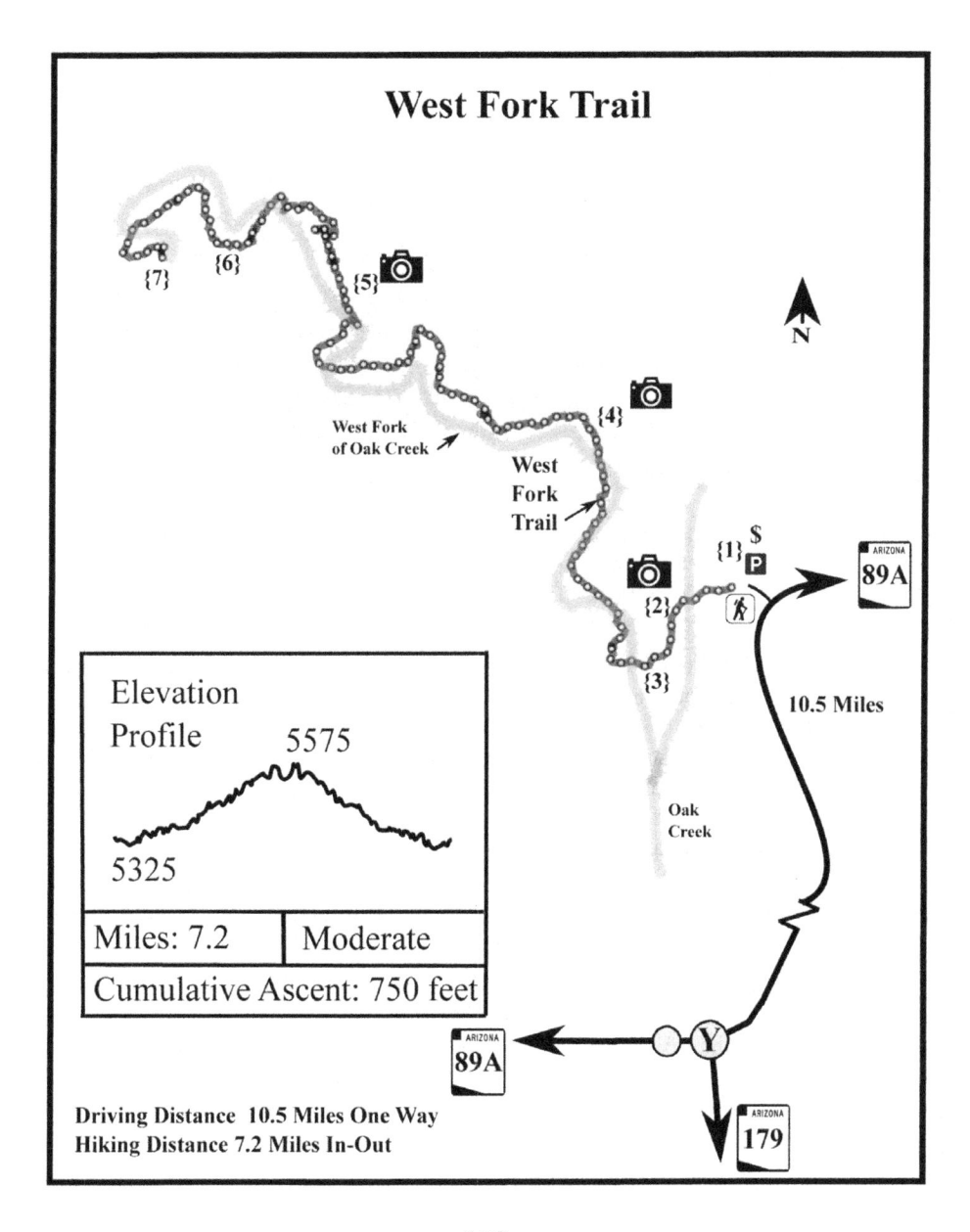

Color Photos: Scan the QR code below for additional color photos of this trail

West Fork Trail

West Fork of Oak Creek

West Fork Trail

Oak Creek

10.5 Miles

Elevation Profile
5575
5325

Miles: 7.2	Moderate
Cumulative Ascent: 750 feet	

Driving Distance 10.5 Miles One Way
Hiking Distance 7.2 Miles In-Out

Wilson Canyon Trail ★

Summary:
A favorite in-out hike in a shaded canyon with limited red rock views

Challenge Level:
Moderate

Hiking Distance:
About 1.3 miles each way or 2.6 miles round trip

Hiking Time:
About 2 hours round trip

Trail Popularity: 🚶🚶🚶

Trailhead Directions: From the "Y" roundabout (see page 7), drive north on SR 89A to Midgley Bridge. The trailhead parking is on your left just after you cross the bridge {1}. (34°54.023'N; 111°44.901'W) There are only 13 parking spots plus 1 handicapped spot so the parking area can fill up quickly. There is a toilet near the parking area.

Description: The trail begins away from SR 89A at the far end of the parking area, just beyond the picnic table pavilion. In about 100 feet, just past the toilet, you'll come to the beginning of the Wilson Mountain (South) Trail on the right {2}. Continue straight ahead for about 0.1 mile then bear right at the fork in the trail and the signpost {3}. At first, the trail is wide but narrows further on. At about 0.5 mile, you'll come to a second, wooden sign for the Wilson Mountain Trail on the right {4}. You'll intersect the end of the Jim Thompson Trail in another 300 feet {5}.

The Wilson Canyon Trail crosses the wash at the bottom of the canyon 13 times as it winds back and forth for 1.3 miles. You'll be hiking among scrub oak and small Arizona cypress. The trail becomes somewhat narrow with large drop offs about 1 mile in.

After 1.3 miles, you'll come to a 3 foot tall cairn (and is the only cairn you'll find after passing the Jim Thompson Trail {5}) that sometimes has a sign End of Trail on it marking the end of the official trail. Stop here or continue up the wash for another 75 feet. Watch for a steep side trail on your right {6}. Scramble up onto the nearby rock outcropping for some terrific views all around {7}. About 20 paces beyond the cairn, you'll see what looks like a continuation of the trail. But it only goes 50 feet or so then drops back into the wash.

160

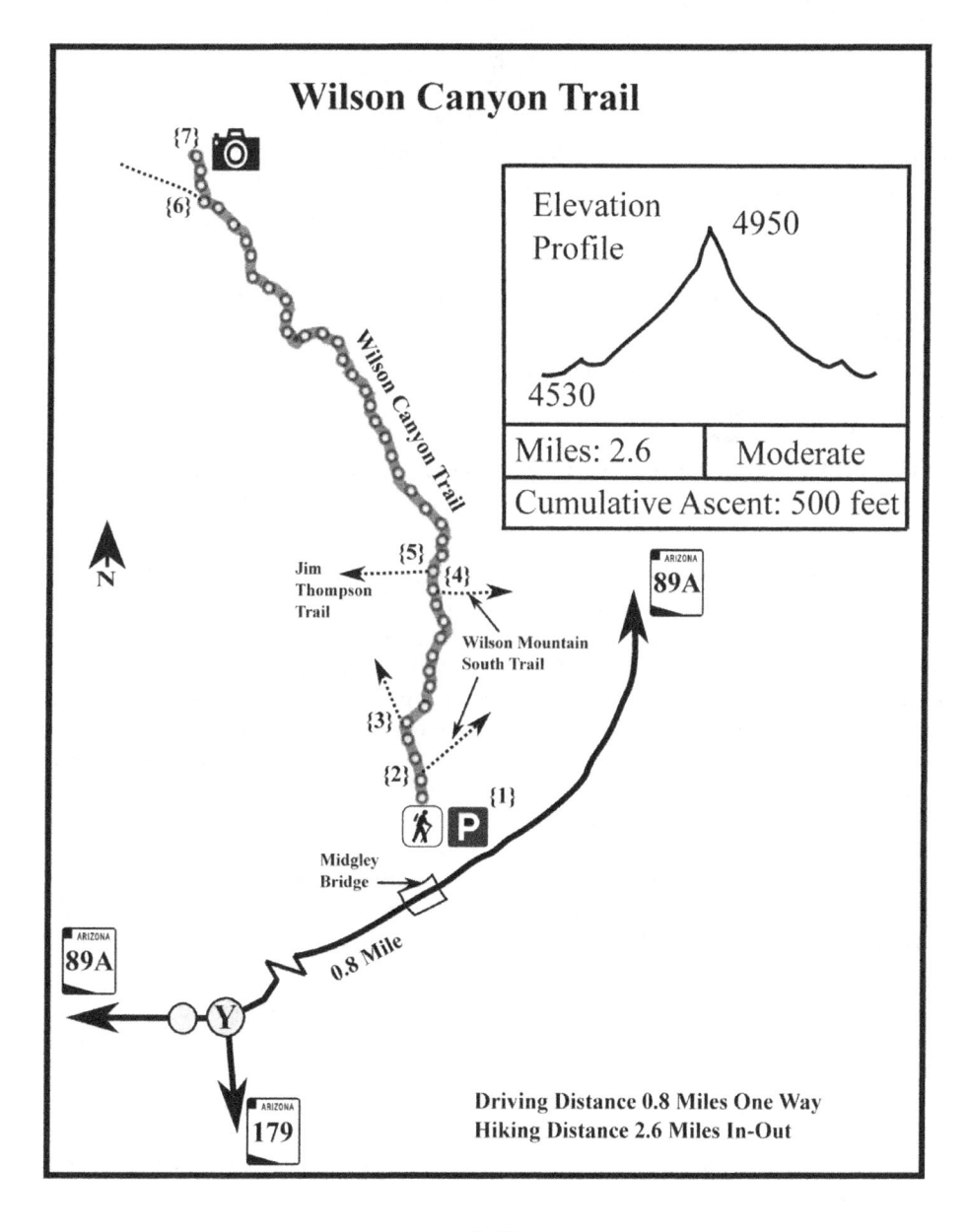

Color Photos: Scan the QR code below for additional color photos of this trail

Wilson Canyon Trail

{7}
{6}

Wilson Canyon Trail

Elevation Profile
4950
4530

Miles: 2.6 Moderate
Cumulative Ascent: 500 feet

{5} Jim Thompson Trail {4}
ARIZONA 89A
Wilson Mountain South Trail
{3}
{2} {1}
Midgley Bridge

ARIZONA 89A
0.8 Mile
Y
ARIZONA 179

Driving Distance 0.8 Miles One Way
Hiking Distance 2.6 Miles In-Out

161

Wilson Mountain North Trail

Summary: A hike up the north face of Wilson Mountain, the highest peak in the Sedona area

Challenge Level: Hard

Hiking Distance: 2.25 miles each way to a view of Sedona or 4.5 miles round trip; 3.8 miles each way to the Sedona Overlook or 7.6 miles round trip

Hiking Time: About 5 hours to the Sedona Overlook round trip

Trail Popularity:

Trailhead Directions: From the "Y" roundabout (see page 7), drive north on SR 89A for 5.3 miles to the Encinoso Picnic Area. Turn left into the parking lot. (34°55.513N; 111°44.133'W)

Description: After parking at the Encinoso Picnic Area {1}, walk north past the entrance drive. You'll see two parking spots in front of you. The trail begins in front of those two parking spots. In about 100 feet, you'll come to the sign that says, Trail 123 Wilson North. Continue parallel to SR 89A, in about 200 feet you make a left turn then begin gently climbing. You'll be hiking through a ponderosa pine forest. In 0.4 mile, you'll come to a sign indicating you are entering the Red Rock Secret Mountain Wilderness. After 1 mile {2}, the trail becomes narrow with a steep drop off for another 0.5 mile. After 1.8 miles, you'll come to the edge of the first bench of Wilson Mountain {3}. If you look to the north, you'll see the San Francisco Peaks in Flagstaff in the distance. Continue across the large open area to intersect the Wilson Mountain South Trail at a sign post, which is 2.25 miles from the parking area {4}. If you hike a few hundred feet south, you'll have a nice view of Sedona below {5}. You can begin the return trip here for a 4.5 mile hike.

Or, return to the signpost {4} then follow the Wilson Mountain Trail to the northwest. You'll steadily climb then after another 1.2 miles, you'll come to a sign and a fork in the trail {6}. If you go to the right, you'll be going to the Boynton Canyon Overlook, about 2 miles to the northwest. If you go to the left, you'll be hiking to the Sedona Overlook. You'll see the remains of a tool shed, which contained fire-fighting tools at one time. Vandals have pretty much destroyed the shed. You'll need to climb over fallen trees for the first 0.1 mile. Follow the trail for 0.4 mile to the edge of Wilson Mountain {7} for a view of Sedona similar to that from the view at waypoint {5}.

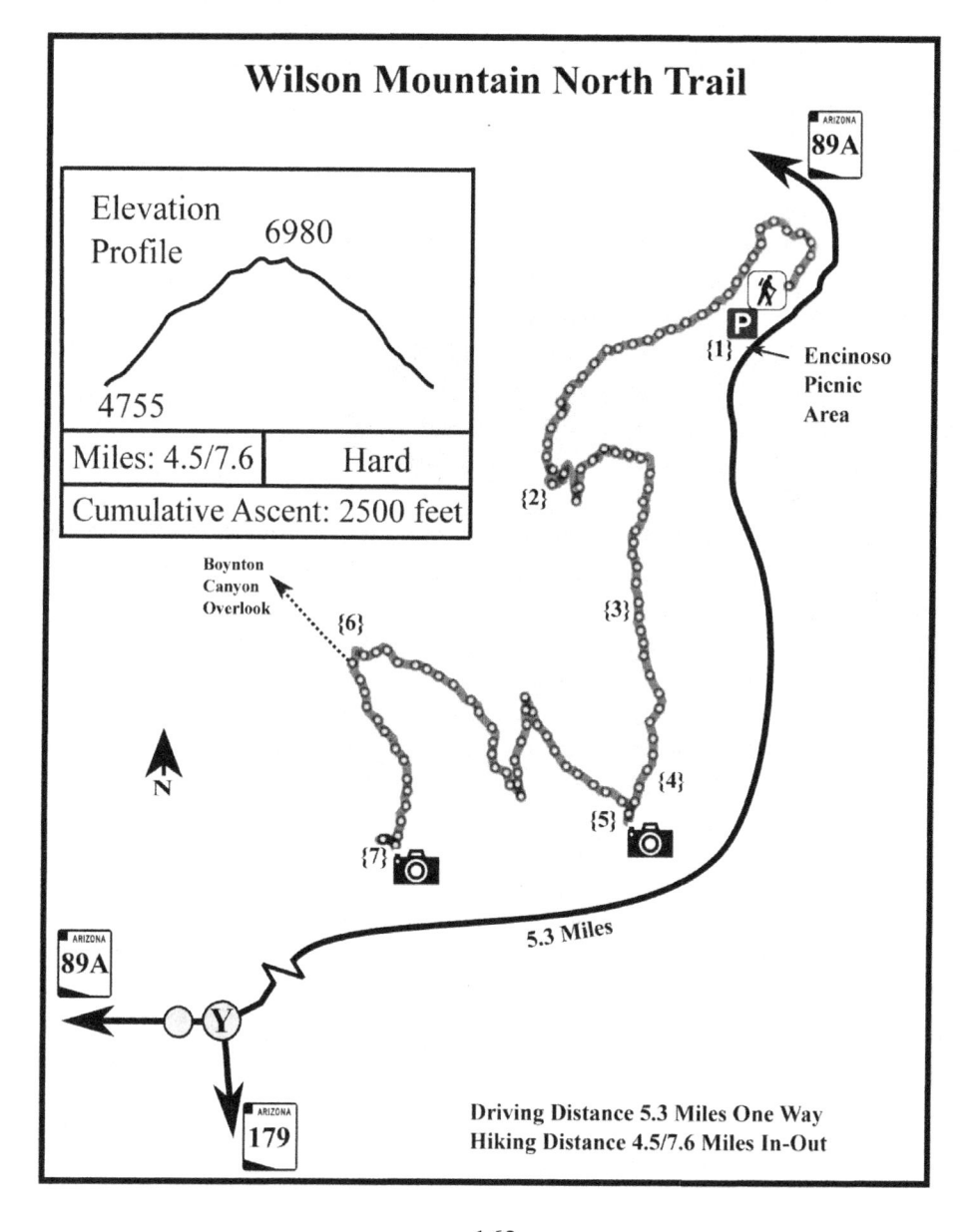

Color Photos: Scan the QR code below for additional color photos of this trail

Wilson Mountain North Trail

Elevation Profile
6980
4755

Miles: 4.5/7.6 | Hard
Cumulative Ascent: 2500 feet

Boynton Canyon Overlook

{1} Encinoso Picnic Area
{2}
{3}
{4}
{5}
{6}
{7}

89A
179

5.3 Miles

Driving Distance 5.3 Miles One Way
Hiking Distance 4.5/7.6 Miles In-Out

163

Woods Canyon Trail

Summary: A sunny in-out hike along Dry Beaver Creek

Challenge Level: Moderate

Hiking Distance: About 2.5 miles each way or 5 miles round trip

Hiking Time: About 3 hours round trip

Trail Popularity:

Trailhead Directions: From the "Y" roundabout (see page 7), drive south on SR 179 about 8.8 miles then turn left into the Red Rock Ranger Station {1}. Follow the drive a short distance then turn right at the first road rather than following the road to the left to the Visitor Center. Make a left then a right turn into the parking lot ahead. The trailhead is at the far south end of the parking area {2}. (34°45.374'N; 111°45.801'W

Description: Just after you begin the trail, you will go through a gate then cross a large wash that sometimes has water in it. Cross this area and look for a trail sign to the northeast.

You'll shortly come to a second gate {3}. The trail becomes very rocky as it proceeds up a canyon and parallels the path of Dry Beaver Creek.

You'll cross a wash after 1.1 miles {4}. After about 2 miles, you'll pass through a rustic, barb wire third gate {5} and begin a moderate climb up to the intersection of the Hot Loop Trail {6}. Continue straight on the Woods Canyon Trail for another 0.3 mile then make a right turn to go down to Dry Beaver Creek {7}. Here you'll see large river rocks, which are deposited when Dry Beaver Creek floods {8}. The creek usually flows in the springtime because of the snow melt from the north. I usually stop here, but the trail continues on and becomes more difficult the further you go. Wildflowers are in abundance in April most years. What little shade there is on this trail begins about 1.6 miles into the hike so can it be a hot hike in the summer.

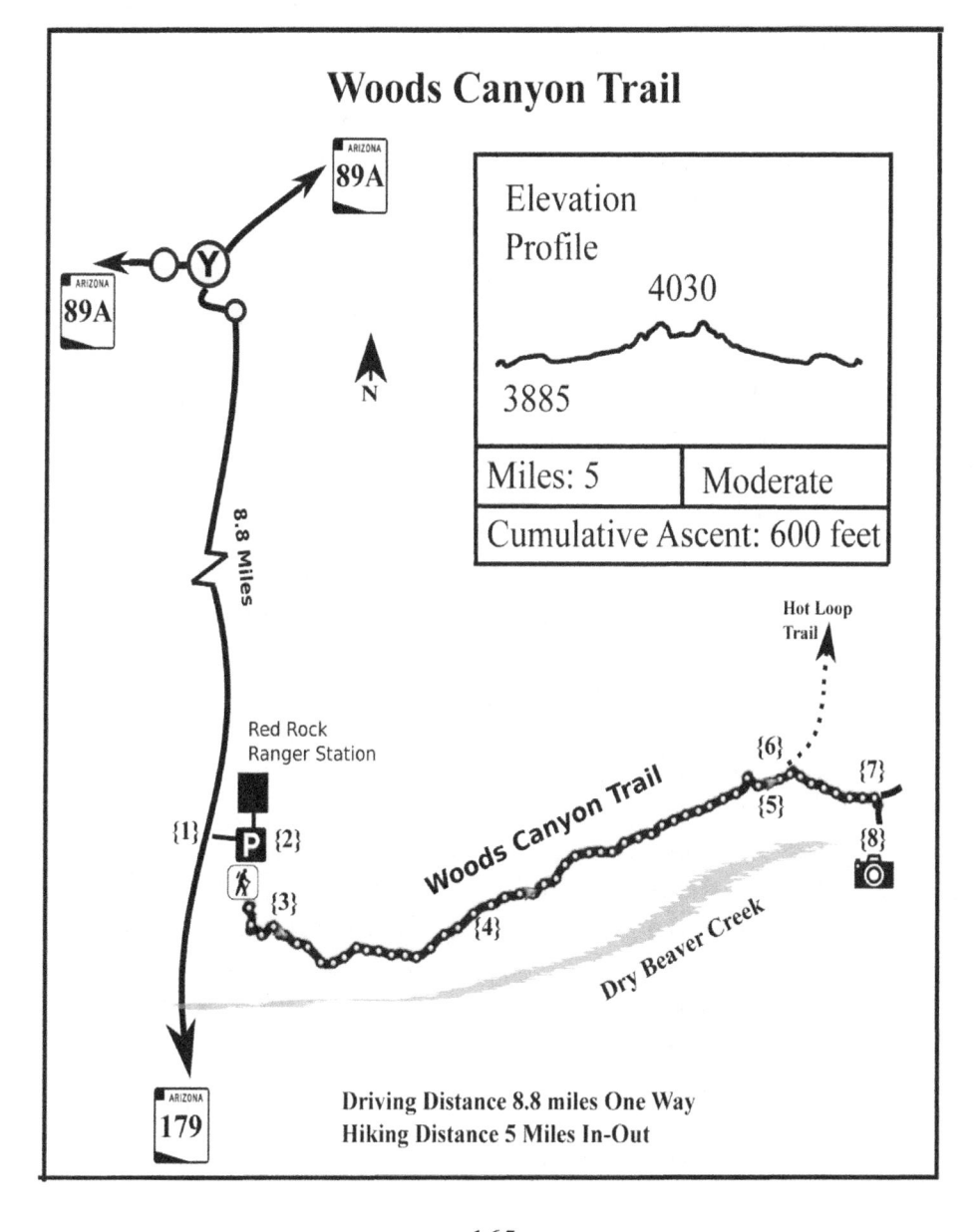

Color Photos: Scan the QR code below for additional color photos of this trail

Woods Canyon Trail

Elevation Profile

4030

3885

Miles: 5 | Moderate

Cumulative Ascent: 600 feet

8.8 Miles

Red Rock Ranger Station

{1} {2} {3} {4} {5} {6} {7} {8}

Woods Canyon Trail

Hot Loop Trail

Dry Beaver Creek

Driving Distance 8.8 miles One Way
Hiking Distance 5 Miles In-Out

165

GPS Data

WP	Latitude; Longitude	Elevation	WP	Latitude; Longitude	Elevation
	Aerie Trail			**Bear Mountain Trail**	**(Cont'd)**
1	34° 53.139'N; 111° 52.194'W	4560 ft.	5	34° 54.759'N; 111° 52.715'W	6010 ft.
2	34° 53.545'N; 111° 51.847'W	4670 ft.	6	34° 54.772'N; 111° 52.793'W	6150 ft.
3	34° 53.954'N; 111°51.353'W	4555 ft.	7	34° 54.886'N; 111° 52.990'W	6480 ft.
4	34° 54.355'N; 111° 50.988'W	4540 ft.			
5	34° 54.456'N; 111° 50.928'W	4560 ft.		**Bear Sign Trail**	
			1	34° 56.236'N; 111° 47.678'W	4805 ft.
	Airport Loop and Airport	**Vortex**	2	34° 56.723'N; 111° 47.680'W	4875 ft.
1	34° 51.345'N; 111° 46.804'W	4590 ft.	3	34° 57.656'N; 111° 49.054'W	5270 ft.
2	34° 51.196'N; 111° 47.372'W	4810 ft.	4	34° 57.655'N; 111° 49.179'W	5490 ft.
3	34° 51.328'N; 111° 46.780'W	4630 ft.			
4	34° 51.350'N; 111° 46.741'W	4660 ft.		**Bell Rock Climb and Bell**	**Rock Vortex**
5	34° 50.773'N; 111° 47.724'W	4710 ft.	1	34° 48.350'N; 111° 46.009'W	4325 ft.
6	34° 50.448'N; 111° 47.959'W	4680 ft.	2	34° 48.227'N; 111° 45.963'W	4350 ft.
7	34° 51.172'N; 111° 47.716'W	4500 ft.	3	34° 48.177'N; 111° 45.869'W	4445 ft.
			4	34° 48.153'N; 111° 45.851'W	4480 ft.
	Baldwin Loop		5	34° 48.069'N; 111° 45.791'W	4495 ft.
1	34° 49.309'N; 111° 48.493'W	4025 ft.	6	34° 48.137'N; 111° 45.934°'W	4475 ft.
2	34° 49.334'N; 111° 48.438'W	4025 ft.	7	34° 48.063'N; 111° 45.954'W	4525 ft.
3	34° 49.390'N; 111° 48.176'W	3975 ft.	8	34° 48.182'N; 111° 46.008'W	4410 ft.
4	34° 49.347'N; 111° 47.984'W	3985 ft.			
5	34° 49.401'N; 111° 47.812'W	3985 ft.		**Bell Rock Loop**	
6	34° 49.091'N; 111° 48.043'W	4050 ft.	1	34° 48.350'N; 111° 46.009'W	4325 ft.
7	34° 48.969'N; 111° 48.071'W	4130 ft.	2	34° 48.227'N; 111° 45.963'W	4380 ft.
8	34° 48.844'N; 111° 48.228'W	4080 ft.	3	34° 48.177'N; 111° 45.869'W	4445 ft.
9	34° 48.953'N; 111° 48.476'W	4020 ft.	4	34° 48.167'N; 111° 45.803'W	4430 ft.
10	34° 48.762'N; 111° 48.589'W	3970 ft.	5	34° 48.141'N; 111° 45.751'W	4435 ft.
			6	34° 47.875'N; 111° 45.578'W	4270 ft.
	Bear Mountain Trail		7	34° 47.860'N; 111° 45.778'W	4260 ft.
1	34° 53.596'N; 111° 51.945'W	4605 ft.	8	34° 48.063'N; 111° 45.954'W	4375 ft.
2	34° 54.004'N; 111° 52.165'W	5100 ft.			
3	34° 54.215'N; 111° 52.500'W	5520 ft.			
4	34° 54.386'N; 111° 52.560'W	5675 ft.			

GPS Data

WP	Latitude; Longitude	Elevation	WP	Latitude; Longitude	Elevation
	Bell Rock Pathway/Templeton Loop			**Brins Mesa Overlook Trail**	
1	34° 49.433'N; 111° 46.555'W	4280 ft.	1	34° 53.287'N; 111° 46.098'W	4520 ft.
2	34° 49.301'N; 111° 46.308'W	4260 ft.	2	34° 54.022'N; 111° 46.765'W	5085 ft.
3	34° 49.256'N; 111° 46.238'W	4200 ft.	3	34° 54.157'N; 111° 47.567'W	5155 ft.
4	34° 48.838'N; 111° 45.909'W	4310 ft.	4	34° 54.147'N; 111° 46.542'W	5170 ft.
5	34° 48.538'N; 111° 45.885'W	4320 ft.	5	34° 54.507'N; 111° 46.374'W	5455 ft.
6	34° 48.582'N; 111° 45.961'W	4275 ft.			
7	34° 48.877'N; 111° 46.256'W	4215 ft.		**Brins Mesa/Soldier Pass Loop**	
			1	34° 53.287'N; 111° 46.098'W	4520 ft.
	Bell-Weir Trail		2	34° 53.524'N; 111° 46.427'W	4645 ft.
1	34° 40.457'N; 111° 42.795'W	3860 ft.	3	34° 53.834'N; 111° 46.502'W	4700 ft.
2	34° 40.727'N; 111° 41.942'W	3925	4	34° 53.928'N; 111° 46.560'W	4825 ft.
3	34° 40.831'N; 111° 41.136'W	3995 ft.	5	34° 54.022'N; 111° 46.765'W	5085 ft.
4	34° 40.700'N; 111° 40.692'W	4045 ft.	6	34° 54.305'N; 111° 47.297'W	4940 ft.
5	34° 40.605'N; 111° 40.577'W	4055 ft.	7	34° 54.226'N; 111° 47.461'W	4875 ft.
6	34° 40.498'N; 111° 40.334'W	4025 ft.	8	34° 54.096'N; 111° 47.394'W	4710 ft.
7	34° 40.449'N; 111° 39.630'W	4130 ft.	9	34° 53.865'N; 111° 47.269'W	4580 ft.
8	34° 40.485'N; 111° 39.580'W	4115 ft.	10	34° 53.781'N; 111° 47.240'W	4565 ft.
			11	34° 53.418'N; 111° 47.149'W	4480 ft.
	Boynton Canyon & Vortex		12	34° 53.182'N; 111° 46.944'W	4480 ft.
1	34° 54.456'N; 111° 50.928'W	4530 ft.	13	34° 53.188'N 111° 46.663'W	45520 ft.
2	34° 54.623'N; 111° 50.987'W	4525 ft.			
3	34° 54.706'N; 111° 50.885'W	4690 ft.		**Broken Arrow/Submarine Rock Loop**	
4	34° 55.169'N; 111° 51.233'W	4680 ft.	1	34° 50.738'N; 111° 45.424'W	4280 ft.
5	34° 55.435'N; 111° 52.697'W	5250 ft.	2	34° 50.429'N; 111° 45.307'W	4365 ft.
			3	34° 50.261'N; 111° 45.226'W	4430 ft.
	Brins Mesa Trail		4	34° 50.245'N; 111° 44.784'W	4485 ft.
1	34° 53.287'N; 111° 46.098'W	4520 ft.	5	34° 49.794'N; 111° 45.240'W	4570 ft.
2	34° 54.022'N; 111° 46.765'W	5085 ft.			
3	34° 54.305'N; 111° 47.297'W	4940 ft.			
4	34° 55.008'N; 111° 48.525'W	4630 ft.			

GPS Data

WP	Latitude; Longitude	Elevation	WP	Latitude; Longitude	Elevation
	Canyon of Fools/Mescal Loop			**Chimney Rock Pass Loop**	
1	34° 53.758'N; 111° 50.206'W	4440 ft.	1	34° 52.325'N; 111° 48.735'W	4550 ft.
2	34° 54.095'N; 111° 50.075'W	4544 ft.	2	34° 52.405'N; 111° 48.781'W	4600 ft.
3	34° 54.265'N; 111° 50.329'W	4575 ft.	3	34° 52.535'N; 111° 48.561'W	4640 ft.
4	34° 54.317'N; 111° 50.369'W	4615 ft.	4	34° 52.659'N; 111° 48.557'W	4690 ft.
5	34° 54.317'N; 111° 49.876'W	4615 ft.	5	34° 52.718'N; 111° 48.589'W	4700 ft.
			6	34° 52.728'N; 111° 48.741'W	4875 ft.
	Cathedral Rock & Vortex Trail		7	34° 52.846'N; 111° 48.658'W	4960 ft.
1	34° 49.523'N; 111° 47.303'W	4050 ft.	8	34° 52.728'N; 111° 48.773'W	4865 ft.
2	34° 49.335'N; 111° 47.369'W	4165 ft.	9	34° 52.768'N; 111° 48.893'W	4750 ft.
3	34° 49.330'N; 111° 47.400'W	4165 ft.	10	34° 52.636'N; 111°48.936'W	4710 ft.
4	34° 49.154'N; 111° 47.538'W	4800 ft.	11	34° 52.492'N; 111° 48.935'W	4660 ft.
	Chimney Rock Lower Loop			**Chuckwagon In-Out Trail**	
1	34° 52.325'N; 111° 48.735'W	4550 ft.	1	34° 53.425'N; 111° 49.240'W	4670 ft.
2	34° 52.405'N; 111° 48.781'W	4600 ft.	2	34° 53.728'N; 111° 49.211'W	4665 ft.
3	34° 52.535'N; 111° 48.561'W	4640 ft.	3	34° 54.115'N; 111° 49.603'W	4490 ft.
4	34° 52.659'N; 111° 48.557'W	4690 ft.	4	34° 54.100'N; 111° 49.667'W	4515 ft.
5	34° 52.718'N; 111° 48.589'W	4700 ft.	5	34° 54.172'N; 111° 48.833'W	4585 ft.
6	34° 52.728'N; 111° 48.741'W	4875 ft.	6	34° 54.024'N; 111° 49.474'W	4495ft.
7	34° 52.846'N; 111° 48.658'W	4960 ft.	7	34° 54.114'N; 111° 49.239'W	4575 ft.
8	34° 52.728'N; 111° 48.773'W	4865 ft.	8	34° 54.209'N; 111° 48.941'W	4620 ft.
9	34° 52.768'N; 111° 48.893'W	4750 ft.	9	34° 54.249'N; 111° 48.876'W	4580 ft.
10	34° 52.636'N; 111° 48.936'W	4710 ft.	10	34° 54.909'N; 111° 48.687'W	4600 ft.
11	34° 52.559'N; 111° 48.891'W	4710 ft.		**Chuckwagon Loop**	
12	34° 52.492'N; 111° 48.935'W	4660 ft.	1	34° 54.100'N; 111° 49.667'W	4515 ft.
13	34° 52.257'N; 111° 48.965'W	4550 ft.	2	34° 54.115'N; 111° 49.603'W	4490 ft.
14	34° 52.297'N; 111° 48.735'W	4555 ft.	3	34° 54.024'N; 111° 49.474'W	4495 ft.
			4	34° 54.114'N; 111°49.239'W	4575 ft.
			5	34° 54.209'N; 111° 48.941'W	4620 ft.
			6	34° 54.172'N; 111° 48.833'W	4505 ft.
			7	34° 54.249'N; 111° 48.876'W	4580 ft.

GPS Data

WP	Latitude; Longitude	Elevation	WP	Latitude; Longitude	Elevation
	Chuckwagon Loop (Cont'd)			**Cookstove to Harding Springs**	
8	34° 54.909'N; 111° 48.687'W	4600 ft.	1	35 00.877'N; 111° 44.256'W	5575 ft.
9	34° 54.831'N; 111° 48.841'W	4570 ft.	2	35 00.717'N; 111° 43.997'W	6330 ft.
10	34° 54.587'N; 111° 49.023'W	4580 ft.	3	35 00.599'N; 111° 44.009'W	6300 ft.
11	34° 54.395'N; 111° 49.444'W	4520 ft.	4	35 00.593'N; 111° 43.983'W	6280 ft.
12	34° 54.269'N; 111° 49.630'W	4555 ft.	5	35 00.457'N; 111° 43.828'W	6240 ft.
13	34° 53.425'N; 111° 49.240'W	4670 ft.	6	35 00.532'N; 111° 43.705'W	6260 ft.
	Cibola Pass/Jordan Loop		7	35 00.351'N; 111° 43.590'W	6250 ft.
1	34° 53.287'N; 111° 46.098'W	4520 ft.	8	35 00.274'N; 111° 43.577'W	6235 ft.
2	34° 53.281'N; 111° 46.138'W	4550 ft.	9	35 00.231'N; 111° 43.727'W	6265 ft.
3	34° 53.283'N; 111° 46.422'W	4680 ft.	10	35 00.122'N; 111° 43.881'W	6200 ft.
4	34° 53.188'N; 111° 46.663'W	4520 ft.	11	35 00.099'N; 111° 43.947'W	6175 ft.
5	34° 53.182'N; 111° 46.944'W	4480 ft.	12	35 00.026'N; 111° 44.226'W	5455 ft.
6	34° 53.418'N; 111° 47.149'W	4480 ft.	13	35 00.039'N; 111° 44.253'W	5455 ft.
	Cockscomb/Aerie Loop			**Courthouse Butte Loop**	
1	34° 53.139'N; 111° 52.194'W	4560 ft.	1	34° 48.350'N; 111° 46.009'W	4325 ft.
2	34° 52.887'N; 111° 51.231'W	4520 ft.	2	34° 48.232'N; 111° 45.961'W	4375 ft.
3	34° 53.141'N; 111° 51.263'W	4530 ft.	3	34° 48.257'N; 111° 45.693'W	4400 ft.
4	34° 53.473'N; 111° 50.936'W	4495 ft.	4	34° 48.332'N; 111° 45.012'W	4500 ft.
5	34° 53.954'N; 111° 51.353'W	4555 ft.	5	34° 47.904'N; 111° 44.891'W	4280 ft.
6	34° 53.545'N; 111° 51.847'W	4670 ft.	6	34° 47.851'N; 111° 45.448'W	4285 ft.
			7	34° 47.860'N; 111° 45.778'W	4265 ft.
	Coffeepot Trail		8	34° 47.501'N; 111° 45.699'W	4185 ft.
1	34° 52.458'N; 111° 47.793'W	4560 ft.			
2	34° 52.712'N; 111° 47.843'W	4635 ft.		**Courthouse Butte Alternate Loop**	
3	34° 52.736'N; 111° 47.798'W	4655 ft.	1	34° 47.501'N; 111° 45.699'W	4185 ft.
4	34° 52.793'N; 111° 47.673'W	4685 ft.	2	34° 47.851'N; 111° 45.448'W	4285 ft.
5	34° 53.025'N; 111° 47.621'W	4810 ft.	3	34° 47.875'N; 111° 45.578'W	4270 ft.
6	34° 53.024'N; 111° 47.515'W	4810 ft.	4	34° 48.177'N; 111° 45.869'W	4445 ft.
			5	34° 48.227'N; 111° 45.693'W	4380 ft.
			6	34° 48.257'N; 111° 45.780'W	4400 ft.

GPS Data

WP	Latitude; Longitude	Elevation	WP	Latitude; Longitude	Elevation
	Courthouse Butte Alternate Loop (Cont'd)			**Dry Creek Trail**	
7	34° 48.332'N; 111° 45.649'W	4500 ft.	1	34° 56.236'N; 111° 47.678'W	4810 ft.
8	34° 47.904'N; 111° 44.891'W	4280 ft.	2	34° 56.723'N; 111° 47.680'W	4875 ft.
9	34° 47.838'N; 111° 45.206'W	4260 ft.	3	34° 56.934'N; 111° 47.622'W	4390 ft.
			4	34° 56.324'N; 111° 47.455'W	5085 ft.
	Cow Pies Trail		5	34° 56.566'N; 111° 47.418'W	5190 ft.
1	34° 52.318'N; 111° 42.779'W	5060 ft.	6	34° 57.760'N; 111° 47.526'W	5235 ft.
2	34° 52.411'N; 111° 42.884'W	5030 ft.			
3	34° 52.568'N; 111° 42.914'W	5050 ft.		**Fay Canyon Trail**	
4	34° 52.417'N; 111° 43.193'W	5065 ft.	1	34° 54.101'N; 111° 51.450'W	4570 ft.
5	34° 52.321'N; 111° 43.248'W	5050 ft.	2	34° 54.507'N; 111° 51.771'W	4650 ft.
			3	34° 54.586'N; 111° 51.673'W	4885 ft.
	Devil's Bridge		4	34° 54.892'N; 111° 52.082'W	4770 ft.
1	34° 53.425'N; 111° 49.240'W	4670 ft.			
2	34° 54.172'N; 111° 48.833'W	4585 ft.		**Hangover/Munds Wagon Loop**	
3	34° 54.100'N; 111° 49.667'W	4515 ft.	1	34° 52.318'N; 111° 42.779'W	5060 ft.
4	34° 54.115'N; 111° 49.603'W	4490 ft.	2	34° 52.411'N; 111° 42.884'W	5030 ft.
5	34° 53.728'N; 111° 49.211'W	4665 ft.	3	34° 52.568'N; 111° 42.914'W	5050 ft.
6	34° 54.024'N; 111° 49.474'W	4495 ft.	4	34° 52.637'N; 111° 42.929'W	5170 ft.
7	34° 54.209'N; 111° 48.941'W	4620 ft.	5	34° 52.643'N; 111° 43.001'W	5150 ft.
8	34° 53.875'N; 111° 48.497'W	4885 ft.	6	34° 52.510'N; 111° 43.508'W	5125 ft.
9	34° 53.859'N; 111° 48.462'W	4985 ft.	7	34° 52.548'N; 111° 43.620'W	5235 ft.
	Doe Mountain		8	34° 52.536'N; 111° 43.753'W	5180 ft.
1	34° 53.596'N; 111° 51.945'W	4605 ft.	9	34° 52.229'N; 111° 43.704'W	4650 ft.
2	34° 53.545'N; 111° 51.847'W	4670 ft.	10	34° 52.254'N; 111° 43.414'W	4750 ft.
3	34° 53.505'N; 111° 51.643'W	5050 ft.	11	34° 52.297'N; 111° 42.946'W	4965 ft.
4	34° 53.697'N; 111° 51.568'W	5050 ft.	12	34° 52.285'N; 111° 42.773'W	5070 ft.
5	34° 53.459'N; 111° 51.476'W	5060 ft.			
6	34° 53.406'N; 111° 51.572'W	5070 ft.			
7	34° 53.288'N; 111° 51.862'W	5130 ft.			

GPS Data

WP	Latitude; Longitude	Elevation	WP	Latitude; Longitude	Elevation
	HiLine Trail			**HT/Easy Breezy Loop**	
1	34° 48.442'N; 111° 46.174'W	4370 ft.	1	34° 49.433'N; 111° 46.555'W	4280 ft.
2	34° 48.383'N; 111° 46.254'W	4405 ft.	2	34° 49.301'N; 111° 46.308'W	4260 ft.
3	34° 48.414'N; 111° 46.293'W	4405 ft.	3	34° 49.256'N; 111° 46.238'W	4200 ft.
4	34° 48.279'N; 111° 46.278'W	4490 ft.	4	34° 49.005'N; 111° 46.379'W	4180 ft.
5	34° 48.280'N; 111° 46.433'W	4550 ft.	5	34° 48.973'N; 111° 46.580'W	4205 ft.
6	34° 48.619'N; 111° 46.643'W	4600 ft.	6	34° 49.268'N; 111° 47.34°9'W	4195 ft.
7	34° 48.628'N; 111° 46.835'W	4625 ft.	7	34° 49.335'N; 111° 47.369'W	4165 ft.
8	34° 48.617'N; 111° 46.122'W	4650 ft.			
9	34° 48.821'N; 111° 47.224'W	4500 ft.		**Huckaby Trail**	
10	34° 48.804'N; 111° 47.697'W	4400 ft.	1	34° 52.000'N; 111° 44.925'W	4465 ft.
11	34° 48.969'N; 111° 48.071'W	4130 ft.	2	34° 51.982'N; 111° 45.086'W	4415 ft.
12	34° 48.953'N; 111° 48.476'W	4030 ft.	3	34° 52.168'N; 111° 45.228'W	4410 ft.
13	34° 48.899'N; 111° 48.468'W	4025 ft.	4	34° 52.533'N; 111° 45.101'W	4420 ft.
14	34° 48.762'N; 111° 48.589'W	3980 ft.	5	34° 52.687'N; 111° 44 903'W	4350 ft.
			6	34° 53.033'N; 111° 44.610'W	4325 ft.
	Honanki and Palatki		7	34° 53.022'N; 111° 44.413'W	4335 ft.
1	34° 51.672'N; 111° 48.948'W	--	8	34° 54.023'N; 111° 44.901'W	4530 ft.
2	34° 53.915'N; 111° 49.733'W	--			
3	34° 54.376'N; 111° 51.023'W	--		**Jim Thompson Trail**	
4	34° 53.292'N; 111° 54.379'W	--	1	34° 53.287'N; 111° 46.098'W	4520 ft.
5	34° 53.422'N; 111° 54.358'W	--	2	34° 53.324'N; 111° 46.078'W	4525 ft.
6	34° 54.396'N; 111° 54.747'W	--	3	34° 53.073'N; 111° 45.883'W	4470 ft.
7	34° 56.193'N; 111° 56.078'W	--	4	34° 53.357'N; 111° 44.726'W	4735 ft.
8	34° 54.891'N; 111° 54.136'W	--	5	34° 53.551'N; 111° 44.507'W	4590 ft.
	HS Canyon Trail			**Jordan Trail**	
1	34° 55.797'N; 111° 48.391'W	4660 ft.	1	34° 53.287'N; 111° 46.098'W	4520 ft.
2	34° 56.281'N; 111° 48.578'W	4720 ft.	2	34° 53.019'N; 111° 46.040'W	4470 ft.
3	34° 56.299'N; 111° 48.631'W	4720 ft.	3	34° 52.983'N; 111° 46.123'W	4505 ft.
4	34° 56.268'N; 111° 48.773'W	4770 ft.	4	34° 52.881'N; 111° 46.259'W	4560 ft.
5	34° 56.536'N; 111° 50.023'W	5410 ft.	5	34° 53.188'N; 111° 46.663'W	4520 ft.
			6	34° 53.182'N; 111° 46.944'W	4480 ft.
			7	34° 53.418'N; 111° 47.149'W	4480 ft.

GPS Data

WP	Latitude; Longitude	Elevation	WP	Latitude; Longitude	Elevation
	Kelly Canyon Trail			**Llama /Bail Loop and**	
1	35° 03.200'N; 111° 43.960'W	6525 ft.		**Llama/Little Horse Loop**	
2	35° 03.517'N; 111° 43.140'W	6405 ft.	1	34° 48.350'N; 111° 46.009'W	4325 ft.
3	35° 03.517'N; 111° 43.020'W	6315 ft.	2	34° 48.227'N; 111° 45.963'W	4380 ft.
4	35° 03.531'N; 111° 43.001'W	6330 ft.	3	34° 48.322'N; 111° 45.703'W	4380 ft.
5	35° 03.688'N; 111° 42.635'W	6440 ft.	4	34° 48.334'N; 111° 45.651'W	4400 ft.
6	35° 03.840'N; 111° 42.301'W	6535 ft.	5	34° 48.574'N; 111° 45.182'W	4440 ft.
7	35° 03.989'N; 111° 42.378'W	6500 ft.	6	34° 48.952'N; 111° 45.660'W	4410 ft.
8	35° 04.163'N; 111° 42.335'W	6575 ft.	7	34° 48.838'N; 111° 45.909'W	4310 ft.
9	35° 04.697'N; 111° 41.854'W	6770 ft.	8	34° 49.508'N; 111° 45.889'W	4330 ft.
10	35° 04.862'N; 111° 41.820'W	6845 ft.	9	34° 49.301'N; 111° 46.308'W	4260 ft.
			10	34° 48.441'N; 111° 45.893'W	4325 ft.
	Little Horse Trail				
1	34° 49.433'N; 111° 46.555'W	4280 ft.		**Long Canyon Trail**	
2	34° 49.301'N; 111° 46.308'W	4260 ft.	1	34° 54.408'N; 111° 49.452'W	4500 ft.
3	34° 49.508'N; 111° 45.889'W	4330 ft.	2	34° 54.671'N; 111° 49.633'W	4565 ft.
4	34° 49.705'N; 111° 45.489'W	4430 ft.	3	34° 55.040'N; 111° 49.880'W	4635 ft.
5	34° 49.921'N; 111° 45.938'W	4480 ft.	4	34° 56.175'N; 111° 51.044'W	5010 ft.
6	34° 49.794'N; 111° 45.240'W	4570 ft.			
				Marg's Draw Trail	
	Llama/Baby Bell Loop		1	34° 50.738'N; 111° 45.424'W	4280 ft.
1	34° 48.350'N; 111° 46.009'W	4325 ft.	2	34° 51.238'N; 111° 45.460'W	4285 ft.
2	34° 48.441'N; 111° 45.893'W	4325 ft.	3	34° 51.427'N; 111° 45.677'W	4280 ft.
3	34° 48.512'N; 111° 45.859'W	4355 ft.	4	34° 51.399'N; 111° 45.286'W	434°5 ft.
4	34° 48.481'N; 111° 45.767'W	4385 ft.	5	34° 51.982'N; 111° 45.086'W	4415 ft.
5	34° 48.428'N; 111° 45.639'W	4375 ft.	6	34° 52.000'N; 111° 44.925'W	4465 ft.
6	34° 48.334'N; 111° 45.653'W	4420 ft.			
7	34° 48.324'N; 111° 45.710'W	4405 ft.		**Mescal/Long Canyon Loop**	
8	34° 48.224'N; 111° 45.967'W	4400 ft.	1	34° 54.100'N; 111° 49.667'W	4515 ft.
			2	34° 54.115'N; 111° 49.603'W	4490 ft.
			3	34° 54.269'N; 111° 49.610'W	4555 ft.
			4	34° 54.319'N; 111° 49.876'W	4620 ft.
			5	34° 54.359'N; 111° 49.876'W	4630 ft.
			6	34° 54.317'N; 111° 50.369'W	4615 ft.

GPS Data

WP	Latitude; Longitude	Elevation	WP	Latitude; Longitude	Elevation
	Mescal/Long Canyon Loop (Cont'd)			**Rabbit Ears Trail**	
7	34° 54.587'N; 111° 50.539'W	4615 ft.	1	34° 47.501'N; 111° 45.669'W	4185 ft.
8	34° 54.688'N; 111° 50.618'W	4530 ft.	2	34° 47.081'N; 111° 43.941'W	4285 ft.
9	34° 55.040'N; 111° 49.880'W	4530 ft.	3	34° 47.525'N; 111° 45.610'W	4190 ft.
10	34° 54.412'N; 111° 49.475'W	4525 ft.	4	34° 47.525'N; 111° 45.570'W	4175 ft.
	Munds Wagon Trail		5	34° 47.449'N; 111° 45.383'W	4225 ft.
1	34° 52.000'N; 111° 44.925'W	4465 ft.	6	34° 47.858'N; 111° 44.868'W	4270 ft.
2	34° 52.098'N; 111° 44.088'W	4545 ft.	7	34° 47.953'N; 111° 44.512'W	4425 ft.
3	34° 52.229'N; 111° 43.704'W	4650 ft.	8	34° 48.028'N; 111° 43.910'W	4685 ft.
4	34° 52.254'N; 111° 43.414'W	4750 ft.	9	34° 48.012'N; 111° 43.824'W	4700 ft.
5	34° 52.248'N; 111° 43.176'W	4850 ft.	10	34° 47.474'N; 111° 43.768'W	4440 ft.
6	34° 52.297'N; 111° 42.946'W	4965 ft.		**Scheurman Mountain Trail**	
7	34° 52.285'N; 111° 42.773'W	5070 ft.	1	34° 50.762'N; 111° 49.716'W	4450 ft.
			2	34° 50.719'N; 111° 49.752'W	4460 ft.
	Old Post/Carroll Canyon Loop		3	34° 50.458'N; 111° 49.902'W	4765 ft.
1	34° 49.990'N; 111° 48.618'W	4020 ft.	4	34° 50.283'N; 111° 49.677'W	4815 ft.
2	34° 50.196'N; 111° 48.695'W	4075 ft.	5	34° 50.542'N; 111° 50.143'W	4890 ft.
3	34° 50.419'N; 111° 48.956'W	4140 ft.			
4	34° 50.566'N; 111° 48.726'W	4275 ft.		**Scorpion Trail**	
5	34° 50.865'N; 111° 48.818'W	4365 ft.	1	34° 50.762'N; 111° 49.716'W	4450 ft.
6	34° 51.187'N; 111° 48.406'W	4275 ft.	2	34° 49.982'N; 111° 48.801'W	4060 ft.
7	34° 50.862'N; 111° 48.117'W	4250 ft.	3	34° 50.719'N; 111° 49.752'W	4460 ft.
8	34° 50.732'N; 111° 48.165'W	4200 ft.	4	34° 50.043'N; 111° 49.461'W	4310 ft.
			5	34° 49.986'N; 111° 49.34°2'W	4240 ft.
	Pyramid Loop		6	34° 49.943'N; 111° 49.205'W	4085 ft.
1	34° 49.982'N; 111° 48.801'W	4050 ft.	7	34° 49.964'N; 111° 49.169'W	4190 ft.
2	34° 49.946'N; 111° 48.850'W	4060 ft.	8	34° 49.946'N; 111° 48.850'W	4060 ft.
3	34° 49.964'N; 111° 49.169'W	4190 ft.		**Secret Canyon Trail**	
4	34° 49.986'N; 111° 49.34°2'W	4240 ft.	1	34° 55.797'N; 111° 48.391'W	4660 ft.
5	34° 50.043'N; 111° 49.461'W	4310 ft.	2	34° 56.299'N; 111° 48.631'W	4720 ft.
6	34° 49.777'N; 111° 49 410'W	4240 ft.	3	34° 56.590'N; 111° 48.929'W	4775 ft.
7	34° 49.779'N; 111° 49.320W	4175 ft.	4	34° 57.111°'N; 111° 49.211'W	4940 ft.
			5	34° 56.971'N; 111° 49.484'W	4900 ft.

GPS Data

WP	Latitude; Longitude	Elevation	WP	Latitude; Longitude	Elevation
	Secret Canyon/ Bear Sign Loop			**Soldier Pass Trail**	
1	34° 55.797'N; 111° 48.391'W	4660 ft.	1	34° 53.057'N; 111° 47.028'W	4460 ft.
2	34° 56.299'N; 111° 48.631'W	4720 ft.	2	34° 53.182'N; 111° 46.944'W	4480 ft.
3	34° 56.590'N; 111° 48.920'W	4775 ft.	3	34° 53.418'N; 111° 47.149'W	4480 ft.
4	34° 57.111°'N; 111° 49.211'W	4960 ft.	4	34° 53.865'N; 111° 47.269'W	4580 ft.
5	34° 57.656'N; 111° 49.054'W	5270 ft.	5	34° 54.068'N; 111° 47.125'W	4850 ft.
6	34° 56.723'N; 111° 47.680'W	4875 ft.	6	34° 54.300'N; 111° 47.388'W	4950 ft.
7	34° 56.236'N; 111° 47.678'W	4805 ft.	7	34° 54.305'N; 111° 47.297'W	4940 ft.
			8	34° 54.265'N; 111° 47.388'W	4955 ft.
	Skywalker/Herkenham Loop		9	34° 52.215'N; 111° 47.013'W	4527 ft.
1	34° 50.762'N; 111° 49.716'W	4450 ft.		**Adobe Jack/ Javelina Loop**	
2	34° 50.822'N; 111° 49.708'W	4460 ft.	1	34° 51.908'N; 111° 46.593'W	4375 ft.
3	34° 50.931'N; 111° 49.454'W	4510 ft.	2	34° 51.941'N; 111° 46.605'W	4350 ft.
4	34° 50.856'N; 111° 49.192'W	4580 ft.	3	34° 52.359'N; 111° 46.604'W	4320 ft.
5	34° 50.810'N; 111° 48.998'W	4410 ft.	4	34° 52.424'N; 111° 46.629'W	4395 ft.
6	34° 51.865'N; 111° 48.818'W	4365 ft.	5	34° 52.586'N; 111° 46.563'W	4400 ft.
7	34° 50.566'N; 111° 48.726'W	4275 ft.	6	34° 52.682'N; 111° 46.406'W	4380 ft.
8	34° 50.419'N; 111° 48.956'W	4140 ft.	7	34° 52.669'N; 111° 46.552'W	4475 ft.
9	34° 50.579'N; 111° 49.262'W	4215 ft.	8	34° 52.920'N; 111° 46.617'W	4575 ft.
			9	34° 52.976'N; 111° 46.648'W	4650 ft.
	Slim Shady/Hermit Loop		10	34° 52.792'N; 111° 46.298'W	4475 ft.
1	34° 48.442'N; 111° 46.174'W	4370 ft.	11	34° 52.814'N; 111° 46.255'W	4510 ft.
2	34° 48.431'N; 111° 46.193'W	4360 ft.	12	34° 52.452'N; 111° 46.190'W	4435 ft.
3	34° 48.413'N; 111° 46.166'W	4375 ft.	13	34° 52.060'N; 111° 46.148'W	4260 ft.
4	34° 48.219'N; 111° 46.218'W	4435 ft.	14	34° 52.097'N; 111° 46.289'W	4280 ft.
5	34° 48.415'N; 111° 46.295'W	4400 ft.		**Grand Central/Javelina Loop**	
6	34° 48.695'N; 111° 46.503'W	4305 ft.	1	34° 51.908'N; 111° 46.593'W	4375 ft.
7	34° 48.973'N; 111° 46.580'W	4210 ft.	2	34° 52.088'N; 111° 46.283'W	4285 ft.
8	34° 48.876'N; 111° 46.254'W	4235 ft.	3	34° 52.976'N; 111° 46.648'W	4650 ft.
9	34° 48.698'N; 111° 46.148'W	4280 ft.	4	34° 53.038'N; 111° 46.721'W	4550 ft.
			5	34° 53.066'N; 111° 46.575'W	4590 ft.
			6	34° 52.881'N; 111° 46.259'W	4555 ft.
			7	34° 52.060'N; 111° 46.148'W	4255 ft.

GPS Data

WP	Latitude; Longitude	Elevation	WP	Latitude; Longitude	Elevation
	Sterling Pass to Vultee Arch Trails			**Templeton Trail**	
1	34° 56.201'N; 111° 44.826'W	4845 ft.	1	34° 48.350'N; 111° 46.009'W	4375 ft.
2	34° 56.062'N; 111° 45.583'W	5955 ft.	2	34° 48.441'N; 111° 45.893'W	4325 ft.
3	34° 56.389'N; 111° 46.147'W	5200 ft.	3	34° 48.538'N; 111° 45.885'W	4320 ft.
4	34° 56.500'N; 111° 46.123'W	5350 ft.	4	34° 48.973'N; 111° 46.580'W	4205 ft.
			5	34° 49.335'N; 111° 47.369'W	4165 ft.
	Sugarloaf Trail		6	34° 49.34'7'N; 111° 47.984'W	3985 ft.
1	34° 52.458'N; 111° 47.793'W	4560 ft.	7	34° 49.309'N; 111° 48.493'W	4015 ft.
2	34° 52.471'N; 111° 47.787'W	4560 ft.			
3	34° 52.712'N; 111° 47.843'W	4635 ft.		**Thunder Mountain/Andante Loop**	
4	34° 52.736'N; 111° 47.798'W	4655 ft.	1	34° 52.325'N; 111° 48.735'W	4550 ft.
5	34° 52.793'N; 111° 47.673'W	4685 ft.	2	34° 52.405'N; 111° 48.781'W	4600 ft.
7	34° 52.841'N; 111° 47.581'W	4680 ft.	3	34° 52.535'N; 111° 48.561'W	4640 ft.
8	34° 52.735'N; 111° 47.689'W	4700 ft.	4	34° 52.659'N; 111° 48.557'W	4690 ft.
			5	34° 52.671'N; 111° 48.490'W	4655 ft.
	Teacup Trail		6	34° 52.690'N; 111° 48.417'W	4650 ft.
1	34° 52.458'N; 111° 47.793'W	4560 ft.	7	34° 52.734'N; 111° 48.025'W	4670 ft.
2	34° 52.712'N; 111° 47.843'W	4635 ft.	8	34° 52.823'N; 111° 48.363'W	4765 ft.
3	34° 52.736'N; 111° 47.798'W	4655 ft.	9	34° 52.718'N; 111° 48.589'W	4700 ft.
4	34° 52.841'N; 111° 47.581'W	4680 ft.			
5	34° 52.993'N; 111° 47.502W	4600 ft.		**Transept Trail**	
6	34° 53.101'N; 111° 47.369W	4625 ft.	1	34° 47.428'N; 111° 47.572'W	4180 ft.
7	34° 53.165'N; 111° 47.066W	4490 ft.	2	34° 47.447'N; 111° 47.368'W	4310 ft.
8	34° 53.216'N; 111° 46.999'W	4525 ft.	3	34° 47.492'N; 111° 47.264'W	4445 ft.
9	34° 53.182'N; 111° 46.944'W	4480 ft.	4	34° 47.635'N; 111° 46.739'W	4640 ft.
	Telephone Trail		5	34° 47.615'N; 111° 46.727'W	4650 ft.
1	34° 59.457'N; 111° 44.150'W	5380 ft.	6	34° 47.612'N; 111° 46.692'W	4700 ft.
2	34° 59.528'N; 111° 44.141'W	5400 ft.	7	34° 48.621'N; 111° 47.170'W	4610 ft.
3	34° 59.709'N; 111° 44.149'W	5620 ft.			
4	34° 59.769'N; 111° 44.014'W	5830 ft.			
5	34° 59.733'N; 111° 43.882'W	5955 ft.			
6	34° 59.658'N; 111° 43.831'W	6140 ft.			
7	34° 59.575'N; 111° 43.780'W	6355 ft.			

GPS Data

WP	Latitude; Longitude	Elevation	WP	Latitude; Longitude	Elevation
	Vultee Arch Trail			**West Fork Trail (Cont'd)**	
1	34° 56.236'N; 111° 47.678'W	4805 ft.	4	34° 59.772'N; 111° 44.942'W	5360 ft.
2	34° 56.258'N; 111° 47.336'W	4870 ft.	5	35 00.154'N; 111° 45.603'W	5520 ft.
3	34° 56.354'N; 111° 46.492'W	5090 ft.	6	35 00.158'N; 111° 45.768'W	5560 ft.
4	34° 56.384'N; 111° 46.148'W	5195 ft.	7	35 00.106'N; 111° 46.017'W	5575 ft.
5	34° 56.416'N; 111° 46.122'W	5215 ft.			
6	34° 56.492'N; 111° 46.114'W	5415 ft.		**Wilson Canyon Trail**	
			1	34° 54.023'N; 111° 44.901'W	4530 ft.
			2	34° 53.162'N; 111° 44.499'W	4540 ft.
	Centennial Trail		3	34° 53.248'N; 111° 44.522'W	4540 ft.
1	34° 51.150'N; 111° 49.889'W	4505 ft.	4	34° 53.517'N; 111° 44.464'W	4575 ft.
2	34° 51.213'N; 111° 49.894'W	4470 ft.	5	34° 53.551'N; 111° 44.507'W	4590 ft.
3	34° 51.224'N; 111° 49.903'W	4500 ft.	6	34° 53.961'N; 111° 44.880'W	4830 ft.
4	34° 51.245'N; 111° 49.968'W	4455 ft.	7	34° 54.022'N; 111° 44.891'W	4950 ft.
5	34° 51.292'N; 111° 50.085'W	4460 ft.			
				Wilson Mountain North Trail	
			1	34° 55.513'N; 111° 44.133'W	4755 ft.
	Girdner/Remnant/ Roundabout Loop		2	34° 55.205'N; 111° 44.645'W	5380 ft.
1	34° 51.150'N; 111° 49.889'W	4505 ft.	3	34° 54.971'N; 111° 44.448'W	6215 ft.
2	34° 51.224'N; 111° 49.903'W	4500 ft.	4	34° 54.626'N; 111° 44.460'W	6315 ft.
3	34° 51.249'N; 111° 49.918'W	4490 ft.	5	34° 54.600'N; 111° 44.470'W	6315 ft.
4	34° 51.303'N; 111° 49.964'W	4480 ft.	6	34° 54.883'N; 111° 45.045'W	6950 ft.
5	34° 51.448'N; 111° 50.232'W	4445 ft.	7	34° 54.559'N; 111° 44.960'W	6980 ft.
6	34° 51.544'N; 111° 50.440'W	4410 ft.			
7	34° 51.576'N; 111° 50.504'W	4395 ft.		**Woods Canyon Trail**	
8	34° 51.346'N; 111° 50.501'W	4420 ft.	1	34° 45.371'N; 111° 45.890'W	3935 ft.
9	34° 51.238'N; 111° 49.970'W	4480 ft.	2	34° 45.374'N; 111° 45.801'W	3885 ft.
			3	34° 45.325'N; 111° 45.709'W	3885 ft.
			4	34° 45.400'N; 111° 44.919'W	3910 ft.
	West Fork Trail		5	34° 45.693'N; 111° 43.968'W	4065 ft.
1	34° 59.446'N; 111° 44.570'W	5325 ft.	6	34° 45.702'N; 111° 43.949'W	4075 ft.
2	34° 59.301'N; 111° 44.753'W	5315 ft.	7	34° 45.645'N; 111° 43.649'W	4030 ft.
3	34° 59.310'N; 111° 44.879'W	5315 ft.	8	34° 45.628'N; 111° 43.642'W	4000 ft.

Beyond the Hike

Here's a list of things to see and do around Sedona when you aren't out on the trail.

Airport Overlook - Atop Airport Mesa is a scenic overlook, which provides magnificent views of Coffeepot Rock, Thunder Mountain, Sugarloaf and Chimney Rock. Looking west across the Verde Valley, you'll see the Black Hills; on a clear day you can even see the "J" above Jerome, Arizona to the west.

From the "Y" roundabout, drive west toward Cottonwood on SR 89A for 1 mile then turn left onto Airport Road. Proceed up Airport Road for 1.1 miles to the parking area on your left. Once you have parked, cross the road and enjoy the view. There is a $3 parking fee here.

Chapel of the Holy Cross - The Chapel of the Holy Cross is a local landmark and a must see. It was opened in 1956 and serves as a place to meditate and enjoy the beauty that is Sedona. There is no charge to park or enter but they gladly accept donations.

From the "Y" roundabout, proceed south on SR 179 to the Chapel Road roundabout. Take the third exit and proceed east on Chapel Road to the end. The driveway and sidewalk up to the Chapel are somewhat steep. The Chapel has a gift shop located in the lower level.

Oak Creek Canyon - The drive up Oak Creek Canyon is a world-famous route. It can be very busy on weekends and holidays. You begin in Sedona and drive toward Flagstaff to the Scenic View Area, just past the Switchbacks. This beautiful canyon, created over millions of years, features beautiful views. Cell phone reception can be limited in Oak Creek Canyon. You'll climb in elevation from about 4500 feet (Sedona) to about 6400 feet (at the Scenic View Area).

From the "Y" roundabout, proceed north on SR 89A through Uptown Sedona. If taking photographs, be sure you pull off the road far enough to let vehicles pass by. Drive up Oak Creek Canyon for 16 miles then turn right into the Scenic View Area.

Crescent Moon Ranch/Red Rock Crossing - Crescent Moon Ranch/Red Rock Crossing is where you can stroll along the banks of Oak Creek and take amazing photographs of Cathedral Rock with the creek in the foreground, one of the most recognized photographic settings in Sedona. Be sure to go in the afternoon for the best photographs. This is a special fee area (see page 11).

From the "Y" roundabout, drive west on SR 89A about 4.25 miles then turn left onto the Upper Red Rock Loop Road. Follow the Upper Red Rock Loop Road for about 1.9 miles for the best views. If you want to continue to Crescent Moon Ranch/Red Rock Crossing, turn left onto Chavez Ranch Road then follow it about 1 mile to the end until you reach the entrance gate.

V-Bar-V Heritage Site - There are more than 1000 images created by the Native peoples from about AD 1100 to 1300 at V-Bar-V. It is an easy 0.5 mile hike from the Visitor Center to the rock art. Note: The site is normally open Friday through Monday, 9:30 am to 3:00 pm, but you should check with the Sedona Chamber of Commerce Visitor Center, the Red Rock Ranger Station or call (928) 592-0998 for days of operation. A Red Rock Pass or equivalent is required to park. Pets are not allowed on the site.

From the "Y" roundabout, drive south on SR 179 about 14.75 miles to the intersection of Interstate 17. Drive under I-17 then continue for another 2.75 miles on the paved Forest Road 618. Turn right into the parking area.

Sedona Heritage Museum – The Sedona Heritage Museum is housed in the former orchard and home of Walter and Ruth Jordan. Here you can learn about the pioneers of the Sedona area, from the 1870s through the heyday of western film-making in the 1950s.

From the "Y" roundabout, drive north on SR 89A about 0.3 mile to the Jordan Road roundabout. Take the third exit onto Jordan Road then drive ¾ mile to the parking area on the left. Call (928) 282-7038 for information on special programs. Leashed pets permitted.

Other Titles by the Author

Hiking the Vortexes, B & W Edition   *Hiking the Vortexes, Color Edition*

Sedona Relocation Guide

Index

Acknowledgements	2	Muffin Rock	66, 68
Alphabetical List of Trails/Loops	12-14	Palatki Heritage Site	84
Alphabetical List of Loop Hikes	14-15	Pumphouse Wash	96
Angel Falls	40	QR Code Technology	4
Arch Trails	17	Red Rock Pass	11
Buddha Beach	22	Required Parking Pass	11
Chapel of the Holy Cross	98	Scenic Overlook Parking	20
Chicken Point	44, 98	Sedona Average Weather	10
Crack, The	34	Seven Sacred Pools	42, 58, 132
Definition of Cumulative Ascent	4	Shaded Trails/Loops	17
Definition of the "Y"	7	Soldier Pass Arches	42, 132
Devil's Dining Room	44	Submarine Rock	44
Devil's Kitchen	42, 58, 132	Sunrise/Sunset Data	10
Favorite Trails/Loops	15	Trail Popularity	4
Features of this Edition	4	Trailhead Shuttle Service	5
GPS Data	10	Trails/Loops by Feature	17
Hiking Time	4	Trails/Loops by Difficulty	16-17
Hiking Tips	7	Trails/Loops for Muddy Conditions	17
Honanki Heritage Site	84	Transept Trail	150
Indian Ruin Trails	17	Turkey Creek Parking Area	22, 82
Loop Hikes	14-15	UFO Rock	66, 68
Master Trail/Loop Hike Locator	8-9	Vortex Information	6
Mayan Maiden	150	Vortex Trails	17
Mayhew's Lodge	158	Water Hikes	17
		"Y," Definition	7

The Author and Niece Standing on Devil's Bridge

Hiking Record

Here's a page to record the name of the trail, the date you hiked it and notes from your hike. I'd appreciate any comments you'd like to share by emailing me at hikebook@greatsedonahikes.com

Name of Trail	Date Hiked	Comments/Notes

Made in the USA
Middletown, DE
02 September 2024